FERGUS McCANN v DAVID MURRAY

FERGUS McCANN
v DAVID MURRAY

How Celtic Turned the Tables
on Their Glasgow Rivals

STEPHEN O'DONNELL

First published by Pitch Publishing, 2020

Pitch Publishing
A2 Yeoman Gate
Yeoman Way
Worthing
Sussex
BN13 3QZ
www.pitchpublishing.co.uk
info@pitchpublishing.co.uk

ISBN 978 1 78531 643 2

Typesetting and origination by Pitch Publishing

Printed and bound in India by Replika Press Pvt. Ltd.

Contents

Acknowledgements

THE author would like to thank the following people for their help during the writing of this book: Tom Boyd, Colm Clancy, Gregor Clark, David Faulds, Tom Grant, Sandy Jamieson, David Kelly, Steve Fitzpatrick and friends, Matthew Leslie, Richard McGinley, Matt McGlone, Ally Palmer, David Potter, Andy Ross, Brendan Sweeney and Alf Young. Additional thanks to the staff of the Mitchell Library in Glasgow and the National Library of Scotland in Edinburgh, and to everyone at Pitch Publishing, especially Jane Camillin. Writing is a solitary activity but a book is always a combined effort, so thanks again guys.

Foreword

A GENERATION ago, British football clubs were British owned. Owners tended to be local butchers, bakers and candlestick makers. Turnstile income was all that mattered and the larger the population of the town, the bigger the club tended to be. Banks didn't lend to football clubs and, consequently, everyone lived within their means.

All of that changed in the 1980s following the elections of Margaret Thatcher and Ronald Reagan. Both promoted deregulation of financial markets, cultures of easy money and increased corporate activity.

Football clubs started to change hands, and in 1988 David Murray acquired a controlling interest in the old Rangers, which valued the club's share capital and bank debt at £12.5m. The club's new parent company, Murray International, was already carrying bank debt of circa £40m, meaning the whole Rangers enterprise was entirely dependent on bank borrowing from the outset and well before it was liquidated 20-odd years later.

Across the city at Celtic, the financial climate change passed unnoticed until it was almost too late. The directors lacked vision, commercial acumen and money, and were eventually forced out after a two-year war of attrition with shareholders and supporters. Fergus McCann arrived and acquired a controlling interest in a deal that valued the club at £13.5m before the share issue to supporters at the end of 1994.

In late 1992, I had flown to Montreal to meet Fergus McCann. The purpose was to try to persuade him to back my plan for removing the Celtic board and to support a substantial capital investment. In his apartment his first words to me were, "Hello, Mr Low, who are you, why are you here, and what do you want?" I loved that, straight to the point, no bullshit and a characteristic that was not always appreciated during his time in Scotland.

Fergus had always been adamant that any investment he made would go straight to Celtic and that he was not prepared to buy shares from the outgoing directors, given their mismanagement of the club's affairs. However, on 4 March 1994 he was confronted with that very dilemma; the old board had no choice but to surrender their positions if the club was to avoid receivership, but the change in control would not take place without acquiring their shares. Protracted negotiations ensued over the course of the day and Fergus eventually agreed to set aside some money to buy the directors' shares. It was the only time I can recall getting him to change his mind about anything. That deal sealed the change in control. It was a momentous day in Celtic's history. The game was over and the rebels had won!

This book deals with two contrasting styles of personality and management: Rangers under the control of the risk-taking and bank-financed David Murray, always living on the edge and pitted against Celtic, now controlled by Fergus McCann, and with a business plan that promoted financial stability, steady improvement and operating within its means.

The Murray model was always going to be popular with fans, as it appeared to provide limitless amounts of money to buy better players, greater football success and never-ending football domination over their oldest rivals. McCann's plan was more difficult to implement and required focus, discipline and patience.

Rangers dominated the 1990s and won nine league titles in a row. Celtic supporters, manipulated by a Rangers-leaning media, became increasingly agitated at the Celtic board's refusal to pursue the risky 'buy now, pay later' policy of their rivals. Despite this, and against the financial odds, Celtic managed to win the league and prevent Rangers from winning its coveted tenth league title in a row. However, that didn't stop a section of the Celtic support booing McCann when he unfurled the league championship flag at the start of the following season.

The other major and often overlooked difference between the two clubs was in the calibre of experience of their boards of directors. Unlike Rangers, Celtic was listed on the London Stock Exchange and had a board of directors that understood the importance of good governance and sound financial practice. These characteristics were important in providing the continuity of management needed after McCann's departure in 1999. McCann's real legacy was a management structure and ownership profile that provided continuity of philosophy to this day.

Under Murray, Rangers fared less well. During his ownership, the Bank of Scotland continued to lend his companies seemingly endless amounts of money, but all that stopped with the financial crash in 2008 and the takeover of Halifax Bank of Scotland by Lloyds TSB the same year. The lending stopped and the club had to start downsizing and paying off bank debt. The whole debt orgy had lasted an exceptional 20 years. Financial profligacy and greed had dominated the sporting landscape, distorted on-field performance and ended with a trail of insolvencies and, in the case of Rangers, liquidation. Extraordinarily, it wasn't the bank debt that finally brought about the death of the club, but unpaid taxes due to Her Majesty's Revenue and Customs (HMRC).

The Murray years should have been recognised as exceptional, and the current, more stable financial landscape as the norm. Lessons should have been learned, but that wasn't to be in the case of Rangers. A new club was formed in 2012 with the assets of the liquidated club; it successfully applied for membership of the Scottish Football Association (SFA) and the then Scottish Football League (SFL), but after a difficult birth the new club has inherited the worst financial attributes of the old one and continues to live outwith its means and is financed by directors' loans.

Celtic now has a considerable and embedded economic advantage over Rangers, as well as everyone else in their domestic league. This can all be traced to the structures put in place by Fergus McCann in 1994 and followed by successive boards since. However, at the time of writing, a new and unforeseen financial threat has emerged that's indiscriminate in nature. The coronavirus is a human tragedy and a financial catastrophe for spectator-based sports, which has the capability to redefine the football industry's entire financial model.

David Low
May 2020

1.

Before the Flood of Money

URING the 1990s, the seemingly eternal rivalry in Glasgow between the city's two great football teams, Celtic and Rangers, appeared to take on a new, ultra-modern dimension in the shape of the two institutions' recognised and successful owners, Fergus McCann and David Murray. Over the course of the decade, these two businessmen came to be considered among the most well-known public figures in Scotland, due almost entirely to their roles at their respective clubs, and to outside observers, certainly at first glance, it may have seemed as if Murray and McCann had been hewn from the same rock. Both were driven, headstrong, self-made men, ready to trample over anything or anyone who had the misfortune to get in their way, and in coming to prominence when they did, the pair also found themselves favourably positioned to exploit the commercialisation and corporatisation of football that was taking place over the period of their involvement in the game.

Yet the two men could hardly have been more different. Murray, the Rangers chairman, at times appeared to be on a never-ending mission to indulge his ego, an unabashed showman, who was prepared to take extraordinary risks with his own, and in particular with other people's money, in the unshakeable belief that his plans would always come to fruition in the end. McCann, by contrast, Murray's counterpart at Celtic Park, gave the impression of a relatively low-key figure, who was happy to beaver away behind the scenes at his club while displaying almost no interest in the dubious distractions of the PR game or in manipulating his public profile in any way. His primary concern, it seemed, was with making money, and in March 1994 he invested almost his entire fortune in Celtic in a bid to effectively relaunch the struggling Parkhead outfit over the course of a five-year plan, by the end of which he had more than quadrupled his initial stake in the club. Murray, the 'impresario', as one of his former directors described him, would throw cash around in order to make himself look good, whereas for McCann, a meticulous trained accountant, who was in for virtually all he was worth, every penny was a prisoner.

As a keen follower of Celtic in his youth before he emigrated to Canada in the mid-1960s, McCann had acquired at first hand a thorough knowledge and understanding of the importance of the club to its community of fans. He knew that Celtic, still under the archaic and stubborn control of the three dynastic families who had dominated the Parkhead boardroom since the Victorian age, was a sleeping giant of the global game, which, if awoken, held within it the potential to return to its former glories. By comparison, prior to his association with Rangers, football held little interest for Murray, who seemed to have been more of a rugby buff in his formative years, thanks to his time at the posh Fettes College in Edinburgh, before his father's bankruptcy and other associated family issues saw him relegated to the nearby local Broughton High School. McCann's insight furnished him with the initial confidence to proceed with his takeover and turnaround of the Parkhead club, which, over the course of his short allotted timescale, he ultimately saw through to a successful conclusion. Conversely, Murray's connection with Rangers eventually extended to almost 23 years, at times with no apparent end in sight, until in 2011, with financial catastrophe looming, he finally bailed out, handing over the reins at Ibrox to a doomed and incompetent successor.

Perhaps the most striking contrast between the two rivals, however, lay in the way in which they were treated by an outrageously partisan mainstream media. At one stage, McCann was compared unfavourably with the international *bête noire* of the day, the maligned Iraqi president Saddam Hussein, while many of these same journalists who were perpetually haranguing the Celtic supremo were simultaneously being invited to dine, and almost choking themselves with flattery, on Murray's fine wine and 'succulent lamb', a notorious phrase that eventually came to define everything that was increasingly wrong and improper with sports journalism in Glasgow and the west of Scotland at this time.

Hard as it may seem to consider, but before the revolution in how football clubs were run in the 1990s, when the game was effectively taken over by corporate and media interests, Scottish football had already enjoyed a long and distinguished history. In particular, Celtic and Rangers, the two 'Old Firm' sides, had from the very earliest days of competitive professional football in Scotland established an effective duopoly over the national game, regularly annexing all the available major domestic trophies and marking themselves out as two of the biggest and most renowned clubs in the global game. Even as far back as the turn of the 20th century, this dual power-base in Glasgow had begun to arouse the suspicion and indignation of rivals and outsiders who, with some justification, began to see the Glasgow clubs as an effective cartel, as much partners as adversaries in the matter of pursuing their own financial best interests. Over the course of the following few decades, however, the religious and ethnic tensions between the clubs, as reflected in the wider society, would tear them asunder, placing the two institutions at opposite ends of an at times ghastly, but always compelling rivalry.

Celtic, for their part, had enjoyed an undeniably glorious history long before the arrival of Fergus McCann in the east end of Glasgow, although sadly for the club's fans, glory and success didn't always go hand in hand for the Parkhead men. The club was founded by a group of prominent Irishmen, most notably Brother Walfrid of the Marist religious order, shortly after Sunday Mass on 6 November 1887 at a meeting in St Mary's Hall in the Calton area of the city. To notify the press about his venture into the popular game of football, Walfrid popped into the offices of the *Scottish Umpire* on Jamaica Street and told them all about his plans and ideas for the proposed new club, with the paper subsequently reporting, 'We learn that the efforts which have lately been made to organise in Glasgow a first-class Catholic football club, have been successfully consummated by the formation of the "Glasgow Celtic Football and Athletic Club," under influential auspices. They have secured a six-acre ground in the east-end, which they mean to put in fine order. We wish the "Celts" all success.'

The team played its first match at the new, purpose-built ground in Parkhead the following May and celebrated a 5-2 win over Rangers, establishing in the process an early friendship with the Ibrox side. Celtic had arrived relatively late on the scene, at a time when professionalism in football had already been legalised in England and was on the verge of being officially accepted in Scotland too. The old amateur ethos of earlier in the century, under which the ex-public school and university boys had popularised and codified the game, was now being purged away as football swept across the industrial communities of England and Scotland, with ordinary working people flocking to support their local teams in increasingly astonishing numbers and embracing Saturday afternoon football as an enjoyable digression from the toil and routine of the working week.

One of Celtic's founding principles, its *raison d'être* in the early years, was to raise money through the charitable St Vincent de Paul Society for the children of impoverished Irish immigrants in the main Catholic parishes of Glasgow's east end. To fulfil the purpose of its foundation, therefore, Celtic had to be both financially viable and successful on the field straight away, and the club's early movers and shakers went to great lengths to persuade some of the best footballers of the age to join their new enterprise. A key factor in convincing others of their credibility and strength of purpose was the procurement from the West Dunbartonshire village side Renton of half-back James Kelly, a Scotland international and one of the greatest players of his day. Kelly's arrival precipitated an influx of *fin de siècle* footballing talent to Parkhead, including a sizeable contingent from fellow Irish side Hibernian, the Edinburgh club founded in 1875, who were fleeced for as many as six players, an outcome which left the Easter Road men understandably vexed. Meanwhile, other recruits to Celtic's cause arrived from teams as far afield as Everton, the champions of England, who lost Dan Doyle to the Glasgow club in 1891, and Aston Villa, the Double winners, from whom the Parkhead side took three players in 1897.

With so many other Catholic representative teams in Glasgow having already fallen by the wayside, this single-mindedness on the part of Walfrid and his colleagues in their dealings with other clubs reveals how resolute and determined they were to ensure that Celtic, in its early, formative years, didn't wither on the vine in a similar fashion. As author Graham McColl observes in *The Official Biography of Celtic*, 'Celtic became renowned for a rapacious ruthlessness that would have made many a Dickensian factory owner's heart sing. Charity may have been at the club's core but it was set aside when dealing with other clubs.' Kelly himself would be named Celtic's first-ever captain and, after his retirement from the game, his move into the directors' box, following the club's incorporation in 1897, established a dynasty in the Parkhead boardroom that would ultimately only end with McCann.

From very early on, Celtic were identified in the contemporary press as 'the team of Irishmen'; although, initially at least, such a label didn't necessarily imply suspicion or disrespect. Nevertheless, when Celtic and Hibernian moved to the top of the league in 1896, the *Scottish Sport* observed with some alarm, 'The two Irish teams are at the top of the table. Is this not a reflection on Scotland?' Evidence suggests, though, that despite their clear Irish Catholic roots, the early founders of Celtic saw the club as a proposed link between Ireland, the ancestral homeland, and Scotland, the new country of residence, as Dr Matthew L. McDowell points out in his book *A Cultural History of Association Football in Scotland, 1865–1902*: 'From the outset, Celtic looked outwith the Catholic community for inspiration ... [The club] was intended as a bridge to Protestant Scotland rather than as an "Irish" organisation, and as such did not restrict themselves to Catholic players.'

This notion of a dual identity within the club represented a clear departure from the policy of Hibernian, which only extended its membership to practising Catholics and whose popularity among the Glasgow Irish community, particularly after their Scottish Cup Final victory over Dumbarton at Crosshills in February 1887, had helped to spark the idea for Celtic's foundation. It has even been suggested that the chosen name for the new club was a reference to the 'Keltic' traditions of both nations, with the Catholics-only suggestion dismissed as parochial and restrictive by the founders of the ambitious Glasgow side. Ultimately, however, the idealistic notion of a pan-'Keltic' club, which linked the communities of Scotland and Ireland, would be undermined in the 1890s by the sporting press's nomination and adoption of Rangers as the club of true Scottish heritage, as the men from Govan emerged as the leading rival to the overnight success story that Celtic had become.

Clearly, however, the efforts of the early Parkhead committee members hadn't been in vain, and within a few short years of the club's foundation there were not many followers of the game in Scotland who could fail to acknowledge their success, as in 1892 Celtic claimed all three major cup competitions, namely the Glasgow Cup, the Glasgow Charity Cup and the Scottish Cup, although they had to settle for second place in the league behind the champions, Dumbarton. Nevertheless, the Parkhead side had now established themselves as one of the greatest teams in the country, and in the new, upgraded Celtic Park, where the club relocated in 1892, they had a splendid, purpose-built ground that was in regular use as the preferred venue for the Scotland versus England international fixture for most of the 1890s.

The establishment of Rangers as a perennial rival to Celtic around the turn of the century slowed the Parkhead club's progress, and by the end of the First World War, as Scottish football and society found itself enveloped in religious bigotry, Celtic's status as the foremost club in the land was challenged and overcome by Bill Struth's regimented and unyielding Rangers sides of the 1920s and 30s. Hampered by external prejudices in the game's governance and in the press, who largely refused to call out Rangers over their anti-Catholicism, it would take until the mid-1960s before Celtic would properly find their feet again. Free from chairman Robert Kelly's tiresome and counterproductive meddling in team affairs, Celtic won the league for the first time in 12 years in 1966 and, under the transformative leadership of new manager Jock Stein, bettered that success the following year with the most coveted prize of all, the European Cup, in a season in which the Parkhead club managed to win every competition they entered.

With Stein in charge, Celtic subsequently went on to lift an unprecedented nine consecutive titles, and in the process re-established themselves as the number-one team in the country. From that position, however, the club entered a slow period of decline, which didn't manifest itself fully until the late 1980s. By early in the following decade, Celtic had become a mere shadow of their former selves, heavily indebted to their bankers and in the midst of a fallow period, which harked back to the pre-Stein era. There was one man, though, who promised to restore the club's ailing fortunes, if only the incumbent board, still dominated by James Kelly's descendants, would allow him … Fergus McCann.

Meanwhile, over on the other side of the city, and predating Celtic by some 16 years, Rangers were founded as far back as

1872 by a group of four teenagers – three from Garelochhead in Argyll and one from Callander in Perthshire – who, like so many of their contemporaries, had migrated towards Glasgow in search of work during the industrial boom of the mid-Victorian period. It was a rocky road for the boys' club at first, with Rangers a nomadic, cash-strapped and controversy-dogged institution in the early years, but by the time of the formation of a Scottish league in 1891, Rangers appeared to have put their earlier troubles behind them and, under the assiduous leadership of secretary-manager William Wilton, had grown into one of the biggest and best-supported clubs in the country. Moving into a new, permanent home on the south side of Glasgow, Ibrox Park, and aided by the sudden appearance of a brash and ambitious new local rival in Celtic, Rangers successfully exploited the era of professionalism and the extraordinary, exponential growth in football's popularity over this period to form a limited liability company in May 1899, just as Celtic had two years earlier. The club's incorporation meant the end of the old committee structure, with posts, such as match secretary and treasurer, elected from the membership lists, to be replaced instead by a board of directors, with the ownership of the club now transferred into the hands of its small shareholders.

Following the club's incorporation, the new Rangers board, led by Baillie James Henderson, was made up largely of prominent citizens, including future chairmen Baillie Joseph Buchanan and Sir John Ure Primrose, an ardent and campaigning opponent of Irish home rule, which for some years now, dating back to Prime Minister William Gladstone's proposed legislation of the 1880s, had been one of the most contentious and sensitive political issues of the day. In time, the number of club administrators at Ibrox was whittled down, and for most of the first half of the 20th century, the Rangers board consisted of a tight group comprising a chairman and two directors, all unwaged, made up almost exclusively of ex-players, including such long-serving and notable figures as Alan Morton and James Bowie. This informal, pseudo-amateur structure served the club well and brought unprecedented levels of on-field success to Ibrox, as Rangers grew into the biggest and best-supported club in the country during the inter-war period. Things changed in the summer of 1947, however, when Bowie, a capable administrator who had previously served as president of both the SFA and the Scottish League, lost out in a bitter dispute over control of the boardroom and was ousted by the club's all-powerful manager, Bill Struth.

In a largely unreported but nevertheless acrimonious and divisive coup, Bowie had suggested to Struth that he might consider retirement and the acceptance of a place on the club's board in return for relinquishing his position as team manager. Struth at the time was 71 years old, the same age at which his great contemporary, Willie Maley, had been ushered towards the exit door at Celtic Park in 1940 after 52 years' service to the Parkhead club, but the veteran Rangers manager appeared to be in no mood to give way and submit himself to the same indignity. Since his appointment in 1920, Struth had been slowly accumulating shares in Rangers, mostly on the cheap in partnership with club secretary, William Rogers Simpson, and by 1947 the manager was the club's largest individual shareholder, owning a total of 1,097 shares. As a paid employee, however, Struth was forbidden by the club's articles of association from becoming a director, but in Bowie's unwelcome suggestion that he should stand aside and move upstairs, Struth sensed an opportunity.

Over the course of a heated extraordinary general meeting (EGM) and annual general meeting (AGM) held on the night of 12 June 1947, the manager used his overwhelming proxy vote to not only vote down Bowie's own attempt at re-election but also to pass an amendment that allowed both he and Simpson to become directors while remaining paid employees of the club, safe in their respective positions as manager and club secretary, with Simpson eventually going on to take over the vacant chairman's seat at the club. Bowie, on the other hand, strode out of the AGM around midnight having been completely defeated, and despite his lengthy association with the club – not least as a player under Struth in the early 1920s – he was never heard of in connection with Rangers again.

It was a momentous day in the club's history, although as Struth's biographer, David Mason, noted, 'The outcome of the meeting that Bowie had construed as being the most important in the history of Rangers Football Club was reported in half a column in the *Glasgow Herald* ... The Bowie camp lamented that the issue was of passive interest to the fans and not one supporter awaited the outcome at the doors to Ibrox.' Similarly, the coverage in *The Scotsman* amounted to just a few lines on page six of the paper, just above an equal-sized column bearing news of a yacht race around Ailsa Craig. The press had offered limited information, and almost no analysis, while the club's supporters seemed entirely nonplussed by the tumultuous off-field events. Bowie had argued passionately at the EGM that the proposed changes would cede control of the club to those with 'financial interests, as against an administration solely concerned with maintaining the [club's] high sporting traditions', but ultimately his pleas had fallen on deaf ears.

The eventual outcome allowed Struth to continue as manager while increasing his stranglehold on power at Ibrox by becoming a fully waged director. However, as an almost unnoticed consequence, control of the club had now passed from those who had a history of previous service with Rangers, or whose shares held a merely passive, emotional value, to investors whose interest in the company might be entirely pecuniary, with directors now likely to have a financial stake in the club or to have bought their way on to the board. One leading club historian later described Struth's boardroom coup as 'the day Rangers became a business', while Mason offered an insight into the far-reaching repercussions of the club's change of direction: 'In many ways, [Bowie's] fears were prophetic of the dangers that would ultimately cause the club such grief in more recent times.'

As a result of Struth's drastic efforts at self-preservation, Rangers shares, and ultimately the control of the club, were now a commodity that could be traded openly, and in 1954 the builder John Lawrence joined the board at Ibrox. Lawrence, famous throughout Scotland for his housebuilding, served as chairman from 1963 until 1973, but his board largely comprised like-minded small businessmen of similar age, who by the early 1970s seemed to be overwhelmed by the club's catastrophic misfortunes. After losing the hegemony of the domestic game to Jock Stein's Celtic, which provoked the panicked and mishandled dismissal of manager Scot Symon in November 1967, Rangers suffered the trauma of the second Ibrox Park disaster, when 66 supporters were fatally injured in a crush on the steps of Ibrox after a 1-1 draw with Celtic on 2 January 1971. The directors, almost all of them well into their dotage by this stage, seemed utterly overtaken by events and, as a group, they were severely criticised at a subsequent private prosecution, in which the wife of one of the disaster victims was awarded more than £26,000 in damages. In giving his verdict, the civil suit judge castigated the Rangers board for their failure to heed the warnings of several previous crushes on the same Ibrox stairway and found that their inaction and incompetence was a contributing factor in the tragedy.

Nevertheless, perhaps surprisingly in the midst of such woe, the high-water mark of the club's on-field achievements soon followed, when Willie Waddell's cautiously defensive side triumphed in the Cup Winners' Cup, with a 3-2 victory over Dynamo Moscow in the Barcelona final in May 1972. The occasion was marred by events at the end of the game, however, when rioting fans prevented captain John Greig from being properly presented with the trophy, with the cup eventually handed over to the Rangers skipper deep within the bowels of the Camp Nou rather than against the customary backdrop of dignitaries and celebrating fans. As a result of the travelling supporters' conduct on the night, Rangers were eventually banned from European competition for a year, denying the team the opportunity of defending their title.

Most of the sitting Rangers directors would be dead by the end of the decade, including Lawrence, who bequeathed his shareholding to his grandson Lawrence Marlborough in 1977. Marlborough had joined the board in 1973, aged just 30, and eventually sat alongside chairman Rae Simpson, a Kilmarnock surgeon, who had himself inherited his shares from his grandfather James Henderson, the incorporated club's first chairman, and from his father, another former chairman, W. R. Simpson, once Bill Struth's seditious ally. Marlborough's and Simpson's fellow directors included a cast of small business owners – builders, proprietors of haulage firms, taxi companies and garage dealerships – who had built up their stakes in the club with small purchases over many years following the coup of 1947. These small-time wheelers and dealers also found themselves largely out of their depth when it came to providing the stability and leadership that Rangers required and, amid frequent and prolonged internal disputes, the club endured a painful, drawn-out spell of on-field mediocrity, which, with the notable exception of two memorable Trebles won by Jock Wallace's rumbustious sides of 1976 and 1978, extended over a 20-year period from the mid-1960s through to the mid-1980s.

In November 1985, Marlborough moved to straighten out the club's affairs and put a stop to the financial losses at Ibrox, which were draining money from his parent company, the Lawrence Building Group. Now based in Lake Tahoe, Nevada, where he had relocated after resigning from the Rangers board in 1983, Marlborough appointed David Holmes, managing director of his operation in Falkirk, to the club's board with instructions to be his eyes and ears in Glasgow. Between them, Marlborough and Holmes then put together a plan to gain a controlling interest in the company with the intention of trying to reinvigorate the underachieving institution and making Rangers more financially viable once again. However, it soon became clear that, if their ideas were to come to fruition, there would first have to be blood on the carpet in the Ibrox boardroom.

In the end, Marlborough's bitter and protracted takeover saw three directors ousted, including Rae Simpson, with 53-year-old Holmes, Marlborough's man on the ground, appointed as the club's new chief executive officer on 14 February 1986. The decisive factor in engineering the coup came when an agreement was secured with disgruntled former vice-chairman Jack Gillespie, one of the warring factions in the old set-up, who agreed to a staggered sale of a significant proportion of his 81,000 shares, sufficient in the end to give Marlborough a 52 per cent stake and outright control of the club. Gillespie was rewarded with a lifetime directorship, although his abiding ambition of one day occupying the chairman's seat at Ibrox would ultimately elude him.

It was another seismic day of seminal and irrevocable change in the way Rangers was governed as an institution. For the first time in its history, the club was now effectively a one party state, wholly beholden to a single majority shareholder and dependent for the sound and capable administration of its affairs on the aptitudes and calibre of one individual. If there were any concerns or reservations being expressed at the time, however, they were soon set aside as, under the incoming regime, Rangers were transformed from a staid, directionless cabal of factional and competing self-interests into a thriving model of speculate-to-accumulate capitalism in Margaret Thatcher's new Britain. The wage structure was dismantled, and the cherished Presbyterian values of thrift and moderation were swept aside; finance was now king, and Rangers would recover their former glories by simply outspending any opponent who dared to put up a challenge against them. Money was borrowed from the bank to pay for expensive new signings and, based on the sound economic principles of supply and demand, ticket prices were immediately ratcheted up to double the level of the previous era. Regardless of the escalating cost, however, supporters came flooding back to the club, with the number of season ticket holders at Ibrox increasing from fewer than 3,000 in 1986 to approximately 30,000 by 1991. In addition, on top of the increased gate receipts, Rangers were one of the first clubs in Britain to identify and exploit the potential revenue from matchday hospitality, with a new executive lounge soon opened in the main stand, equipped with facilities to cater for 240 corporate guests.

Elsewhere in the stadium, refurbished as an almost fully seated arena after the 1971 disaster, the ordinary fan also couldn't help but notice the smaller, subtler modifications around the club, as the matchday programme was given a glossy makeover, electronic scoreboards were installed behind the goals for the first time and a proper DJ was hired to provide the pre-match entertainment, lending Ibrox Park an unmistakeable sense of modernity and change. Only the less affluent supporter was overlooked in the upgrades that were taking place at the club, it seemed, as all tickets sold on the day of a game were now full price, with no concessionary rates available to non-season ticket holders, making it very difficult for children, students, pensioners and the less well-off to follow Rangers on a regular basis.

Key to the club's resurrection was the appointment of a new manager to replace the discarded Jock Wallace, and the candidate David Holmes and his colleagues eventually identified would prove to be perfectly in tune with the new direction that the club was embarking upon. Graeme Souness was a man who freely admitted that he had no idea what he was letting himself in for when he agreed to become the Ibrox club's new player-manager in March 1986, but with his outspoken adherence to the Thatcherite ideal, he seemed to anticipate and exemplify the changes that were taking place in football and in society at the time. Under their new manager, Rangers outspent every other club, not just in Scotland but in Britain, over the next few years. Thanks to Holmes's readiness to take the club deep into debt, a raft of top-quality English internationals agreed to join the Ibrox side, including, initially, Terry Butcher, the England captain, and Chris Woods, followed not far down the line by Gary Stevens, Trevor Steven, Mark Walters, Trevor Francis, Ray Wilkins and Mark Hateley.

Scottish football was utterly stunned; the self-seeking, monetarist principles of Thatcherism had been widely rejected north of the border, particularly in the industrial Labour heartlands of west central Scotland, yet here was the country's leading club transforming itself and indeed the Scottish game with a strategy that the Iron Lady herself could have readily prescribed for the ailing Ibrox institution. Two games, played a year apart, against the same opponent, perhaps provided the clearest illustration of the changes that had taken place at Ibrox over the intervening 12 months. In January 1986, just 12,371 fans watched a Rangers team featuring the underwhelming talents of Hugh Burns, Craig Paterson and Bobby Williamson labour to an eventual 4-2 win over Clydebank, the league's perennial strugglers. Almost exactly a year later, an Ibrox side including such luminaries as Souness, Woods, Butcher and new signing Graham Roberts, again faced the hapless Bankies, who had only been reprieved from relegation through league reconstruction, and routed them 5-0 in front of 36,397. Over a three-month stretch between February and April 1986, Rangers won a total of just one league game, eventually finishing the season without a trophy and in a lowly fifth place in the Premier Division. Over the same period the following year, the Ibrox men won ten games out of 12 en route to the title.

The directionless and anachronistic institution of earlier in the decade was now attractive to investors, and by October 1988 the City had already been made aware of the potential availability of Marlborough's shareholding in the club. Because of stock market rules, Marlborough had been obliged to make an offer for all the remaining shares after his takeover in 1986, and, as a result, he had eventually acquired 66 per cent of the stock. The following month, on 23 November 1988, Marlborough finally sold up, ending his family's 44-year involvement with the Ibrox institution, which led one anonymous ex-player to observe at the time that former chairman John Lawrence, the so-called 'benign bishop' whose name had become associated with Rangers over the many years of his involvement at Ibrox, would be 'spinning in his grave' at the discontinuation of his family's interest in the club. Marlborough, son of Lawrence's daughter Alice, was the anointed successor, after John Lawrence Junior, known as Jack, predeceased his father and brother William showed no interest for the fray, but now the favoured grandson and nominated heir was cashing in the family jewels, receiving £25 per share, roughly double what he had paid less than three years earlier. David Holmes, by then the club chairman, denied that Marlborough had been forced into a sale and that the sustained overspending at Ibrox was contributing to the Lawrence Group's ongoing financial problems, insisting instead that the company was merely 'streamlining' its operation.

The buyer was 37-year-old David Edward Murray, who saw off a late, clandestine move to acquire Rangers by the doomed and subsequently disgraced media baron, Robert Maxwell, to become the new owner of the famous old Ibrox club. Murray, immediately described in the tabloids as a 'metals and property tycoon' and a 'sports car enthusiast', a hobby he apparently retained despite having lost both his legs in a high-speed roll-out while driving home from a rugby match in 1976, was already one of Scotland's best known and mostly highly regarded young businessmen. 'He is, quite simply,' opined Alf Young, economics editor of the broadsheet *Glasgow Herald*, who had done a bit more digging into Murray's background, 'one of the most aggressively successful deal doers the Scottish corporate scene has ever seen.' Murray paid just over £6m for Rangers, acquiring as part of the transaction Marlborough's 240,713 ordinary shares, which included options on the remaining stock still held by Jack Gillespie, due to be obtained by Marlborough, under the terms of the 1986 takeover, over the next two years.

With the stadium valued at £22m and the player registrations worth an estimated £10m, Young made the obvious point in his piece for *The Herald* when he noted, 'Many will be pondering over a deal where a company can buy a club for substantially less than the estimated value of its players.' But with Murray obliged under stock market rules to make an offer for all the remaining shares, which was forecast to see his stake rise to around 75 per cent of the total holdings, Young accounted for the apparent anomaly in the purchase price by also noting the substantial overdraft that had been taken on by the new owner, estimated at around £9m, and by quoting a leading financial analyst, who observed that while the deal 'looks like a very good bargain ... perhaps there will be a lot more to pay out before the matter is finished'.

Murray acquired Rangers through his parent company Murray International Holdings (MIH), which he had grown from a one man and a secretary operation when the firm was set up in Edinburgh's Alva Street in 1974 into a multinational conglomerate of 36 companies with a turnover of £90m and an estimated workforce of 1,200 people, trading in steel, electronics, office systems and equipment, leisure, other metals and, most recently, property, making MIH one of the top three private businesses in Scotland. Also coming in on the deal was manager Graeme Souness, who contributed £600,000 for a 10 per cent 'lifetime' stake in Murray's majority share of the club, adding a directorship to his already joint roles of manager and player, although the former Scotland international midfielder's influence on the field at Ibrox would be limited from this point onwards.

It was Souness, in fact, who originally brought Murray, his friend and fellow Tory ideologue, to the table with Rangers and brokered the agreement with Marlborough, after the industrialist, in May 1988, had failed in his attempted takeover of home town club Ayr United, whose directors had judged Murray to be too hotheaded, and a 'most volatile' and 'very unpredictable' individual. Despite being offered almost four times what their shares were then worth, when they dug down into the detail of his bid, the seven-man board of the Somerset Park club had come to the conclusion that Murray was trying to gain control of the business on the cheap, in effect for a mere £125,000 of his own money. Led by chairman George Smith, a local farmer, and majority shareholder Sandy Loudon, a Girvan accountant, the board subsequently declined his offer, claiming that the prospective purchaser was looking for 'too much, too soon and at too little a price', a rejection that left Murray incandescent.

By November, just six months later, the steel tycoon couldn't resist a sideswipe at those who had earlier spurned his advances: 'Perhaps Ayr United will now realise what I could have done for them. I think they will be inquiring among themselves about what they've missed,' Murray offered immodestly, once his takeover of Rangers was complete. Described as the 'sports deal of the year' – by Murray – the *Daily Record* reported how the new owner, on acquiring Rangers, 'became the most powerful figure in Scottish football with a single flourish of his pen'. It seemed an odd turn of phrase even at the time; how could the majority shareholder of one of the country's clubs, however big, be regarded as the most important and powerful person in the game? Regardless, it was an accolade that Murray would live up to over the coming years, after he expressed the view that no institution, other than the Church of Scotland, was more important in the country than Rangers.

All this was pretty much par for the course, and the open-arms welcome that Murray received from the media after his purchase of Rangers was largely to be expected. On closer inspection, however, behind the multimillionaire, swashbuckling captain of industry public persona, there was a young man with a very chequered background. In the 1960s, Murray's father, David Ian Murray, known as Ian, had reinvented himself as a flamboyant professional gambler and racehorse owner after failing his exams as a trainee veterinary surgeon and then dropping out of the family coal merchant business. Murray Snr subsequently emerged as something of a local celebrity in Ayr and was so successful and prominent for a period that he became known within the community, ironically, as 'Lord Beresford' in reference to his numerous business interests on the town's swanky Beresford Terrace. After amassing a small fortune on the horses, however, Ian subsequently lost the lot, and when bankruptcy and court action ensued, the result was a two-year prison sentence in 1968, after he was convicted of illegal business transactions and intent to defraud his creditors.

Around the same time, the young David witnessed the break-up of his parents' marriage, which was followed almost immediately by his forced removal from Fettes College in Edinburgh, an upmarket, fee-paying boarding school, and his enrolment instead, due to his family's now considerably reduced circumstances, at the altogether more affordable Broughton High School just around the corner. It couldn't have been easy – a posh boy from Fettes, from a broken home and with a jailbird dad, being obliged to go down the road and mix in at the local, state-funded secondary. Later in life, Murray loved to recount the story of how his father, after being cleaned out and left effectively penniless by his gambling habit, was paid a substantial sum of money by a Sunday tabloid for the exclusive rights to his life story. Murray Snr immediately staked the entire fee he received from the paper on a horse, which romped home at outrageously long odds.

In addition to the unstable environment of his childhood, Murray then suffered a life-changing trauma just as his fledgling business career was beginning to take off, when he was involved in a near-fatal car accident, smashing his Lotus into a tree at high speed and only waking up in hospital after both his legs had been amputated. At roughly the same time, in September 1975, his father Ian died aged just 50, and the young entrepreneur also had to write off a substantial bad debt, which left him £100,000 out of pocket – not an easy position for a young man with a wife and two baby sons to support.

Nevertheless, now hyper-motivated as a result of these setbacks and with a portfolio of viable businesses to occupy his time and energy, Murray found the economic climate of the 1980s very much to his liking. At the age of 33 he was named 'Young Scottish Businessman of the Year' at the Scottish Business Achievement Awards in 1984, a recognition of his talents, which afforded Murray the opportunity to air his views on what he perceived was going wrong with British industry in the early 1980s. 'There are too many people in business who spend all their time talking about it. Too many maybes, would-haves and could-dos,' the young entrepreneur complained while berating the upper-crust, old-guard business community in Scotland and Britain, whom he dismissed as 'the four-hour lunchers'. 'As a nation, we're not hungry enough any more. Today it's the Taiwanese and the Mexicans who are hungry, and just look what that's doing to sections of our industry,' Murray lamented. 'In the United States they applaud it, but here the climate's all wrong and the incentives are all wrong.'

The 1980s, generally, was a decade when aspirational, lower-middle-class men such as Murray were rising to prominence, regardless of mediocre levels of academic attainment or whether or not they had the right background or connections, and Murray was entirely typical of the new breed of businessman who was becoming involved in football around the time of his acquisition of Rangers. But even considering the abrupt, no-nonsense manner of well-known figures such as Alan Sugar at Tottenham or Martin Edwards at Manchester United, Murray often appeared to be in a category of his own when it came to the sheer belligerence of his bearing and disposition. Describing himself as 'abrasive, arrogant and full of self-confidence', his management style was characterised by an obvious disdain for boardroom consensus or for laboriously long meetings, which he admitted left him feeling bored. 'The very important yes or no decisions are made by me right here in this office. People can walk in and see me and if I need to I can go and see them,' he explained. It was an approach that appeared to fit with the times, but perhaps augured less well for Murray's ability to navigate the waters of more stormy economic conditions ahead.

At times, though, such was the extent of his haughtiness and self-absorption, that it almost seemed as if there was a screw loose somewhere with Murray, and over the next few years, as the chairman and his club went crashing recklessly forward, his notorious ego would eventually get the better of him. With the banking community and the media favourably aligned to his cause, Murray's Rangers soon set off in their quest to emulate Celtic's record nine consecutive domestic league titles as well as, most ruinously of all, the Parkhead side's elusive capture of the European Cup in 1967, with ultimately catastrophic consequences for the Ibrox club and for Murray's business empire overall. Unfortunately, however, with all the eulogising and the media profiling that was going on, which would only increase in the magnitude and volume of its obsequiousness as the years went by, nobody appeared to notice until it was too late.

2.

High Noon

FERGUS McCann's association with Celtic already extended back over several years by the time he flew into Glasgow, overnight from the States, wearing his trademark bunnet, to rescue the distressed Parkhead club from almost certain insolvency. As early as 1988, he had offered to provide the funds, via a low-interest loan, to increase the capacity at Celtic Park to 72,000, which would have included an expansion of the number of seats in the ground from 8,700 to 24,000. With McCann's background in golf tourism lending him a valuable insight into the increasing importance in top-level sport of repeat business and corporate hospitality, he also hoped to install an array of executive boxes in the new, two-tiered main stand. His plans, however, were rebuffed, and whenever he sought to revisit his interest in an increasingly forlorn and financially stricken Celtic, he was dismissed by the Parkhead club's beleaguered and inflexible board with the perennial question, 'When are you going back to Montreal, Fergus?'

With their persistent refusal to entertain his offers of assistance, which were largely viewed by the sitting directors as a threat to their own positions, McCann was becoming increasingly aware that the Parkhead club's board was out of its depth. He believed that the traditional idea of largely indolent custodian-directors, whose main role was to oversee a reliable and steady income from a captive audience of supporter-customers, was a dangerous anachronism, which could lead an organisation to the brink of ruin in the competitive world of commercialised sport in the 1990s. Football was changing, and despite the justifiable reservations that were held by many over the direction the modern game seemed to be taking, the Celtic board were effectively allowing the tide of commercialism to wash over them while never quite managing to learn how to swim in such troubled waters.

By 1992, McCann's frustration with the Parkhead executives was exacerbated by the determination of a majority of the senior figures to hold on to their posts due to their families' history of involvement with Celtic. Chairman Kevin Kelly and his younger cousin Michael were nephews of Sir Robert Kelly, who had served as chairman from 1947 until 1971 and been knighted after the club's European Cup win in Lisbon in 1967, while their grandfather was James Kelly, Sir Robert's father, Celtic's first-ever captain and another former chairman of the club. In addition, club secretary Christopher White, Celtic's largest individual shareholder, was the son of former chairman Desmond White, who succeeded Sir Robert in 1971, remaining in his post until his death in 1985, and the grandson of Tom White, the club's long-standing chairman from 1914 until 1947, who also served as head of the SFA from 1919 to 1927. Finally, stadium director Tom Grant was the great-grandson of James Grant, who was elected on to the board of the newly incorporated Celtic in April 1897. Although it was never the intention among Celtic's numerous and varied early movers and shakers that the club should become a dynastic affair, the Kellys and Whites, in particular, had over the years come to dominate the club's boardroom and they had also amassed a significant percentage of the company shares, which, as their determination to remain in their positions increased, even as the spectre of financial implosion loomed over Celtic Park, made them almost impossible to dislodge.

In many ways, Rangers were at the forefront of the developments that were taking place across British football at this time, with the increasing importance of financial power-brokers in the game leading to a new, more complicated relationship between clubs and their supporters. Even before Gazza's tears at Italia 90 and the formation of the breakaway English Premier League (EPL), which put the British game on a new commercial footing, the Ibrox club had been reorganised on a more businesslike structure, which involved cultivating relationships with financial institutions, chiefly the Bank of Scotland in Rangers' case, and recognising the importance of the power of the chequebook as the quickest and surest means to sporting success. Under the partnership of Marlborough and Holmes, the cosy cartel, operated with Celtic, of paying players relatively low wages and expecting them to get by on loyalty to the cause, was abandoned in favour of a more mercenary approach, and Rangers were now offering some of the best players in Britain, including the England captain Terry Butcher, some of the highest salaries available anywhere in the country.

Celtic initially responded slowly, but after defender Mick McCarthy was signed from Manchester City in May 1987 and put on £1,000 per week, becoming the best-paid player in the club's history, the Parkhead men subsequently went on to win a celebrated league and cup Double in their centenary year. The club failed to build on their success, however, with manager Billy McNeill later acknowledging his frustration over the refusal of the Celtic board – still debt-free at the time – to release more funds to invest in the team and, in the end, the Double of 1987/88 proved to be only a temporary interruption in Rangers' revival under Souness and the Ibrox side's gathering dominance of the Scottish domestic scene. The decline set in with startling alacrity; after taking seven points out of eight against Rangers in the centenary season, Celtic suffered 5-1 and 4-1 losses at Ibrox the following year, with midfielder Tommy Burns admitting that he had been lying awake on the night after the first heavy defeat, worried and relieved that his team hadn't been beaten by a wider margin, and that the record 7-1 scoreline between the sides, achieved by Celtic in the 1957/58 League Cup Final, hadn't been surpassed.

The Parkhead men eventually rallied to win a tense Scottish Cup Final over Souness's side, 1-0 at Hampden, thanks to a goal from Joe Miller, but when over the summer the club tried to flex their financial muscles once more and make a statement signing with the anticipated purchase of Maurice Johnston from Nantes for £1.2m, Celtic were outmanoeuvred again when the former Parkhead striker rebuffed his old employers at the last moment and decided, shortly after pledging his immediate future to the club, that he would in fact prefer to join Rangers, where a more lucrative contract was on offer.

To many, it was a shocking act of betrayal by the one-time Celtic idol, made particularly egregious by Johnston's professed love for his boyhood side, which included recent statements to the effect that there was no other team in Britain he could consider playing for, such was his emotional attachment to the

Parkhead club's cause. To others, however, it was simply a sign of the times. 'Mo got a million in his hand, he couldn't turn it down, says father,' explained *The Sun* some years later, while the *Daily Record* had previously noted that Souness's out-of-the-way home in Colinton, Edinburgh, vacated by the manager after the break-up of his marriage and which Johnston would now be occupying, 'comes complete with a tennis court, sauna, gymnasium, stables, impressive gardens and a trout stream'. The mansion would later be bought by the subsequently disgraced former knight of the realm, Fred Goodwin, during his heyday as the chief executive of the out-of-control Royal Bank of Scotland. Football players, it seemed, for so long considered to be working-class heroes of their local communities, were even by the late 1980s starting to inhabit an altogether different financial world from the supporters who traditionally idolised them.

Johnston had also claimed in the weeks leading up to the transfer and in his autobiography, co-authored with the journalist Chick Young and published in October 1988, that he could never have anything to do with Rangers due to the ongoing issue of anti-Catholicism at Ibrox. This malaise was perhaps most apparent in Rangers' long-standing exclusionary employment policy, the controversial embargo on Catholic players at the club, which Johnston himself had just spectacularly ended. Footballers' autobiographies are usually an outlet where players can get some issue off their chest, speak honestly for a pleasant change and dispense with the media training that often characterises so much of the jejune platitudes that are routinely uttered by sportsmen in post-match interviews or during formally arranged press conferences. Free from any duties and responsibilities to the club that employed him, Johnston certainly wasn't afraid to speak plainly in his book and let his feelings be known on certain matters, for example on Glasgow's divided footballing loyalties.

'Let me just spell out where I stand here,' the player took the trouble to explain. 'I am a Celtic man through and through and so I dislike Rangers because they are a force in Scottish football and therefore a threat to the club I love. But more than that, I hate the religious policy which they maintain. Why won't they sign a Roman Catholic? I hate religious bigotry … The whole thing is just crazy.' By contrast, Johnston's feelings for Celtic could be summed up in another one of the player's heartfelt sentiments. 'I nurse a dream deep inside me and it is this: that as I take my last breath on this earth my memory bank will be filled with pictures of that day I made my debut for Celtic,' vowed the striker, never one to miss an opportunity to indulge in such hyperbole when it came to expressing his feelings for the Parkhead club. Earlier in the book, however, in an apparent jokey aside, Johnston had offered the view, 'I might even agree to become Rangers' first Catholic if they paid me £1 million CASH [his capitalisation] and bought me Stirling Castle to live in!' In the end, metaphorically at least, given the plushness of Souness's Colinton residence, that's almost exactly what he got.

While it's clear that the Johnston case may have been exceptional, it was also becoming increasingly evident by now that, when it came to matters financial, the Parkhead board seemed curiously encumbered and were unwilling or unable to match the wages on offer to one of their former players by free-spending Rangers. In addition to the failure to agree a deal with Johnston, Celtic also lost, over the course of the following campaign, both their captain and vice-captain, Roy Aitken and Tommy Burns, mainstays of the team since the 1970s, leaving 25-year-old Paul McStay as the club's longest-serving player.

The cumulative effect saw the Parkhead men finish in a lowly fifth position in 1990, a season that included 12 defeats and a total of 15 matches without a goal scored. Celtic did, however, manage to reach the Scottish Cup Final again, eliminating Rangers along the way, but after a goalless draw with Aberdeen at Hampden, McNeill's side lost 9-8 in a penalty shoot-out, with Dutch goalkeeper Theo Snelders making the decisive save from Anton Rogan's spot kick.

In response, over the summer Celtic signed Martin Hayes from Arsenal for £650,000 in what looked an intriguing move, but turned out to be an unmitigated disaster, with the Englishman making only 12 appearances for the Parkhead side and departing 18 months later on a free transfer after a succession of injuries and a series of poor displays for McNeill's men. Charlie Nicholas returned to the club from Aberdeen and proved to be a useful option for the manager at least over the short term, while the youthful John Collins arrived from Hibernian but was said to have needed a period of adjustment for his skills to translate into an effective weapon for his new team. Rangers were not exactly trembling in their boots; the only highlight of another abject, trophy-less campaign for the Parkhead club came after back-to-back wins over their city rivals in the Scottish Cup and league on 17 and 24 March, with the first victory made all the more gleeful for the Celtic Park crowd by the sight of three Rangers players being ordered off, as the home side raced into a 2-0 lead, in a match that became known among Celtic fans as the 'St Patrick's Day massacre'. Anticipating a similar outcome the following week, the fans were able to produce their own red cards and display them to Scott Nisbet, as the defender became the fourth Rangers player to be dismissed against Celtic in a week, with the Parkhead men this time notching up a 3-0 win. Once again, however, the supporters' joy was cut short as Celtic lost 4-2 to Motherwell in a replayed Scottish Cup semi-final, a match that they had twice led, with the Lanarkshire side going on to lift the trophy after a memorable 4-3 extra-time victory over Dundee United in the final.

The unmistakeable sense of stagnation at Parkhead around this time was complicated considerably in January 1990 with the publication of the Taylor Report, commissioned in the wake of the Hillsborough disaster the previous April when 96 Liverpool fans lost their lives in a devastating crush on an overcrowded and poorly policed section of terracing at the start of an FA Cup semi-final against Nottingham Forest. The report called for top-flight football grounds around Britain to be converted to all-seater stadiums, a recommendation that was quickly accepted by the government, and the requirement for the ageing terraces to be torn down and replaced with new seated stands was universally adopted, with a deadline imposed for the upgrades to be completed by the start of the 1994/95 season.

It was an unwelcome development and a shock to the system for Celtic; aside from the main stand, constructed in the early 1970s, the interior of the ground had remained largely unaltered for decades, with former chairman Desmond White noting, perhaps with a degree of truth, but also betraying the lack of vision that came to characterise his and subsequent Celtic boards, 'Our supporters prefer to stand.' With its vast sprawling terraces, Celtic Park had been compared to 'paradise' in the 1890s when it was first constructed, a nickname that had stuck, but 100 years later the Parkhead stadium was indisputably showing signs of age and had been dubbed, ironically, 'the finest 19th century ground in Britain'.

Celtic's response, in May 1990, was to co-opt on to the board Michael Kelly and Brian Dempsey, men with acknowledged expertise in, respectively, public relations and property development, in what was described at the time as a 'dream ticket' move by the club's board. It proved to be anything but. Kelly was a former Lord Provost, or mayor, of Glasgow, best known for bestowing the freedom of the city on Nelson Mandela, the leader of the ANC in South Africa, who was still at the time imprisoned on Robben Island, and for his work in developing the successful 'Glasgow's Miles Better' campaign, which had been devised by one of the city's leading advertising agencies and inspired by the similar 'I Love New York' promotion of the late 1970s. Featuring children's author Roger Hargreaves's Mr Happy character encircled by a neat, ambiguous slogan – was it Glasgow Smiles Better? – the campaign had helped to transform the city's unhealthy image by the early 1980s and reinvigorate its declining economy.

Kelly was also a former Labour councillor, a Justice of the Peace and a lecturer in economics at Strathclyde University, as well as an honorary graduate and former rector of Glasgow University, who had been awarded a CBE, which, in addition to his PhD, had one wag observing around the time of his appointment to the Celtic board, 'The list of letters after his name stretched halfway across the foot of his company notepaper.' He had later formed his own PR firm, Michael Kelly Associates, and it was hoped that his knowledge and experience could similarly help to market the flagging Parkhead club and in particular portray its unpopular board in a more favourable light, not just with the media, but also with the club's increasingly frustrated fans.

Dempsey, a very different character, was the son of the Labour MP, Jimmy Dempsey, a former haulage firm clerk who had held off a Tory surge across Scotland in the 1950s to narrowly retain the seat of Coatbridge and Airdrie for the party, defeating his Conservative, or 'Unionist', opponent, Catherine Morton, sister of the Rangers director and legendary winger Alan Morton, by fewer than 800 votes at the 1959 general election and eventually going on to hold the seat until his death in 1982. Despite being something of an outsider at Parkhead, in that he was neither a scion of one of the established families nor a former Celtic employee, it was intended that Dempsey, who had made his fortune in property and construction, would provide assistance to the club over its dilemma with the condition of the stadium in the post-Hillsborough era. Following their appointment, a photo of Kelly and Dempsey in an embrace, holding a cake and a placard reading 'Celtic's miles better' was circulated among the press, although as Matt McGlone of *Celts for Change* later noted, 'I bet neither of them has that picture on their mantelpiece at home anymore.'

Almost as soon as he became involved with Celtic, Dempsey came forward with an ambitious plan to deal with the stadium issue by relocating the club to a new, purpose-built ground in the Robroyston area of the city on a site where he happened to have a stake in the ownership of the land. It soon became clear, however, that the two nominated directors didn't get along and, using Dempsey's alleged conflict of interests over the proposed new stadium site as his pretext, Kelly, in partnership with club secretary Christopher White, engineered his colleague's removal from the board just five months later at the club's AGM in October, when Dempsey's proposed ratification as a director was voted down.

The attempted move against Dempsey was originally defeated by shareholders on a show of hands, 17 votes to 13, but

White then called for a rarely used poll vote, a system that put the decision in the hands of the largest individual shareholders, and when the auditors had completed their calculations the decision not to ratify was carried by 733 votes to 472 with 20 abstentions. It was an unusual, rarely used strategy, but White was within his rights as the club's largest shareholder to call for the poll vote, the same method that Bill Struth had employed in 1947 when he successfully removed Ibrox chairman Jimmy Bowie from his post. The defeated Dempsey was forced to withdraw and consider his options, but as he gathered allies to his cause over the next few years, frequently appearing at supporters' rallies as an outspoken critic of the board and an advocate of regime change at Parkhead, it soon became clear that, in the struggle for control of Celtic Football Club, the battle lines had been drawn.

Shortly after Dempsey's departure, moves were undertaken to make Celtic a more commercially savvy operation with the appointment of Terry Cassidy to the newly created position of chief executive officer at the club in January 1991. Cassidy had experience in successfully recapitalising struggling companies by increasing their turnover, including in the often volatile newspaper industry, while his other career pursuits had included spells as a nightclub bouncer and, briefly in his teens, a professional football player. It was never a match made in heaven, however; one of Cassidy's first acts as CEO was to advise Celtic's bankers, Bank of Scotland, not to increase the club's overdraft as he saw no viable business plan by which the money could be repaid.

This earned him the mistrust of his employers right from the start, and Cassidy became an even more controversial figure after a memo that he had written, outlining the best way to handle the dismissal of manager Billy McNeill, including a draft press release, was leaked to the media and reported in *The Sun*. McNeill subsequently described Cassidy as a 'thoroughly unpleasant, untrustworthy, overbearing, offensive individual', while director Jimmy Farrell noted that he was 'the master of the gratuitous insult'. Another executive figure at the club, stadium manager Tom Grant, was at one point almost reduced to tears by Cassidy, as the tensions in the boardroom reached breaking point, and he had to be talked out of resigning his directorship. Following McNeill's eventual dismissal, Cassidy then fell out with his replacement, Liam Brady, after the Irishman had been in his post for all of one game. Brady had given the board an ultimatum regarding Cassidy shortly after his appointment in the summer of 1991, but when the board stood by their controversial CEO, the club's inexperienced new manager backed down, possibly undermining his position and authority right from the start.

In another episode, Cassidy quarrelled with the club's shirt sponsor, the garage dealership Peoples Ford, owned by prominent Celtic-supporting businessman Brian Gilda, with the result that the Parkhead club was left without the income generated by the appearance of a sponsor's logo on their kit for a year, although as fanzine *Not the View* later noted, 'We had a season of unpolluted hoops. The press attempted to stir this up, but were oblivious to the fact that for once the fans were pleased with the board's incompetence. Shirt sales went through the roof. It was a move of unintentional marketing genius.' Cassidy was himself eventually sacked in October 1992, which proved to be the prelude to a wrongful dismissal suit, played out in a very public and damaging court case. It was obvious to everyone, including the board, that change was required at Celtic, but what seemed less clear was the directors' ability to implement the necessary solutions effectively, and with Cassidy's appointment, in hindsight, it appears that they were groping about in the dark, trying to adapt to the changes and developments in the modern game but never fully embracing or understanding how football was evolving. As Brian Wilson noted in *Celtic: The Official History*, 'Some of the appointments made by the old regime as it sought to shore up its position merely poured fuel on the fire,' while Cassidy himself later remarked, perhaps in recognition of the chaos that was enveloping Celtic Park at the time, 'If I had reported what happened at board meetings, no one would have believed me. They would have said Basil Fawlty wrote that.'

Brady, the graceful former Arsenal and Juventus midfielder, tried to encourage his Celtic team to play a more fluid, technical game, after he took over from McNeill as the club's manager in the summer of 1991. With Paul McStay so often the talisman in midfield, alongside the fast-developing John Collins, Brady's side was pleasing on the eye and, initially at least, appreciated by supporters, especially when the attacking style brought about some eye-catching results, such as a 3-2 aggregate win over Bundesliga stalwarts Cologne in the UEFA Cup, achieved at Parkhead on the back of a 2-0 first-leg deficit. Early in the previous season, however, Brady's first at the club, Celtic had suffered a humiliating 5-1 defeat at the hands of the unheralded Swiss outfit Neuchâtel Xamax in the same competition, with Egyptian striker Hossam Hassan helping himself to four goals in one of the worst defeats on the Continent in the club's history. The result couldn't be retrieved in the return leg at Celtic Park despite a 1-0 win, after Celtic's hopes of an unlikely comeback were dashed when an early penalty awarded to the home side was squandered by Nicholas. Celtic in truth were a contrary team under Brady, and for all the highs, such as Cologne, the occasional win against Rangers and the attractive style of football, there were also the lows, including the baffling signings of players such as Tony Cascarino and Stuart Slater.

Brady's appointment represented new territory for the Parkhead side in that the Irishman was the first Celtic manager never to have previously played for the club, the first with no managerial experience since Willy Maley in 1897 and, significantly, the first to have his employment ratified with a formal contract, which reportedly saw him earn double what his predecessor, McNeill, had been taking home. His initial signings, expensively assembled, included Gary Gillespie, an injury-prone defender, Gordon Marshall, a second-choice goalkeeper, as well as Cascarino, a startlingly ineffective forward, and with none of the new players able to make a meaningful contribution to the team's cause, Celtic's off-field position worsened as Brady's spending, without really strengthening the side, helped to push the club's overdraft up by over £2m towards a looming total of £5m, the agreed limit.

If the spending strategy was an attempt by the board to move with the times, it ultimately ended in failure, as Walter Smith's solid Rangers side kept Brady's more fluent team at arm's length, most notably in the Scottish Cup semi-final of 1992, when the Light Blues somehow managed to emerge victorious from the Hampden encounter, despite taking a pummelling on the night from Brady's men. And with Celtic eventually finishing in third place in the league, behind Rangers and Hearts, progress on the field at Parkhead was vanishingly difficult to detect. The campaign ended on another downbeat note when Brady's side, needing only a draw in the final fixture of the season to secure the runners-up spot, lost 2-1 at home to Hibernian, throwing the club's European aspirations into jeopardy. Only the fractious situation in the Balkans allowed Celtic a reprieve, after Scotland were awarded an extra UEFA Cup place at the expense of war-torn Yugoslavia.

On the day before the ultimately forlorn Scottish Cup semi-final with Rangers, a tumultuous EGM took place at Celtic Park at which the former director Brian Dempsey and his allies, who he had been gathering to his cause since his acrimonious departure from the club in October 1990, successfully blocked a bid by the Kelly-White board to remove fellow directors James Farrell and Tom Grant from their posts. Farrell, Dempsey's lawyer, had originally been appointed to the Celtic board as far back as 1964, but in recent years he had been a forthright critic, and at the EGM he spoke passionately about what he believed to be the wrong direction the club was now pursuing, reserving particular condemnation for the role currently being played by Michael Kelly in the club's affairs. 'All that I have done … is resisted Michael Kelly, because he is the man who, in my view, should be ejected from this board,' Farrell declared. 'If I am voted off today, those directors who are with him, unless he changes his tune completely, will find him a most uneasy bedfellow, and they will not rest in their beds at night for imagining what he is up to.' Noting that Kelly was being paid a handsome fee by the club for his role as a PR consultant, Farrell also lamented how Celtic's image and reputation were presently being dragged through the dirt, in noted contrast to how the club had been perceived in earlier times: 'In my view the public relations of this football club in the past 18 months or two years have never been lower … Celtic were always a class act. Celtic were something different, where the directors and shareholders of Celtic Football Club were a fine body of men and women, and even on bad days when we were not doing so well on the field everybody throughout the length and breadth of Scotland, and internationally, respected the Celtic for being a class apart.'

The EGM, the club's first since 1948, had originally been requisitioned by the board in a bid to try to outmanoeuvre Dempsey and his band of supporters, led by financial adviser David Low and by now known collectively as 'the rebels', who had for some time been agitating for a takeover of the club and demanding seats on the board. Recently, the rebels had been buying up shares and acquiring proxies that were held in far-flung corners of the globe by, in many cases, descendants of Celtic's early stakeholders at the time of the club's foundation in 1888 and incorporation in 1897. Because Celtic was a private limited company and the shares were not traded on the open market, nobody appeared to know their real value and, in theory at least, the board was able to block a transfer of shares to anyone they considered unsuitable.

Nevertheless, orchestrated by Low, and using former European Cup winner Jim Craig as a handy agent, the rebels had tracked down and persuaded a significant number of people to part with their shares or, in case of the board's refusal to accept them, to offer their proxies, while others, such as wealthy Canadian businessman Jim Doherty, refused to sell but agreed to join the rebels' cause. Although they still didn't have the numbers to pursue their plans for a takeover of the club, the Dempsey-led rebels were now in a position, thanks to a successful writ obtained from the Court of Session in Edinburgh that prevented the owners of partly paid shares from using their votes at the EGM, to block the board from removing Farrell. Stadium director Tom Grant meanwhile, a relatively young man with a recent mortgage and two adopted young children, appeared to waver over the direction of his allegiances and his indecision was exploited by Michael Kelly, who persuaded him to sign up with the board at the last minute, at which point the vote to remove him became a merely procedural issue.

The EGM also saw the ratification of the appointment to the board of David Smith, who had been named the club's finance director the previous month and who was now also confirmed in his role as the company's vice-chairman. Smith was a long-standing friend and associate of club secretary Christopher White who had previously been involved in the multibillion-pound acquisition of the Gateway supermarket group, the biggest business deal in European corporate history at the time, and it was hoped that he would bring some much-needed experience and business acumen to the board, particularly in view of the club's escalating debt and the increasing doubts over the feasibility of the proposed new stadium project. Originally from Brechin, but now based in Fulham, Smith had sound Celtic-supporting credentials, travelling up from London on a fortnightly basis to watch the team, but his appointment split the board down the middle, with directors Farrell, Grant and former chairman Jack McGinn all opposing his original nomination and appearing sympathetic to the rebels' cause. White and Michael Kelly, meanwhile, saw Smith as a crucial weapon in their efforts to quash the rebellious faction, and it was only with the casting vote of chairman Kevin Kelly, which tipped the balance in favour of the traditional families, that Smith's nomination was eventually approved.

One of Smith's first acts as finance director, following the ratification of his appointment at the EGM, was to instigate a formal agreement among the board members not to sell their shares to outside parties. With rumours of a potential takeover escalating and having witnessed how the energy and determination of the rebels had scored them such noted successes at the EGM, the directors, working late into the night following the gruelling, eight-hour meeting, put their names to a legally binding shareholders' agreement, or pact, which was intended to preserve the status quo in the boardroom and protect their positions at the club. Under the terms of the pact, which was established through a company called Celtic Nominees Ltd, none of the signatories could legally sell his shares to a third party without first offering them to the other directors. Valid for ten years and requiring the members to vote together on all issues at board meetings, the watertight pact was an unashamedly defensive move by the controlling families on the board, motivated by self-preservation and designed to stop the ongoing attempts by Dempsey and his allies to buy up shares and gain control of the club. With the nominees' combined portfolios accounting for 60 per cent of the club's total holdings, in the short term at least, the pact succeeded in its primary aim, with Michael Kelly observing, 'The shareholders agreement dealt effectively with the takeover tactics of the rebels ... We had slammed the door firmly in their faces and had locked a large amount of their money into a hopeless minority position.'

The nominees were Kevin and Michael Kelly, White, Smith, despite the fact that the new vice-chairman wasn't yet a shareholder, and Grant, although the stadium manager's position continued to be unclear. After seeming to side with the rebels, Grant was persuaded to sign up to the pact by Michael Kelly, but strangely, in response to the failed attempt by the board to remove fellow director Farrell, he noted after the EGM, 'What we have done is try to convince the Kellys and Whites that the others will not go away. They cannot continue with the attitude that it is my ball and you will play my game.' Grant also ratified the appointment of Smith at the EGM, a move he had originally opposed, but he refuted the allegation of flip-flopping, telling the club's in-house publication, the *Celtic View*, 'I do not accept that I jumped ship or took sides in the votes. But for my share of the votes neither David Smith nor Jimmy Farrell would now be directors. I voted for unity and, I believe, for the benefit of Celtic Football Club.' With Grant now signed up to the pact, however, the result was a tortuous stalemate, which rumbled on for a further two years and which propped up the incumbent board almost to the point of the club's insolvency.

Michael Kelly's claim that the outcome of the EGM and the implementation of the pact represented a 'permanent settlement', however, proved to be inaccurate. The *Celtic View* also carried quotes at this time from the other established directors, who lined up to confirm the settled view of how peace and unity had broken out at Celtic Park, when in reality, despite the short-term effectiveness of the pact, the rebels' successes at the EGM had given them confidence and credibility, with Dempsey informing the *Daily Telegraph*, 'The movement towards change is unstoppable now.' Perhaps there was some justification in Dempsey's optimistic tone, because behind the scenes the rebels had been in secret negotiations with another wealthy stakeholder who had been keeping an eye on what was happening at Celtic, and who had his own agenda and ideas for pushing through reform at the club.

In the days running up to the EGM, the press had introduced the Scottish footballing public to Fergus McCann, dispatching their intrepid reporters out to doorstep the Canadian businessman at his hotel in Glasgow and splashing their profiles across the tabloid back pages. McCann, it was revealed, had his own plans for the future of Celtic, which involved injecting £17m of new capital into the club – £5m from fans who would take up shares in a rights issue, £5m from outside investors and £7m of his own money through a separate company called Celtic's Future plc. It was a similar package to what McCann had offered back in April 1989, where minutes from Celtic board meetings at the time state: 'Proposals put forward by Fergus McCann to provide finance for various capital expenditures … were unanimously rejected by the Directors'; and then again in August of the same year: 'Mr McCann's latest proposals were discussed and it was hoped that this was a final discussion on the subject. Latest proposals were rejected by Directors.' Despite these dismissals, McCann was still sounding conciliatory and hopeful that the sitting directors would see sense and approve his plan for a rights issue, which would expand the company's meagre share capital of just 20,000 £1 shares, although such a move would inevitably dilute their own holdings. He denied that his intention was to oust the incumbent board members, telling the media, 'Current shareholders would benefit from that [a new rights issue]. They would become a smaller number of a larger shareholding.' While confirming that he had held talks with some of the rebels, he was at pains to stress his independence and his reluctance to take sides, confirming that, although he was in Glasgow, he would not be attending the EGM.

Perhaps McCann was offering the board one last chance to accept his proposals for fresh investment in the club because it seems that, by 1991, he was already in a tentative alliance with Dempsey, as the Canadian later admitted: 'We became a group at that time. I believed that I needed to work with Brian Dempsey because he was the director who had been removed by the families. He had also established a connection with the supporters.' The rebels, for their part, now that they had been effectively blocked by the five-man pact, began to pin their hopes on McCann as the man with the financial clout to deliver a knockout blow to the existing board. The alliance seemed to be confirmed when, shortly after the EGM, the club's new vice-chairman David Smith met with McCann, but reported back to the board that all offers of financial assistance from the Canadian had now been withdrawn.

Fergus John McCann was born in Stirling on 26 February 1941, the son of the headmaster of the local Catholic secondary school, St Modan's, which the young Fergus attended in the 1950s. Around the same time, his father, Allen, started taking him to see Celtic matches in Glasgow, but with the McCann family living in Kilsyth, a town which, according to its Wikipedia page, 'has a long tradition of radical protestantism' as well as a junior league team called Kilsyth Rangers, it was perhaps unsurprising that Fergus's Celtic-supporting fervour was directed towards the nearby village of Croy, a largely Catholic mining enclave in North Lanarkshire, where, still in his teens, he became treasurer and bus convener of the local Celtic supporters' club. After finishing his education with an accountancy degree from Strathclyde University, he accepted a position with a small firm in Glasgow, but still he seemed restless, even trying his hand as a sports journalist in September 1963 when he reported back from Switzerland for *The Herald* on Celtic's comfortable 5-1 win over FC Basel in the Cup Winners' Cup, the club's first-ever victory in European competition. Later in the year, McCann left Scotland altogether, emigrating to Canada, where he initially found work with accountants Deloitte and Touche (then known as Touche Ross & Co.) and then Seagram's, the drinks conglomerate, at their head office in

Montreal. He was acquiring, as his career progressed, valuable lessons and experience in the key business skills of marketing and financial management, and it wasn't long before the exiled young Scot began to venture out on his own.

After tuning in from afar on an old Grundig shortwave radio to the BBC's coverage of Celtic's victory over Inter Milan in the 1967 European Cup Final, McCann sensed an opportunity five years later when the two teams met again in the semi-final of the same competition. Both clubs by this time were giants of the European game, and McCann believed that there would be interest in the match not only from the large number of expatriate Celtic fans in Canada, but also from the country's sizeable Italian community. With the tie finely poised after the first leg finished goalless at the San Siro, McCann bought airtime to cover the return match at Celtic Park, hiring out Toronto's historic multipurpose sports venue, Maple Leaf Gardens, and selling seats to a delayed, closed-circuit transmission of the match.

McCann had secured the rights for the broadcast from Celtic chairman Desmond White for the reasonable fee of £300, but unfortunately for the budding 31-year-old entrepreneur, neither team managed to find the net over a gruelling 90 minutes of attritional football. When the game subsequently extended into extra time and then a penalty shoot-out, which eventually saw substitute Dixie Deans's wayward spot kick deny Celtic the opportunity of a third appearance in the final in six seasons, McCann realised to his horror that he would be obliged to carry the cost of the required additional satellite time at a rate of $16,000 per hour. With the anticipated interest from the Italian community failing to materialise after what was perceived as a negative result for Inter in the first leg, which left McCann well short of his target of 12,000 paying customers, it seemed highly likely that the young émigré's fledgling business career would be strangled at birth.

The lessons of his failed venture into sports broadcasting were not lost on McCann, as he later admitted. 'The school of hard knocks gives you the best MBA you can get,' he told journalist Kevin McCarra. 'You have to be able to take the knocks. Not many people can handle that, and I found that I could. The short, sharp lesson lasting three weeks in 1972 I value now very highly.' When he did eventually get back on his feet, McCann reinvented himself as a provider of golf tourism, chartering Boeing 707s to fly wealthy North Americans to their dream holidays in Scotland, where as part of a package deal including flights, meals and accommodation, McCann's customers would be able to play rounds at famous Scottish golf courses such as St Andrews and Royal Troon. The business thrived, with McCann's astute marketing skills, honed at Seagram's, as well as an emphasis on customer service and attention to detail, allowing him to gradually build up a healthy database of repeat clients among North America's more well-heeled golfing aficionados. By the time he sold his company in the mid-1980s to Michael Ashcroft, later Lord Ashcroft, the controversial Tory peer, McCann had amassed a tidy if somewhat modest fortune, in strictly business terms, of around £15m, money which he was now free to invest in other projects and opportunities, including in a certain struggling football club on the other side of the Atlantic.

In many ways, as he sought to pursue his interest in Celtic, McCann proved to be an easy target for certain sections of the press, some of whom went to great lengths to rummage around in his background and lifestyle choices in order to dig for dirt on the 50-something bachelor, turning up almost nothing that could be considered worthy of tabloid attention on the clean-living businessman. Others would label him an eccentric, with his transatlantic accent and his brusque, idiosyncratic manner, which led one Canadian journalist to observe of McCann's abruptness, 'He makes getting straight to the point sound like procrastination.' Later, in a profile piece for *The Independent* in November 1993, as English-based newspapers at last began to take an interest in the off-field events at Celtic Park, McCann was labelled 'a small balding man with a ... fierce, corrugated expression'. Marvelling at his almost neurotic attention to detail, the correspondent then went on to describe how McCann, while being interviewed for the feature, chastised a waitress at the Glasgow Hilton for not serving him his breakfast in the correct manner – 'that's four and a half minutes from *cold* water' was apparently how McCann liked his eggs in the morning.

As a boy he also came into contact with the much older Jimmy Farrell, the future Celtic director, who admired McCann's father, but found the young Fergus 'a very cheeky upstart ... he was full of ability but he was also full of habits I would not agree with; just his way of dealing with people'. These and other criticisms relating to his mannerisms and interpersonal skills, justified as they often were, may have led many to underestimate McCann and overlook his qualities and experiences as an astute financier who had built himself up from nothing, enduring occasional hardship along the way, before selling up and emerging as a wealthy gentleman of leisure, involved in charity work and overseeing the activities of his Bermuda-based investment company Firstgreen Ltd, a name which reflected McCann's interest in both golf and Celtic rather neatly, it seemed. Arguably, McCann's key strength, however, lay in his close personal attachment to the Celtic cause and, unusually perhaps among the 90s glut of preening football executives, his first-hand understanding of the emotions that the club was capable of arousing among its enormous, glory-starved fanbase. At a time when others could only see a crippled, directionless institution, once great but now struggling to cope with dwindling attendances and a forlorn capacity for often heartbreaking failure, McCann had the intuition and presence of mind to glimpse a far brighter future for the Parkhead club.

Meanwhile, an important part of David Smith's remit in his new capacity as finance director and vice-chairman of Celtic Football Club was to take forward the board's renewed bid to relocate the stadium to a 30-hectare site on Bogleshole Road, Cambuslang, two miles to the east of Parkhead, a plan that was formally revealed with much fanfare in the *Celtic View* in April 1992. Under the headline 'World's best stadium for the world's best fans', the announcement detailed proposals for the construction of a new, purpose-built 52,000-capacity all-seater stadium with a circular 'space-age' roof and up to 100 executive boxes, which would sit alongside an array of other facilities and commercial enterprises. Described as 'a major property development which will itself contribute to the regeneration of the East End of Glasgow', the site was intended to have 'an economic life of its own beyond Saturday afternoon' and would include, in addition to the stadium as part of an incorporated 'support village', an eight-screen cinema complex, a 30-lane ten-pin bowling alley, a retractable stage, drive-through fast food restaurants, a museum, car showrooms and shops, commercial and office units, a 200-bedroom hotel as well as something called 'integrated sports and leisure facilities'. With construction due to begin by the end of the year, the initial phase of the project required £26m to be raised for a stadium with two

16,000-capacity stands running along the touchlines, which would be ready for the start of the 1994 season, with a further 10,000 seats at each end to be added at a later date.

Perhaps understandably there was scepticism about the Cambuslang project right from the start, with chairman Kevin Kelly admitting that planning permission was still required for the new site and that, more significantly, funding for the complex hadn't yet been secured, with total costs expected to reach £100m and the deadline for compliance with the requirements of the Taylor Report just over two years away. Regardless, Kelly was sounding bullish when he took a snipe at the club's critics, claiming, 'For far too long the Celtic board has faced a non-stop barrage of ill-considered criticism from uninformed people of dubious motivation ... We promised that they [the fans] would be told of our plans first and we are now delivering on that promise.' For some, Kelly was sounding a little too self-congratulatory, when all the board had announced was a set of unfunded and unapproved plans for a new ground, which the chairman conceded that Celtic, as the so-called 'anchor tenant' of the new facility, would not even own.

Veteran director Jimmy Farrell had already expressed his concerns about the project at the EGM in March, claiming that Superstadia Ltd, the firm of consultants whose plan had been accepted by the board, had failed to go into sufficient detail over the feasibility of the project, which had yet to be subjected to independent scrutiny. In a letter to shareholders, he warned that if the scheme backfired or ran into financial problems it could 'lead to the possible liquidation of Celtic'. Regardless, the board ploughed ahead with their plans over the next few years until, perhaps inevitably, the project stalled and became beset with problems, including claims that the proposed site was contaminated with toxic chemicals and susceptible to flooding from the nearby River Clyde.

* * *

With so many unwelcome distractions going on in the background, Liam Brady and his Celtic players might have been forgiven for taking their eye off the ball and allowing all the speculation and issues around the periphery of the club to permeate the dressing room and have a negative effect on the team's performances on the field. Following the defeat to Rangers in the Scottish Cup semi-final and the completion of another trophy-less campaign, however, the manager was sounding upbeat at the start of the new season when he admitted that he was at last, after a lengthy induction process, adjusting to the unique world of Scottish football. Things improved marginally for Brady in his second term at the club as an early ten-game unbeaten run initially offered hope of a credible title challenge from the Parkhead side. Forward Andy Payton was signed from Middlesbrough and looked a capable striker, but it quickly became clear that fellow acquisition Stuart Slater, a former client of Brady when he was working as a player's agent, who was purchased from West Ham for a club record £1.7m, would struggle to adapt to the Scottish game. The diminutive winger never managed to find his feet in Glasgow, with the manager eventually forced to admit that Slater's move to such a high-profile club as Celtic had shattered his fragile confidence and, in all probability, ruined his career.

In Europe, there was the euphoria of Cologne, but hopes of further progress in the competition were dashed by Borussia Dortmund, who inflicted home and away defeats on Celtic for the first time in the Parkhead club's history. The team's domestic form eventually collapsed, with consecutive home losses to Hibernian and Partick Thistle in September coming on top of a semi-final defeat to Aberdeen in the Skol (League) Cup. Brady's side eventually limped home in third position once more, with the team's problems summed up by a clearly exasperated manager following another unlucky loss at Ibrox, 1-0 on 2 January 1993, who reflected after the game: 'The team was magnificent; that's the way football should be played – apart from putting the ball in the net.' Commenting on the gap between the sides that had opened up at the top of the league table, a crestfallen Brady was forced to concede, 'As regards us and the championship, I think the challenge is over.' When Celtic subsequently lost to Falkirk in the Scottish Cup the following month, the Parkhead side was left without a trophy to compete for with still almost four months of the season to play, a position the club hadn't found itself in since the early 1950s.

When the summer eventually arrived, Brady moved to shake up his backroom team by adding former Celtic players Tom McAdam and Frank Connor to his coaching staff and bringing in former Scotland international forward Joe Jordan as his assistant. The plan was to have Jordan take care of coaching and training the players during the week, while Brady assumed a more distant role as an overseer and arbitrator, still in overall charge but retaining a more aloof presence until matchdays. The restructuring of the management team at the club was immediately hailed by chairman Kevin Kelly as a key development that would 'see Celtic back at the top of Scottish football, and hopefully Europe as well'. The new arrangements didn't meet with universal approval in the boardroom, however, as Kelly's cousin, Michael, immediately moved to dismiss Brady, after the manager was hauled in front of the directors and asked to outline his future plans for the team, although the idea wasn't supported at the time.

Perhaps the directors should have paid more attention to Michael Kelly's suggestion, as the season got off to a tortuously slow start for Celtic, with only the form and energy of Pat McGinlay, signed from Hibernian in the summer for £525,000, offering any encouragement, as Brady's team won only two of their first ten league fixtures. In addition, on 22 September, Celtic lost the Skol Cup semi-final 1-0 to a Rangers team who, once again, just as in the Scottish Cup semi-final the previous March, played much of the game with ten men after Huistra was ordered off early in the second half following a confrontation with Boyd. This time, however, Celtic were denied even the consolation of glorious failure, with the manager admitting after the game that his team were going nowhere in the match and that the performance of his players was feckless and uninspired.

The fans had finally run out of patience with Brady, something the manager was intelligent enough to detect, and it seemed that the writing was on the wall when Celtic travelled to Perth for a midweek fixture on 6 October and lost 2-1 to lowly St Johnstone. On the same night, Rangers, who were defending a Treble but who had also made a sluggish start to the new campaign, lost 2-1 at home to Motherwell, meaning that Celtic were still in touch with their old rivals and only four points behind early league leaders Hibernian. Brady's mind was made up, however, and shortly after the team bus arrived back in Glasgow the manager offered his resignation to Kevin Kelly, which was immediately accepted by the chairman.

The board would have been grateful and relieved that, in the end, Brady did the honourable thing and stepped down from his post of his own volition. The Irishman was the first manager in Celtic's history to have signed a formal contract of employment, so to have removed him against his wishes would have been both messy and expensive. The board's problems were becoming increasingly apparent to everyone involved in Scottish football and, following his departure, Brady cited his inability to shield his squad of players from the progressively worsening off-field distractions as an important contributing factor in his decision to quit. With Brady gone, Joe Jordan took training the following day and then decided that he would follow his boss out of the door, claiming that he was unwilling to step into the manager's shoes after only being appointed as an assistant that summer, but perhaps learning in the meantime that the board had no intention of promoting him, after the club's pursuit of Stoke City manager Lou Macari became public.

By the time of Saturday's home game against Dundee, first-team coach Frank Connor was virtually the last man standing, and he oversaw a 2-1 victory for his charges in what, incredibly, was Celtic's first home win of the season. The match was played out in a surreal atmosphere in front of fewer than 17,000 supporters as the organised protests by the fans began to gather momentum, with many expressing vociferous opposition to the board before and throughout the course of the game, much to the consternation of the watching press. 'I have never seen anger like Saturday's from the fans,' Alex Cameron subsequently observed in the *Daily Record*. 'Banners fluttered around the ground demanding resignations. When there was a lull on the park, groups pointed to the directors box shouting "Sack the board",' the veteran tabloid commentator continued. Jack Stewart, writing in *The Independent*, opined, 'People like to say that Celtic are a family club ... Here is a family like the Macbeths or the Lears ... The fans are at war with the board, and the directors ... are at odds with each other.'

Matters came to a head at another momentous EGM, this time held on 26 November 1993, when Fergus McCann and his allies effectively went all in to try to persuade the besieged directors, still stubbornly bound together by their notorious voting pact, to accept the offer of fresh investment that was on the table and allow a rights issue to broaden the ownership of the club. The meeting had been requisitioned the previous month, at the club's stormy AGM, held just two days after Brady's resignation, when directors were jeered as they tried to enter Celtic Park and were confronted with banners, some of which, as witnessed by the media, were still on display the following day at the Dundee game. By now, the rebels and their growing band of associates had switched tactics and were trying to loosen the board's control of the club, not through numbers, which were still stacked against them due to the watertight pact, but by an emotional appeal to the shareholders' judgement and common sense, as they waved millions of pounds in front of the directors of what was, it seemed indisputably clear to everyone by this stage, a desperately struggling institution.

Celtic at the time were still a fairly small, privately run company, whose main fiscal priority down the decades had been to break even over the course of a season, and then roll forward into the next campaign, year after year, in a relatively steady and consistent manner. Now, however, the financial scenery in football had shifted and the directors found that this stable environment in which their forebears had thrived no longer existed, and in quite a short space of time the club had been transformed from a debt-free organisation into a loss-making business whose credit line had all but expired. In addition, the company was grossly undercapitalised, with a current total share value of just £20,000 and debts standing at £7.2m, which prompted one speaker at the EGM to observe, 'I have never come across a company that has survived when its liabilities were 360 times its share capital.' At the time, the assets to debt ratio of Celtic, in effect the value of the club, stood at just £571,000 – the equivalent figure for Rangers was £34.8m – while, if that wasn't enough to set alarm bells ringing, by now the Bank of Scotland had secured a 'floating charge' over the company, meaning that if the club couldn't pay its bills, the bank could seize all its existing viable assets, including the stadium, the pitch and even the players' registrations, and dispose of them as they saw fit.

Despite this clearly precarious predicament, Michael Kelly had sounded worryingly blasé a few days earlier when he told one journalist in reference to the floating charge, 'Most companies have it. Banks like to have these sorts of things.' It was presumably attitudes such as this that allowed Kelly and his colleagues to be so dismissive of McCann and his repeated offers of financial assistance, with Kelly admitting that he was unable to fathom the motives of the Canadian businessman. 'What is McCann trying to prove anyway? He has a house in Montreal, a house in Phoenix, a house in Bermuda. Why does he come to Glasgow and put all his money into Celtic and want to be chief executive?' he pondered in *The Independent*.

On the night of the meeting, McCann pledged to produce funds from various sources totalling £17.9m, described as 'the biggest offer of equity ever made to a British football club', which would pay for the upgrade of the stadium, for strengthening the team and for dealing with the club's perilous financial position. His resolution also proposed to increase the issued number of shares from 20,000 to 250,000, which, working on the assumption that the existing directors couldn't afford to take them up, would then allow McCann and his friends to put up their money and buy their way in. In return for a 50 per cent stake, McCann wanted outright control for five years, during which time his shares would be 'locked in', before being sold to other existing shareholders, ensuring that, at a time when corporate big shots and other grandstanding self-publicists were starting to meddle in the affairs of British football clubs, the ownership of Celtic would instead be kept in the hands of people who held the club dear.

Aware that his plans would need the approval of at least some of the sitting directors, McCann told the meeting, 'I do not think this club was ever intended to be a family business. It was started to improve the lot of poor families in the East End of Glasgow,' an assertion that was greeted with warm applause from the floor. 'The people who are demonstrating outside … are not a rabble agitated by individuals,' McCann continued. 'They are people who feel a great deal for the club. They want to see the club move ahead … On the field, as everyone knows, no success is guaranteed because of money only. However, I can guarantee you one thing: in professional team sports at the level that Celtic are expected to play at, with no money you are guaranteed no success.'

Director Jimmy Farrell, not a member of the pact, pointed out that McCann was a genuine Celtic supporter of long standing and not a merely transient footballing tycoon, or a Robert Maxwell-type figure, in reference to the controversial media baron who just a few years earlier had only narrowly been prevented from buying Rangers. 'I think he falls into a quite different category from … Robert Maxwell and all the rest of them, these people who are big-money people in England,' Farrell offered. He described the McCann-led rebels, whose proposals he had decided to support, as 'a man and a group of people whom I know to be Celtic supporters and not lepers'. Another speaker to back McCann's plan was Dominic Keane, an Edinburgh-based businessman, formerly with the Royal Bank of Scotland, who accused financial director David Smith and the Bank of Scotland of allowing asset stripping to take place at Celtic. The previous month, winger Stuart Slater had been sold to Ipswich Town for £700,000, a full £1m less than the fee that was paid for him barely a year earlier. Keane remarked, 'We now have a situation where players who were bought for fairly expensive transfer fees are now being hived off and I call that asset stripping … Unless we accept Mr McCann's plan, there is no future for Celtic.'

In the end, however, regardless of all the protests and the heartfelt entreaties, the shareholders' pact couldn't be shifted, despite one of its signatories, stadium director Tom Grant, admitting that he would like to see it 'binned', and with a two-thirds majority required for McCann's plans to be accepted, the resolution failed, with 47 votes in favour and the same number opposed on a show of hands. In hindsight, however, and despite their nominal, pyrrhic victory on the night, many of those involved in Celtic's affairs over this turbulent period came to regard the events of the November EGM as effectively the old board's last stand and the moment it finally became clear that their time in charge of the club was coming to a close. Celtic were perilously indebted to an increasingly anxious Bank of Scotland, the club's main creditor, who had just witnessed the directors wave away a potentially life-saving, multimillion-pound package of investment in order to protect their own positions. It would not be long now before the bank stepped in and made a crucial intervention that would determine the future of the Parkhead club.

In the meantime, seemingly undaunted, the beleaguered board limped on into the new year, but by now they had collectively driven the club's long-suffering fans to distraction. On 1 January 1994, Celtic, unbeaten in eight matches and with a clean sheet record extending back over their last six home games, faced a Rangers team who had been struggling in recent weeks after a last-minute defeat to the Parkhead men in Lou Macari's first game in charge following his appointment as Brady's replacement in October. At the Ne'erday game, however, the visitors scored two goals inside the first three minutes and added a third unanswered strike before the half-hour mark, prompting fans in the main stand to start pelting members of the board, seated in the Parkhead directors' box, with improvised missiles, including coins, Mars bars and half-eaten pies.

As Celtic eventually succumbed to a 4-2 defeat, the exasperation of some supporters grew to such an extent that in between outbursts of raucous support for the floundering team on the field, they turned their attention away from the game for long periods in order to sustain the invective that was being directed towards the board. One fan was even seen clambering on to the roof of the dugout, where he tied his scarf into a noose and dangled it menacingly in front of the directors and their guests, who sat in stony silence throughout the unravelling fiasco with some of them, according to match commentator Archie Macpherson, 'looking as impassive as Mount Rushmore'. As if to emphasise the internecine nature of the civil war that was being waged at Parkhead on the day, when Rangers manager Walter Smith paused to survey the seething carnage all around him, one fan in the main stand screamed at him, 'What are you looking at, it's got fuck all to do with you.'

In the end, with Rangers fans gleefully exploiting the turmoil in the stadium by singing 'Happy New Year' and 'Keep the Board', the match perhaps provided the purest on-field indication to wavering supporters of the malaise that was afflicting the club, in contrast to all the financial chicanery and plotting that up to that point had been happening behind the scenes. When Celtic subsequently lost their next two league games, to Partick Thistle and Motherwell, and then exited the Scottish Cup a few weeks later at the hands of the Fir Park side, with the only goal of the game scored by discarded former Parkhead striker Tommy Coyne, it appeared that any lingering sympathy for the Celtic board among the club's long-suffering fans had all but evaporated.

The overwhelming majority of fans were at the end of their tether, but aside from the impromptu expressions of rage, which by now were occasionally starting to spill over into something more unpleasant than just waving banners and jeering, there were also the more formally organised and properly constituted groups, founded with the intention of representing the feelings of the majority of supporters and ultimately bringing about regime change at the club. Unlike at Rangers in the 1980s, where the club's followers had remained largely indolent in the face of adversity and were, in the end, almost wholly absent from the story of seminal change at Ibrox, the involvement of the Celtic fans in bringing about revolution at their club cannot be overstated. As website thecelt015.com noted, 'What the fans lacked in finances they made up for in passion and a love of the club. Their rallies, their demonstrations and even their boycotts would be every bit as important in the fight for Celtic as the millions of McCann.' Evolving out of the fanzine scene, where outlets, including the long-running *Not the View* and *Once a Tim, Always a Tim*, had been voicing criticism of those running the club for some time, the protest movement among ordinary Celtic supporters was now growing, in the face of the board's intransigence, into something altogether more substantial and ultimately effective.

The first group to appear on the scene was an organisation calling itself Save Our Celts, which had held its inaugural meeting, for invitees only, in Shettleston Town Hall as early as February 1991. Convened by a Clydebank-based Celtic supporter named Willie Wilson, the meeting was chaired by Joe Beltrami, the well-known Glasgow lawyer, and attended by two Celtic directors, Tom Grant and Jimmy Farrell, as well as the recently deposed Brian Dempsey, who urged the audience 'to go that extra mile to achieve what we want and deserve as the paying customer'. Other directors were also invited to attend, but club secretary Christopher White sent only a terse letter, read out at the meeting by Beltrami, which stated, 'I would acknowledge receipt of your letter of 24th of January 1991. I do not think that your organisation serves any purpose other than to cause embarrassment to Celtic Football Club. I therefore decline your invitation. Yours sincerely, C. D. White.' Kevin Kelly, meanwhile, who became club chairman later the same year, dismissed the protestors as 'malcontents', a moniker that was quickly adopted by *Not the View*, with the famous fanzine immediately proclaiming itself on the cover of its next issue as 'The Magazine for Malcontents'.

Save Our Celts failed to survive the year, perhaps because of a more optimistic outlook among supporters following an upturn in results, including back-to-back wins over Rangers in the league and Scottish Cup shortly before the departure of Graeme Souness from Ibrox in April 1991, and the mandate for more militant pressure at the time, such as an organised boycott of matches at Celtic Park, was lacking. Two and a half years later, by September 1993, the mantle had passed to Celts For Change, a more determined and serious body with a committee of five young Celtic supporters, led by Matt McGlone, the founder and editor of *Once a Tim, Always a Tim*, the fanzine that had been leading the attacks on the board since its initial publication in November 1990, when it had started running a cartoon strip featuring 'The Board Stiffs'. As was suggested at the time, 'Save Our Celts is a little plaintive; Celts For Change sounds like people with an agenda.'

The founders of Celts For Change freely admit that, initially at least, they were learning on the job and making things up as they went along. Like Willie Wilson of Save Our Celts, the five-man committee were mostly working-class 20- and 30-somethings, who had almost no experience of event management or public speaking between them. Yet within a short space of time they were addressing rallies attended by huge numbers of frustrated Celtic supporters, who were impressed in particular by McGlone's firebrand rhetoric as well as by the depth of the group's concern and the extent of their efforts to bring about reform. The meetings had expanded from just a few dozen or so attendees in the group's formative weeks to roughly 2,000 by the end of the year, with the gang at one point even making the ferry crossing from Stranraer over to Belfast so that they could hold a rally on the return trip with 1,100 vociferous Irish fans en route to Celtic Park. Petitions and demonstrations were organised before Celtic home games, with a 24-foot banner being smuggled into the ground before a match against

St Johnstone, which read 'Back the team, sack the board'. The slogan 'Sack the board' soon became such a ubiquitous refrain that even the Labour leader John Smith appeared to have been paying attention to the fans' campaign when, in March 1994, he urged the Scottish Labour Party conference to 'sack the board' in reference to John Major's Tory government of the day.

Celts For Change's timing was impeccable; the team's form had collapsed, the supporters were generally spitting feathers and, perhaps most worryingly of all from the board's point of view, the bank was now weighing up its options. In a targeted attempt to try to influence the club's main creditor, another move by the group involved an organised march on the Bank of Scotland's Glasgow headquarters in St Vincent Street, with several hundred fans in attendance carrying placards in support of McCann and urging the bank not to prop up a bankrupt board. After entering the bank's premises, accompanied by television crews, McGlone demanded to speak to the manager, but was told he was unavailable. 'If we can't speak to the manager then all of the people outside will be coming in to open accounts and then close them again,' McGlone insisted. Eventually the assistant manager was briefly put at the group's disposal, and the protest leaders were duly informed that the bank's relationship with its customers was a matter of confidence and not something that could be publicly discussed. Nevertheless, despite the brevity of this riposte, the stunt had fulfilled its primary purpose by attracting a great deal of publicity in the mainstream media, which in turn afforded Celts For Change new levels of credibility among wavering and confused fans, particularly when, later that evening, footage from the rally was shown on the main evening news bulletins on both BBC Scotland and Scottish Television (STV). Deep within his ivory towers, Rowland Mitchell, the bank's general manager in Glasgow, blinked.

The group's ultimate weapon of protest, however, was the threat of an organised boycott of home matches at Celtic Park, and with all other avenues seemingly exhausted, drastic action was now called for. In a controversial move, which was criticised even by some sympathisers as going against the group's mantra of 'Back the team, sack the board', the rearranged match against Kilmarnock on Tuesday, 1 March, postponed from the weekend following a blizzard, was identified as the game when Celts For Change would carry out their threat to effectively withdraw their financial support from the club and its besieged board of directors. After discussions with other supporters organisations, McGlone's group put out a call for an official boycott and stationed activists and independent market research agents – paid for, as with all the group's activities, through crowdfunding – around the stadium to make a headcount of those passing through the turnstiles.

The result was a disputed attendance figure, with Celts For Change claiming that only 8,225 people were present at the game, compared to the club's official total of 10,882, but regardless of the exact numbers, the size of the crowd was small. With Kilmarnock having brought up almost 2,000 fans from Ayrshire and with Celtic's 7,000 season ticket holders presumed to be in attendance, paying customers on the night must have been pretty thin on the ground. It seemed there was no way that the club could break even on these numbers, and by the end of the week the struggle for control of Celtic Football Club would finally be settled.

In the meantime, however, a few days in advance of the boycotted match against Kilmarnock, the beleaguered board and the group of directors who were still signed up to the voting pact made a final throw of the dice in a last-ditch attempt to try to cling on to their positions and remain in charge of the club. Announced by finance director David Smith, flanked by chairman Kevin Kelly and Patrick Nally of Stadivarius, the investment arm of Superstadia, to a packed press conference in the Jock Stein suite at Celtic Park, the board revealed its new plan to raise an estimated £4m–£6m by immediately releasing up to 30,000 new shares, valued at approximately £200 each, in order to provide sufficient short-term liquidity to deal with the club's crippling overdraft and provide funds to buy new players.

Based on the Manchester United model, the board would then take the club into public ownership later in the year through the flotation of a new holding company, which would have its own board of directors, including Smith, the only current executive figure with the requisite commercial experience. At the same time, the company would retain a subsidiary or 'Club Board' to ensure the continuation of Celtic's 'traditions, spirit and values', which some of the other existing directors, alongside ex-players and prominent supporters, could expect to be a part of.

Smith also invited anyone with finance, including the various rebel factions, to invest, but he warned that they would not be able to prevent any members of the traditional families who wished to remain involved with Celtic from having a continuing role in the club's affairs. To many it seemed that Smith and his colleagues were asking McCann and some of the other parties interested in Celtic, such as the group fronted by retail tycoon Gerald Weisfeld, who had sold his What Everyone Wants chain of stores in the late 1980s for around £50m, to put their money in without seeing very much in return. Describing the move somewhat ironically, Alf Young, economics editor of *The Herald*, who like the rest of the assembled press pack had turned up at Celtic Park that morning at very short notice anticipating news of the directors' mass resignations, observed, 'Directors, instead of selling out, launched a plan to give everyone who wants one a stake in a glittering new future. Paradise, far from being lost, is to be regained, it seems.'

In addition to the financial restructuring of the company, Smith also announced that the Cambuslang stadium project, which it seemed to the outside world had been mothballed over the previous two years, was now being brought out of cold storage, with £20m 'cornerstone funding already in place' for the new facility, underwritten by a Swiss merchant bank named Gefinor, a distinctly low-profile investment house with offices in Geneva, London and Lebanon. Smith maintained that the board's plans amounted to 'undoubtedly the most exciting proposal that any football club in this country, and indeed in Europe, can have contemplated'. But with the board's plans requiring a two-thirds majority of shareholders to be approved at a future EGM – another one – and with the pact directors holding only 60 per cent of the shares, successful implementation of the new measures seemed far from guaranteed.

More immediately though, there was widespread scepticism following the announcement, both among supporters and, not least, the popular press, who were scathing in their criticism of the club's new proposals. Two days after the media conference, on 27 February, the *Sunday Mail* published one of the most notorious back page headlines ever seen in Scottish tabloid journalism, with a photograph of a hearse parked outside Celtic Park attended by a sombre-looking undertaker below the full font caption 'CELTIC R.I.P.'. On the inside pages, the paper was quick to pour scorn on the idea of the Parkhead club being permitted to go public, carrying quotes from an independent analyst, Robin Woulstenholme, who claimed, 'It seems highly unlikely that Celtic will satisfy Stock Exchange listing requirements ... Any comparison with Manchester United is misleading because they came to the market with a stadium, assets and a healthy financial outlook. Until Celtic's stadium is completed and up and running you cannot really regard it as an asset.' David Low, meanwhile, financial adviser to the McCann-led rebels, declared that there was 'not a cat in hell's chance' of a proposed Celtic plc being awarded a listing on the London Stock Exchange.

Elsewhere, as the world of Scottish football was still trying to take all this in and grappling with the implications of these latest developments, support for Smith's proposals seemed difficult to detect, even among other members of the club's board; the two non-pact directors, Jimmy Farrell and John McGinn, hadn't been informed of the announcement in advance and only learned of the board's intentions when a press release was issued. Farrell immediately derided the new measures, claiming, 'The plan is clearly designed to perpetuate the power of certain members of the board. It does absolutely nothing to address the real problems of the club ... After being treated in such an outrageous manner I should resign – but because of my commitment to Celtic and my duty to our supporters, I intend to remain and fight this battle to its final conclusion.' Matt McGlone of Celts For Change, meanwhile, added to the general tone of scorn and incredulity when he accused the club's directors of insulting the intelligence of supporters with their latest charade, while the former director Brian Dempsey noted of the board's plans, 'In all their announcements, if you check six months later you find that the reality is a different matter. This will be no different.'

The problem with all of this – the main one anyway – was that Gefinor themselves, the publicity-shy investment bank, whom Smith had claimed were underwriting the new stadium project, didn't seem to know very much about it. Their small office in London was attended only by a broken answerphone machine, and when sceptical hacks tried to do a bit more digging, they were met by a wall of silence. Eventually, the following week, the *Evening Times* managed to track down an executive of the bank in New York, Edward Armaly, who confirmed only, 'We met with Patrick Nally and Stadivarius some months back, but nothing has happened. It is not being pursued ... I know there is a lot of debt in Celtic as a club and they don't have the cash flow to borrow £2m, let alone £20m.' Later, it emerged that Gefinor had indeed agreed to provide Superstadia, the club's agents over the Cambuslang venture, with a conditional letter of guarantee, detailing provisional funding for the construction of six new stadiums across the UK, but any deal involving Celtic was dependent on the club itself raising £30m for the project, with Gefinor stepping in only if there was a shortfall.

Superstadia, once memorably described by Fergus McCann as 'a bunch of advertising and promotion people and recession-hit architects', were subsequently left backtracking following the tabloids' investigations, with a spokesman for the company confirming that the finances would only fall into place once detailed planning consent had been obtained. Outline planning permission for the development of Cambuslang had been granted as far back as May 1993, but the details of the scheme had altered so radically by the time of the new announcement that the project was virtually back at square one, with an on-site start date now pencilled in for August 1996. According to the board's latest press release, the venue would also now include a 10,000-seat indoor arena, with Celtic expected to run basketball and ice hockey teams from the facility at some point in the future, but the capacity of the ground was now listed as just 40,000, some 12,000 down from the original estimate published in the *Celtic View* two years earlier. With the total cost of construction now coming in at £50m, roughly half the original sum, it seemed that the club's new stadium, once described in a hard-hitting *Focal Point* documentary as an 'all-things-to-all-men leisure complex with Celtic at the very heart of Cambuslang's Xanadu', had been downgraded considerably over the two-year period since the initial announcement, something that very few people seemed to have noticed.

The debacle over Gefinor was one of the few mistakes that director Michael Kelly later accepted that the board had made. Nally had warned the Celtic directors about the bank's low-profile business culture, insisting that they would prefer a minimum amount of public exposure, but the board, in their desperation, had insisted that their name be brandished about during the press conference and in the accompanying literature, throwing the firm's name out there like a fleshy bone to be fought over and devoured by the rottweilers of the Scottish press. The board's strategy was undermined from the start, Kelly conceded, 'in not having Superstadia's construction guarantors, Gefinor, sufficiently well briefed to withstand the hostile publicity which the announcement of the funding package for Cambuslang received. We should not have disclosed their name before being sure that they would not wilt under fire. But then of course the announcement would have been given even less credibility.' Despite the acknowledged error of judgement, in addition to everything else that was going wrong for the directors at the time, Kelly was still referring to their latest proposals months later as the board's 'masterplan'.

The collapse, or more accurately the non-existence of the arrangement with Gefinor, was the final nail in the board's coffin, and with the success of the organised boycott a few days later, matters now moved forward relatively quickly. Immediately following Smith's dramatic press conference on the Friday, Rowland Mitchell, head of the Bank of Scotland in Glasgow, attended a board meeting at Celtic Park, where he demanded personal guarantees from the directors, including their shareholdings, as collateral for the club's debt. At Michael Kelly's insistence, however, after being brought up to speed with the board's hastily revealed plans, Mitchell then confirmed that he would take a look at the detail in the new proposals over the weekend, in particular at the rights issue, which seemed to represent the only viable means of servicing the overdraft. After agreeing to take stock and crunch the numbers, however, Mitchell returned the following week seemingly unimpressed, and after informing the board that his position remained unchanged, he requested that the directors immediately sign over their shares, so that they could be sold if the cash was required to keep the club afloat.

Time was now running out for the incumbent directors. On Thursday, 3 March an emergency summit was held between Mitchell and the Celtic board, but chairman Kevin Kelly took along only Tom Grant, James Farrell and Jack McGinn to the meeting. With four of the seven board members in attendance, a deliberate majority on the chairman's part, Mitchell spelled out the reality of the situation – Celtic were about to go bust – and he gave the directors until 12 noon the following day to come up with £1m or the receivers would be sent in and the club would cease trading. The chairman and his colleagues were shocked; they apparently had no idea that the club was so imperilled, and Kelly's reaction was to sanction the summary dismissals of finance director David Smith and club secretary Christopher White on the grounds that they had misrepresented the club's financial position to the board.

The four directors in attendance also immediately gave notice of their approval of Fergus McCann's investment plans, in accordance with the terms proposed by the rebels at the previous November's stormy EGM, which allowed Mitchell to stipulate a further demand for a '£5m cash collateralised guarantee which will be made available once Mr Fergus McCann has reached the UK and has had a chance to apprise himself of the situation'. In return, with a clear majority of the board in favour, the bank agreed to deal exclusively with McCann and his allies, precluding the possibility of the other directors selling their shares to the Weisfeld group, who at the time were also still vying for control of the club.

Weisfeld was head of a consortium involving his step-son Michael MacDonald and the Glasgow businessman Willie Haughey, who believed right up until the board's final hours that they had struck a deal to take over a controlling interest in Celtic. Directors White, Smith and Michael Kelly favoured Weisfeld as the 'anyone but McCann' candidate, who, unlike the Canadian at that stage, was proposing to buy the directors out, offering £3.6m for their combined shares, while McCann was still maintaining his position, in his unmistakeable transatlantic twang, that the board members would not receive 'one thin dime' as a result of the takeover transaction. White and Michael Kelly were in fact locked in a meeting with the Weisfeld group even as the summit was going on between the bank and the other directors, where, because a majority of the board were in attendance, including the all-important chairman, a confused Mitchell, who had already heard and accepted Weisfeld's £3m guarantee from the other directors, had no choice but to agree to their desire to bring in McCann.

In the end, the notorious voting pact proved to be the undoing of the other faction on the board who wished to proceed with the Weisfeld offer, because under the terms of the agreement, White and Smith first had to offer their holdings to the other signatories, including Kevin Kelly and Tom Grant. The chairman, who by now had gone over to the rebels and was under the close guidance of David Low every step of the way, could therefore use his veto to block any transfer of shares to third parties, and consequently the deal with Weisfeld, who had earlier been so convinced that he was about to take control of the club that he went on holiday to Australia to celebrate, was prevented. The chairman, along with Farrell, McGinn and Grant favoured the McCann proposal as representing the best way forward for the club, and by the time Weisfeld flew back into Scotland to try to salvage his deal, it was too late.

Arriving at Brian Dempsey's office in Glasgow by 9.30am on Friday, 4 March, after flying in overnight from Phoenix, Arizona, a jet-lagged Fergus McCann began phoning around to see if the money he had wired from America, in accordance with the bank's demands, had arrived in Glasgow, paperwork and all. It seems that in the slow, pre-digital days of early 90s technology, McCann had arrived in Scotland in advance of his money and it took some time before confirmation came through that the funds had been cleared. McCann was then able to take his banker's draft for £1m round from the Clydesdale Bank in St Vincent Street, where he banked, to the Bank of Scotland's office a few yards further up the road. After another lengthy round of paperwork was completed, the cheque was deposited in the Celtic account at 11.52am, eight minutes shy of Mitchell's midday deadline.

The threat of imminent insolvency had receded – for now – but the day's events were still far from over. As McCann, by now the club's largest unsecured creditor, made his way over to Celtic Park, the media scrum outside the stadium, accompanied in the worsening weather by a growing number of jubilant and expectant fans, had developed into such a bunfight that his BMW accidentally ran over a photographer's foot. After pausing only to tell reporters that the financial position of the club had been secured, McCann and his team of lawyers then settled in with the last remaining directors, who were all put into separate rooms, to negotiate the terms of their resignations and the transfer of their shares to the club's new owners. In the end, McCann relented on his 'one thin dime' vow to force the directors to relinquish their shares for a nominal sum and, in return for their resignations, he offered the departing executives a pot of money, totalling up to £1.4m as an 'entry price', for them to share among themselves as they saw fit.

Finally admitting defeat, a spokesman for David Smith, who had already been asked to resign by the chairman, conceded, 'He has no more rabbits to pull out of the hat.' In the end, Smith acknowledged that the game was up and agreed to take a loss on his earlier purchase of £250,000 worth of shares from Michael Kelly. In addition to the figure that he had previously received from his colleague, however, Kelly, the last to agree and holding out for the best price even at the expense of some of his other extended family members, eventually secured £300 per share for his meagre remaining holdings and he walked away, including his wife and children's stake, with a further sum in excess of £200,000.

By now, it wasn't just the usual suspects of Scottish sports journalism who had been alerted to the unfolding events in Glasgow. The story was national news and an overjoyed Matt McGlone of Celts For Change had already been chauffeur-driven round to Celtic Park in a limousine at 6am so that he could speak of his delight via a satellite link-up to GMTV presenter Penny Smith. Later, the main evening news bulletins of the UK-wide networks dispatched their men to the scene of the unfolding drama at Celtic Park, with Scotland correspondents Hugh Pym and Andrew Cassell on the ground, fighting it out for space alongside the Jim Whites and Chick Youngs of this world. Meanwhile, Nick Owen, Peter Sissons and Martin Lewis, among others, were following events over the course of the day from the BBC and ITN studios in London. Around teatime, former banker Dominic Keane emerged from the stadium to confirm that he had been co-opted on to the club's new-look board, with Fergus McCann, the new CEO-in-waiting, also replacing White, Smith and Michael Kelly as directors.

The nature of the negotiations, ensuring that the takeover was legally binding and watertight, meant that the evening dragged on, with the two groups adjourning for a fish tea at 6pm, as the meticulous, small-print documentation of the transaction stretched on into the night. At the rebels' table, the meal was accompanied by cigars and champagne, while just a few feet away, in another corner of the Walfrid restaurant at Celtic Park, the ousted directors and their legal entourage were literally crying into their dinners, with Christopher White barely able to eat a morsel, a reaction that dismayed and annoyed Michael Kelly, who, despite being on a diet in advance of his daughter's wedding, defiantly ordered up some ice cream for dessert just to demonstrate to the celebrating rebel party that they hadn't put him off his food. It wasn't until 10.45pm that Dempsey finally emerged from the ground to announce to the waiting and expectant crowd, 'The game is over, the rebels have won.' It would be the start, not so much of a new chapter in Celtic's history, as of an entirely new volume in the story of the club's affairs; there was the first 106 years of Celtic before McCann's arrival and intervention, and then there was everything else that has come, and continues to come, since.

3.

The Longed-For Breakthrough

THERE are certain aspects of Rangers' history that seem putrid to the modern observer, while other features and qualities of the Ibrox institution fail to offer the necessary redemption. In particular, the issue of anti-Catholicism was associated with the Govan club for most of the 20th century, with Rangers, long before the arrival of David Holmes and Graeme Souness at Ibrox in the mid-1980s, establishing themselves as an exclusive, Protestants-only organisation and feeding off the popularity at the turnstiles as well as the success on the field that this stance helped to confer upon them.

Unforgivably in any sphere, but particularly in a sporting context, Rangers took the decision at some relatively early point in the club's history to exclude the Catholic community in its entirety from their organisation, as a wider social problem, namely anti-Catholicism and anti-Irish sentiments, was allowed to filter into and take hold of every aspect of the club's operations.

For years, there have been all manner of competing theories proposed and discussed in the context of Scottish football, as well as in the broader community, as to exactly how this situation came about at Ibrox, with the difficult process of establishing facts and reliable evidence on the issue impaired by Rangers' long-standing policy of refusing to allow public access to their records. What seems certain, however, is that as early as 1890, just two years on from Celtic's foundation, Rangers patron Sir John Ure Primrose established a lasting association between Rangers and the Freemasons when he recruited the club to a fundraising event for the Grand Lodge of Scotland. Soon afterwards, criticism of Rangers in the sporting press, which had been rigorous and extensive amid continuing controversy during the pre-Celtic era, seemed to evaporate into thin air, as the Ibrox organisation's place in Scottish society was transformed from an errant and wayward, relatively minor sporting body, dogged by controversy and criticism, into 'Scotia's darling club', as elements of the sporting press were moved to describe Rangers in the 1890s.

Later, Ure Primrose, a man who had occasionally shared a platform with Sir Edward Carson, the founder of the Ulster Volunteer Force, to express his zealous opposition to the movement towards Irish home rule, assumed the chairmanship of the Ibrox club in 1912, and around the same time Rangers came to an arrangement with Harland and Wolff, the Belfast-based shipbuilding firm, which had moved on to the Clyde in March of the same year. This controversial and secret agreement between the new neighbours in Govan saw the Ibrox club, struggling at the time financially, receive a loan of £90,000 from the Ulster firm, who themselves had taken a hard line regarding the demographic problems in the north of Ireland

and had been effectively operating a no-Catholics exclusionary and nepotistic employment policy among its skilled Protestant workforce for many years.

At the time of this agreement, William Lord Pirrie, chairman of Harland and Wolff and a former Lord Mayor of Belfast, was convalescing on a yacht in the Baltic Sea after undergoing a complicated and perilous operation in London to remove a swollen prostate gland. While hardly a radical left-wing firebrand, Pirrie was a man who at least seemed to have a more open-minded approach towards the whole home rule conundrum, a stance that on at least one occasion had seen him pelted with flour, rotten eggs and herring back home in Belfast. Pirrie had been instructed to rest and recuperate until the autumn following his operation, somewhat fortuitously as it turned out, as his condition meant that the Harland and Wolff chairman missed the transatlantic maiden voyage of his company's flagship vessel, the RMS *Titanic*, which struck an iceberg and sank while en route to New York in April, with the loss of more than 1,500 lives. It seems certain that under the terms of the loan agreement between Ure Primrose's Rangers and Harland and Wolff, tied up behind the back of the company's more liberal boss, the Ibrox club were exhorted to take a similar stance as their creditors in regard to their employment practices and become a Catholic-free zone. With the adoption of this exclusionary and discriminatory policy, in an era of fraught religious tensions, it's no exaggeration to say that Rangers effectively became Scotland's Catholic-hating football club from this period onwards.

At the same time, the club's image of itself grew ever grander, with Rangers' status as the foremost and most important sporting institution in the country confirmed with an impressive new main stand at Ibrox constructed in the 1920s, including the stadium's famous red-brick façade, which in 1987 was given the status of a Category B listed building. Inside the ground, the layout was even more striking, with visitors to Ibrox greeted by an oak-panelled hallway, chequered flooring and marble staircase leading up to the hallowed shrine of the manager's office, from where Bill Struth ruled the roost over the club during the inter-war period. The design of the interior, by renowned architect Archibald Leitch, also incorporated other elements, more mysterious and intriguing, which revealed Rangers' secret heritage, as journalist Iain Duff helpfully explains in his book *Temple of Dreams: The Changing Face of Ibrox*: 'What probably will not register with most modern-day visitors, however, is the Masonic imagery incorporated into the design. The pillars, the chequered flooring and the staircase are all symbols of King Solomon's Temple, a key part of Freemasonry ... The symbolism of the design definitely would not have been lost on the Rangers players, as the majority, if not all, would have been Masons in that era.'

In 1926, Rangers finished in a lowly and almost unprecedented sixth position in the league, as the team, under the management of a man who, in Struth, didn't fully understand football, struggled to cope with the newly implemented change in the offside rule, which was adopted at the start of the season with the aim of encouraging more attacking football, but in the end seemed to have the opposite effect and led to the introduction of the third defender, with the 'centre-half' becoming the 'centre-back' and playing alongside the two full-backs. It was to be a mere aberration, however, as Rangers, a club with by now, as Duff candidly observed, Masonic allusions and imagery incorporated into its architecture, cemented their position as by far the most successful football club in the country, collecting trophy after trophy, with barely a mention of the issue of religious bigotry and discrimination at Ibrox ever being uttered publicly.

Struth, meanwhile, after a nervous start in the manager's role, had latterly cultivated around himself at Ibrox an air of such absolute authoritarianism that he was able to establish Rangers as a club beyond censure, with the *omertà* on public discussion of the club's sectarian policies persisting down through the decades and into the Murray era, when the unofficial ban on Catholics was finally lifted. More than any other individual, it was Struth who was responsible for the transformation of Rangers from a controversial and disjointed institution in its earliest years – a nomadic, cash-strapped club, hampered by relentless internal bickering – into a beacon of unblemished Protestant respectability and Scotland's establishment club.

Even after Struth's eventual retirement, the situation at Ibrox remained unchanged, as the management of the club passed in 1954 to the aloof and enigmatic Scot Symon, one of Struth's former players. The seamless transition saw Rangers' policies and conventions unaffected under the new manager, as Rangers' secret Catholic, the striker Don Kichenbrand, took extreme measures to disguise his religious upbringing during his short spell at Ibrox after arriving in Glasgow from South Africa, while around the same time Canadian-born full-back Johnny Little was presented with an ultimatum by Symon: 'Your Catholic girlfriend or Rangers.' The prevailing mood shifted slightly in the 1960s, in tandem with the changing social circumstances and attitudes of the new decade, which also witnessed the growth of civil rights movements among oppressed and marginalised communities across the western hemisphere. Gradually, Rangers' policies began to attract murmurings of disapproval and eventually even isolated instances of outright condemnation.

By the middle of the decade, former Ibrox striker Ralph Brand had taken to criticising the club in a series of interviews published in the Scottish edition of the now defunct *News of the World*, in the days before the paper's conversion to a tabloid red-top under the controversial ownership of international media baron Rupert Murdoch and his News Corporation company. By the time his articles were published in the paper, Brand had fled the scene at Ibrox and was plying his trade in England with Manchester City, but the striker was well aware that he was, by his own admission, 'shattering the great Rangers tradition of silence' by opening up and selling his story to a national newspaper.

In the whistleblowing pieces, which extended over six weekly editions of the paper, Brand compared Ibrox's red-brick façade to the 'Iron Curtain' in terms of allowing information from within the club to be publicly disseminated, and he criticised Rangers' arcane training methods, selection policies and parsimonious wage structure. In addition, according to Brand, the club's fans were hubristic glory supporters, 'gorged on success', who 'find it difficult to get very enthusiastic until Rangers are on top'. Importantly, Brand also lamented the club's exclusionary, all-Protestant employment policies, pointing out what seemed to the rest of the outside world to be a version of the bleedin' obvious, when he observed, 'If a large British industry barred Catholics from its employment – as Rangers do – there would be a public outcry,' and the former Ibrox striker also predicted, accurately as it turned out, that the ascendancy of Celtic, for years the black sheep of Scottish football, to a dominant position within the Scottish domestic game was imminent.

By the time Brand was a few weeks into his revealing series of articles with the newspaper, the long-serving Ibrox forward had also gone on to castigate the SFA over its selection policies for the Scotland national team, claiming that international caps were handed out to Rangers players almost as 'one of the "perks" of being an Ibrox player', something that everyone at the club was apparently well aware of. "If you're playing well in the Rangers first team you'll find the caps coming soon enough," was what I was told when I first started. I can state categorically that there always have been better players with less fashionable Scottish sides than some of those from Ibrox who got caps,' Brand admitted with disarming honesty, confirming a favouritism on the part of the game's governing body in Scotland, which at the time was generally considered to be common knowledge anyway. One of the consequences of the SFA's perceived bias towards the Ibrox club, which saw more gifted candidates for international honours overlooked in preference to inferior Rangers players, was that the Scotland national team failed to qualify for three consecutive World Cups between the tournaments of 1958 and 1974, a period in which unparalleled levels of success were being achieved by the country's club sides and when, in players such as Jim Baxter, Billy Bremner and Denis Law, the standard of exported Scottish talent was at an all-time high.

As the revelations continued, Brand, who claimed all along that he believed he was acting in the Ibrox club's best interests and was merely trying to help his inveterate former employers, perhaps by pressurising them into a form of enforced modernisation, lamented the 'thousands of anonymous letter writers who have fouled the postal system' over his series of articles, and he berated the media, who were, the forward acknowledged, confirming another open secret of Scottish football, 'always on the side of the Ibrox management'. Predictably enough, with the club reeling in the face of these unprecedented rebukes, the Ibrox apologists in the press were quick to leap to Rangers' defence, including Allan Herron of the *Sunday Mail*, who lambasted Brand as 'the guy who carries tales out of school'. A spokesman for the Ibrox supporters meanwhile accused the striker of 'vitriolic effrontery and impertinence', to which Brand wrote in reply, 'There you have the whole Ibrox philosophy – a mere player should know his lowly place in life, touch his cap and keep his mouth shout ... I suppose they'll be painting me out of the team pictures and scratching my name out of the records.'

All this was truly astonishing stuff and Ibrox was shaken to its foundations by the manner and extent of Brand's outspokenness, while at the same time the illusion that the club was somehow beyond criticism, an almost unchallenged assumption over the previous 40 years and more, was utterly shattered by the player's forthright and sustained invective. The embarrassing revelations couldn't have come at a worse time for the striker's former club, as the Ibrox hegemony of the Scottish game, following the Treble of 1964, was in the process of being eroded away during this period, while at the same time rivals Celtic, as Brand had indeed predicted, were on the cusp of establishing a new domestic dominance.

The Parkhead side, whose players were being coached and improved from the middle of the decade onwards by the modernising methods of manager Jock Stein, were soon elevated from a team of perennial strugglers, almost a laughing stock within certain circles of the Scottish game, to the status of nine-in-a-row champions and a side capable of toppling the giants of European football. The tide had turned, the old order was being swept away and, as Rangers-supporting writer and academic, Graham Walker, later noted of this period, 'Rangers, in a sense, have never recovered their national identity bearings since the culture shocks and political turmoil of the '60s ... The century, in effect, accelerated away from hidebound attitudes from the second half of the '60s, while Rangers did not even break into a jog.'

A further serious issue for the Ibrox club arose over the next few years, as Rangers' image of itself as a bastion of establishment strength and respectability was undermined by a series of hooligan-related incidents involving the team's supporters, which damaged the club's name across Britain and even Europe. In the context of Celtic's re-emergence as a credible and successful force within the Scottish game, alongside the challenges to the accepted traditions and conventions of the day that were taking place across society in the late 1960s, Rangers' reputation and standing were adversely affected by serious outbreaks of fan violence in Newcastle, Barcelona, Birmingham and Manchester in addition to numerous more minor, but no less troubling incidents across Scotland.

By now sections of the press, no doubt emboldened by the frankness and success of the Brand articles, were also on Rangers' case, but the club itself, in the person of general manager Willie Waddell, vehemently rejected the idea that the incidents of fan misbehaviour were related to the club's employment policies, which he considered to be the Ibrox organisation's business and nobody else's, and criticism of Rangers in the media remained largely sporadic. It was only much later on, in the mid-1990s, that one of Graeme Souness's biographers, Sandy Jamieson, acknowledged, 'The sectarian policy and discriminatory employment practice of Rangers Football Club in the 1960s,

1970s and 1980s was a disgrace to a civilised society and should have been regarded by all sections of the community as intolerable. But there was no campaign, ever, and that absence represents a stain of shame.' It was the kind of unequivocal statement on the issue, which for many seemed long overdue.

By the time of Souness's arrival at Ibrox in the mid-1980s, Rangers' sectarian badge of identity was starting to become an albatross around the club's neck. Clearly David Holmes, having helped to engineer a boardroom coup over the old-style Rangers directors, wanted to move the club on from the burden of its own traditions, and in Souness he had appointed a manager who was not only married to a Catholic, but whose two sons, according to the unwritten laws of Ibrox, would not have been eligible to play for the club. Neither Souness nor Holmes, nor either of the two other board appointees following Marlborough's takeover of the club, Hugh Adam and Freddie Fletcher, were from a traditional Rangers-supporting background, so the time seemed ripe enough for the controversial employment practices at Ibrox to be finally done away with. Souness himself was clear from the start, telling journalist Chick Young while he was with the Scotland squad in Santa Fe, New Mexico, preparing for the 1986 World Cup, 'I will sign a Catholic player. There will be no hedging of the bets on this. Supporters either want a successful team my way or not. Rangers are too big a club to be limited to signing only a percentage of the population.'

For years Scottish football held its collective breath in anticipation of the longed-for breakthrough. With every one of Souness's numerous signings for the club, the press were impatient to ascertain the religion of the newest Ibrox recruit, eagerly rummaging around in the player's background and educational history in an increasingly frantic search to find Rangers' first known Catholic employee of the modern era. Often it was one of the first questions asked at press conferences when a new signing was unveiled, usually to the bemusement of the player himself, particularly if he happened to come from, as was the case with most of the manager's acquisitions at this time, an area outwith the unique cultural environment of the west of Scotland. A succession of suitable candidates were linked with Souness's side, including Ian Rush, Ray Houghton, John Sheridan, Derek Statham, Ally Dick and John Collins, but unsurprisingly perhaps, there appeared to be a reluctance on the part of sensible men to step into the role of the first Catholic of the modern era to play for the club. Eventually Holmes and his boss Lawrence Marlborough departed the scene at Ibrox with Rangers still the bastion of unblemished Protestantism that it had always been.

Then in the summer of 1989, eight months after Marlborough had sold the club to David Murray, an opportunity arose that appeared to be too good to turn down. Celtic's putative signing of Maurice Johnston had hit a snag and, armed with a much heavier purse than their rivals had been willing to offer, Souness stepped in and brought the player to Rangers. The news sent Scottish football into a daze; would the laws of nature continue to function now that there was a Catholic plying his trade at Ibrox? Would the world continue to spin? The reaction in the media was predictably over the top, with the signing greeted by what one writer described as 'banner headlines normally reserved for presidential assassinations and royal deaths', but once the eyes had popped back into their sockets and the jaws had collectively been picked back up off the floor, the new regime at Rangers was lauded to the heavens.

Despite Souness being clear in his ambition and his efforts to bring Catholics to Ibrox ever since the earliest days of his spell at Rangers, it was, however, the club's relatively new owner, David Murray, who received the lion's share of the praise from the press, regardless of the comparatively passive role he had played in the whole affair. 'Murray has been in charge of the club only since November, and ... in just under eight months he has achieved what his predecessors have either ducked or secretly supported,' Ian Paul affirmed in *The Herald*. Meanwhile, Alex Cameron, writing in the *Daily Record*, boldly proclaimed that, 'The new Rangers management have wiped out bigotry at Ibrox and are right to do so.'

The press conference that saw Johnston unveiled as a Rangers player in the Blue Room at Ibrox lasted all of seven minutes, during which time the word 'Catholic' wasn't uttered once. This wasn't so much because any mention of Roman faith had traditionally been regarded as taboo at Ibrox, but rather a result of the insistence by Murray, Souness and Rangers CEO Alan Montgomery that the signing was being made purely on sporting grounds, and the press pack, with their accustomed deference towards the Ibrox hierarchy, simply left it at that. The hyperventilating reaction to the transfer did eventually calm down enough over the next few days, however, to allow several journalists to point out that the Johnston signing hadn't been completed merely on moral or ethical grounds, but rather for more practical reasons, as another carefully worded, but no less flattering opinion piece in the *Evening Times* suggested: 'He [Murray] has a vision of Rangers in the 1990s playing in a European super-league. And he knows that dream can never become a reality as long as Rangers could be branded as a sectarian club ... If that means sections of the Rangers support decide to vote with their feet and stay away from Ibrox, he [Murray] is prepared to take that on board.'

Likewise, Paul maintained in *The Herald*, 'The executives ... have grasped the thorn because they believe the club and the game is entering a new era, one in which Rangers cannot afford to be parochial in any fashion. For that they deserve the upmost credit,' although the same writer also pointed out, in an apparent contradiction to the idea that bigotry at Ibrox had been vanquished at a stroke by the signing: 'If anyone imagines that the sight of Johnston in a Rangers strip will ease the pseudo-religious tensions, he is blessed with a beautifully naïve nature.' Only Brian Meek in *The Herald* offered any sympathy in regard to Johnston's previous pledges, now apparently forgotten elsewhere, to his former club Celtic and its manager Billy McNeill. 'This is Carl Lewis running for the Soviet Union, William Wallace putting on a white shirt,' Meek professed, claiming that McNeill and Celtic 'had every right to feel let down' by the player's defection to Ibrox.

This was apparently the crux of the matter. The timing of the transfer was ideal for everyone involved at Ibrox, not least because, as Souness had anticipated, it helped to send their rivals on the other side of the city into a tailspin from which the old board in charge of the jilted Parkhead club would never recover, but it was also advantageous that Rangers were enjoying their most successful period on the field in many years at the time. If the club had signed a high-profile Catholic when the team was struggling, under Jock Wallace or John Greig for example, it could have been a disaster for everyone involved, with the player in question becoming an easy scapegoat for angry supporters frustrated at a lack of success as well as the abandonment of the cherished tradition. Jim McLean's proposed solution to the sectarian conundrum at Rangers, when he was offered the chance to become the club's manager in 1983, was to sign and field several Catholic players at the same time for the Ibrox side, so that the burden and share of the blame for any misfortune would have been shared around, but in the end the Dundee United boss turned down the job offer from Ibrox and decided to remain at Tannadice.

The Johnston signing provoked predictable outrage among hard-line elements of the Rangers fanbase, widely reported in the press at the time, which included supporters burning scarves and tracksuits outside Ibrox, while a wreath mourning the loss of the club's long-standing Protestant heritage was thrown down outside the front doors of the ground. Particular scorn was reserved for Souness, far more so even than Johnston himself, a resentment towards the manager that lingered for many years, perhaps because, with the ex-Liverpool man in charge, as Meek observed in *The Herald* of the Ibrox intransigents, 'They have been slapped down by the very institution that was their rock.' The reaction in Ulster was particularly strong, where effigies of Souness were burned in the streets, but some at least were able to enjoy the manifest way in which Rangers outmanoeuvred and outspent their city rivals. As author and playwright Alan Bisset later noted of the Johnston transfer, 'Even Catholics want to play for us now.'

The signing of Maurice Johnston was the most noteworthy act in Murray's eight months in charge at Ibrox and, regardless of where the allocation of credit was due or what exactly inspired the motivation for the transfer, it was unquestionably the correct move for the club. The Labour Party's spokesman on sport, Brian Wilson, later a director and historian of Celtic, who had been a vocal critic of Rangers' practices for some time and had previously called on UEFA and FIFA to intervene and compel the club to end the ban on Catholics at Ibrox, stated, 'It's a great change for Scottish football and Scottish society – and the important thing is that it has happened.'

In 1990, Souness received the Award for Sport from Glasgow Lord Provost, Susan Baird, for officially ending Rangers' dogmatic policy, while from Murray's point of view, the signing of Johnston represented as encouraging a start to his ownership of the club as could have been envisaged. The chairman had held his nerve while others on his board were expressing concern that supporters would desert the club in droves as a result of the signing, and he had allowed his manager to proceed with the transfer of Johnston, thereby ending Rangers' most controversial and abhorrent tradition, and winning almost universal acclaim from the wider world for doing so. Murray had already been given the red carpet treatment by most of the media following his initial purchase of the club, but after the Johnston signing the new Rangers owner was now confirmed in his position as one of the most highly regarded public figures in Scotland.

With Johnston in their side, Rangers took some time to get up to speed at the start of the 1989/90 campaign, as Souness's men won only two of their first eight league games and were eliminated from the European Cup in the first round after a 3-1 aggregate defeat to Bayern Munich. It was the club's new striker, however, who had scored both the winning goals in the 1-0 home victories over Hearts and Aberdeen, and by the time Johnston repeated the feat, netting the only goal of the game against Celtic at Ibrox on 4 November with just two minutes of the match remaining, Rangers were already well into their stride and on course to retain the league championship for only the second time in 26 years. Johnston, who started every competitive fixture for his new team over the course of the season, had formed a prolific strike partnership with Ally McCoist, with the two forwards, operating together, scoring 29 goals between them during the victorious league campaign, with Johnston finishing as the club's top scorer. In addition, record signing Trevor Steven, a £1.5m purchase from Everton, had proved an effective force for the Ibrox men on the right side of midfield, although in the domestic knockout competitions, Rangers lost the League Cup Final to Aberdeen and were eliminated from the Scottish Cup in the fourth round by Celtic, who, minus Johnston, finished in fifth position in the league with just 34 points collected from 36 games.

Souness's side picked up from where they left off the following season, and things appeared to be going along relatively smoothly during the first half of the 1990/91 campaign, with only home and away defeats to Dundee United tarnishing Rangers' otherwise unblemished domestic record. Behind the scenes, however, tensions and difficulties were beginning to emerge, epitomised by the manager, who seemed to be making enemies and falling out with people everywhere he turned, including at times even his own players, as captain Terry Butcher left the club under a cloud in November to join Coventry City. Souness's relationship with the SFA, meanwhile, was reaching breaking point, with the manager having recently been hit with a £5,000 fine and a two-year touchline ban for his latest in a series of disciplinary transgressions. Then there was the notorious and unseemly episode with the St Johnstone tea lady, Aggie Moffat, whose favourite jug the manager was suspected of having smashed during a post-match rant following a disappointing draw at McDiarmid Park in February. The confrontation soon escalated and threatened to become potentially more serious for the Rangers manager when the Perth club's chairman, Geoff Brown, became involved, as he and Souness, by now on his final warning, almost came to blows over the incident.

Despite their continuing dominance on the home front, the strains behind the scenes at Ibrox were further exacerbated and seemed to reach boiling point following the club's elimination at the hands of Red Star Belgrade in the second round of the European Cup. The eventual winners of the competition had handed Souness's side a technical and tactical lesson during their 3-0 win in the first leg in Yugoslavia, a result that amounted to nothing short of a humiliation for a club more used to throwing its weight about back home and lording it over domestic opposition in an aggressively overweening manner. Following the defeat, which left no one in any doubt about the gap in quality that still existed between Rangers and the top European teams, one of the Ibrox side's players noted, 'Afterwards Souness had the look of a man who knew basically that he was fucked. He had been given a fantastic chance by Rangers, but he had also been told by David Murray that it wasn't enough for the Gers to be strong in Scotland; they had to be a major force on the Continent as well, and I don't think he had a clue as to how to make that happen … [He] seemed to be all over the place by 1991.' The confusion in the manager's mind was perhaps best illustrated when he lamented to the press after the defeat, 'How can I win the European Cup with 11 Scots in the side?' – despite his team against Red Star containing only five native players.

Early in the new year, Souness was linked with the managerial vacancy at his former club Liverpool, following the unexpected resignation of Kenny Dalglish from the post in February. After being privately offered the job by the Anfield club's board, Souness discussed the opportunity with his assistant Walter Smith, who initially persuaded his boss that the Merseysiders were a declining force in the English game and that it would be a mistake for him to return to Anfield. Souness subsequently issued a series of repeated and vehement denials that he was on the point of leaving Ibrox, including to the *Rangers News*, the club's in-house periodical, who reported in no uncertain terms the manager's feelings on the matter. 'I've no intention of ever leaving this place. I see my short-term and my long-term future here ... I would never contemplate leaving Ibrox,' Souness told the club's fans, an assertion that allowed Alex Cameron to follow up in the *Daily Record* by announcing that the manager's statement 'refutes finally any lingering doubt about him moving back to Liverpool'.

In addition, Souness had also offered his views at the time of his investment in Rangers, when he contributed £600,000 to purchase shares in the company that Murray had used to buy the club, telling the press, 'When I came to Rangers certain people said it was a jumping off ground for bigger things. Now they will know better. I doubt if I'll ever be involved with another football club. I have said all along that Rangers were the biggest and best club in Britain and I meant it. This looks like me for life ... We're still just scratching the surface and I hope to be involved in even greater things at Ibrox in the future.' Nothing, it seemed, had changed in the two and a half years since Murray acquired the club, and Souness's initial declarations of unequivocal commitment to the Ibrox cause put a temporary end to the speculation linking him with a return to the city where he had enjoyed his greatest success as a player.

In the face of such stonewalling, Liverpool quickly moved on and turned their attention to other candidates, with John Toshack installed as the new favourite for the Anfield hotseat, but it soon became clear that something was eating away at

Souness. To the outside world, it appeared that he was still in the perfect job; he was a successful manager and director of Rangers, very well-paid and, with over three years left to run on a five-year contract, he enjoyed a level of job security that made him almost unsackable, while the manager's overall relationship with his chairman was founded on a close personal friendship that extended well beyond football into politics and other areas. Professionally, Souness and his club found themselves in the fortunate position of being regularly able to challenge for honours, and the manager would have been aware that, as long as the league championship was won, he would be in a position to have a crack at the coveted European Cup with the Ibrox side on an almost annual basis.

After weighing things up, however, over a lengthy period of uncharacteristic hesitancy, which saw further statements and claims from within Ibrox to the effect that Liverpool would be a step down from Rangers, Souness eventually changed his mind and privately agreed to become the Anfield club's new manager. He was at pains to make clear to his prospective new employers, however, that it was his intention to see out the season at Rangers and guide the club over the line in the title race, but crucially Souness had still failed to advise David Murray of his decision. With the rumours of the manager's departure once again beginning to circulate, Murray spoke to assistant manager Walter Smith, who confirmed to the Ibrox chairman that he had been discussing the vacancy at Liverpool with his boss and that Souness was on the verge of formally accepting the position with his former club. Murray's reaction, on learning that his friend and most high-profile employee had chosen to further his career away from Ibrox, was a combination of pique and fury, and the affronted chairman immediately informed Souness that he should clear his desk and leave Rangers at once, despite the club being involved in a tight title race with Aberdeen, which by now was coming down to the wire with only four games of the season remaining.

At the press conference announcing his departure from Rangers on 16 April, Souness became emotional and walked out of Ibrox for good, setting off immediately on his journey to England, leaving Murray to tell the press, 'He's making the biggest mistake of his life.' In fact, despite Murray's glib assertion, which he undoubtedly believed to be accurate, it later became clear that Souness had been storing up serious health problems for himself at Ibrox, given the stressful environment he was operating under at the club, and within a few years his condition had become so severe that he required a complicated triple heart bypass operation to prevent him from suffering a massive heart attack. In the end, rather than a mistake, and regardless of how his career as a manager turned out thereafter, it's no exaggeration to say that Souness's decision to leave Rangers may, in all probability, have saved his life.

The jilted chairman, meanwhile, in addition to admitting that he felt 'personally let down' by Souness's actions, also directed his anger at Liverpool, castigating the Anfield club for 'not having the decency to negotiate on a chairman-to-chairman basis', and eventually chasing them down for £400,000 in compensation for the loss of his manager. Murray had taken characteristically swift and decisive action, telling club captain Richard Gough that 'his [Souness's] feet are not going to touch the floor going out of here', but he also had the insurance of knowing that, if the title race was lost as a result of any short-term disruption over his decision, there would be an easy scapegoat in the person of the departed manager for the club's failure. In the event, Rangers were guided home by the promoted Smith, who stepped out of his boss's shadow and saw off the challenge of Aberdeen after a dramatic, final-day encounter between the two teams at Ibrox on 11 May, which Rangers won 2-0.

At the time, and for many years since, Scottish football has not been short of theories regarding Souness's apparent change of mind and his eventual decision to leave Ibrox, given the strong position he seemed to be in at the club and the level of devotion to the cause that he had shown over the five-year period of his involvement with Rangers. Souness and Murray were a pair of high-flying Thatcherite 30-somethings, who appeared almost to be on a mission together at Ibrox, but now it seemed that the manager was getting fed up with it all, citing family reasons at the press conference but also, more enigmatically, stating his belief that 'I have taken this club as far as I will be allowed to go', a cryptic reference that provoked intense speculation over its precise meaning.

It was undoubtedly the case that Murray was now starting to interfere in recruitment in a way that Souness wasn't used to, stepping in to veto the manager's plan to sign goalkeeper Andy Goram from Hibernian, for example, after refusing to meet the Edinburgh club's financial demands, whereas Souness's accustomed method at tempting footballers to Ibrox was simply to offer to enhance their wages, regale them with a tour of the stadium and then show them where to sign. For the most part it was a strategy that worked, but the haphazard recruitment methods were shown up on at least one occasion when Souness promised to double the salary of a prospective new signing for the club and asked the player about his current wage packet. When he was informed that his target's weekly earnings amounted to £500, the Rangers manager immediately offered £1,000 as an inducement to come to Ibrox, without realising that he was in fact quadrupling the salary of a player who had exaggerated his income and was actually only being paid £250 per week.

Many have also contended that Souness was referring in his statement to the treatment he was continuing to receive at the hands of the SFA who, in May 1990, in addition to several exponentially increasing fines, had banned the Rangers manager from the touchline for two years for his most recent indiscretion. With their latest censure, the governing body were potentially one further offence away from issuing Souness with a *sine die* lifetime ban, a suspension that might well have been incurred had St Johnstone chairman Geoff Brown gone public over the fracas involving the two men following the incident with the tea lady after the drawn game between the sides at McDiarmid Park in February. Souness also felt that, from his earliest days at Rangers, he had become a target both among opposing teams – an odd justification for a player who had built his reputation as a take-no-prisoners hard man – and among the media, with the Ibrox manager admitting, 'Everywhere I went, I was being scrutinised in a negative way.'

There were, however, other reasons for his decision to leave Scotland, such as the bigotry factor at Rangers, which Souness was not born into and that he later claimed in *The Independent*, once he was safely back down south, would 'always be at Ibrox'. Souness may have longed for a return to a healthier, less insular football environment in a country where, even at the time, the league was more competitive and offered a greater sporting challenge. With assurances in place that the Anfield club's extended ban from European football, following the Heysel Stadium disaster in 1985, was coming to an end, he may have been eager to exploit the advantage that Liverpool held over

Rangers in being able to attract a better calibre of player and attain an overall higher standard of football than was available with his Scottish side, particularly after repeated failures on the European scene with Rangers had left Souness flummoxed.

Crucially, he would also have realised that for all Murray's bombast, Rangers were not and, certainly in the modern era, were never likely to become a bigger club than Liverpool. Souness, by his own admission a footballing mercenary, received a hefty pay rise when he eventually, after much soul-searching, made up his mind and joined up with the Anfield club. On leaving Rangers, the now former manager of the Ibrox side was also able to cash in his shares in the club, pocketing £2.4m from the sale of his stake in Murray's company, a healthy profit on what he had paid just two and a half years earlier. Regardless of the precise motivation, journalist and broadcaster Ian Archer labelled his departure from Ibrox, after so many assurances that it would not happen, an 'act of betrayal' and described Souness as 'a product of the yuppie, Thatcherite world'.

Murray didn't take long to find a replacement for the departed boss, not that he was required to look very far, as Walter Smith was invited to make the step up from his role as Souness's assistant, and at a press conference on 19 April, just three days after his predecessor left the club, Smith was confirmed in his appointment as the new manager of Rangers. The chairman had consulted widely over the suitability of the new man in charge and it seemed that the great and the good of Scottish football had been lining up to endorse Smith as the ideal candidate for the vacant position, including such luminaries as Alex Ferguson, Smith's former boss with the Scotland set-up, who was quick to voice his approval of Murray's decision. 'Smith is an absolutely first-class choice. He has a magnificent knowledge of the game,' the Manchester United manager confirmed, while former Rangers captain John Greig observed, 'When David Murray told me he was appointing Walter to take over from Graeme, I told him he couldn't have made a better choice. Walter had worked closely with the players during his time in charge, and he had earned their respect – but he was smart enough to recognise that all good teams need to keep evolving.'

Unlike Souness, Smith was steeped in Rangers and had grown up supporting the club, even admitting, much later in his career, that in his younger days he had made the mistake of singing sectarian or, more precisely, anti-Catholic songs from the terraces of the old Ibrox. He had also been present at the stadium, along with his brother, on the day of the Ibrox Park disaster in 1971, although he didn't witness directly the full effects of the fatal crush at the end of the New Year derby with Celtic and remained unaware of the unfolding tragedy until he had returned safely home. Of his experience that day, Smith later recalled, 'We managed to scramble out over a fence so we must have climbed over the top of other people in order to get out on to Edmiston Drive. We then got on to our bus and went home. Communication back then wasn't what it is today; there was nobody on the bus really talking about it much at all. It was only when we got back to Carmyle, where everybody was congregating and waiting to see if we were all okay, that we realised there had been such a horrible disaster.'

As a young footballer, Smith had initially spent several years working part-time as an electrician during a fairly unremarkable playing career as an orthodox defender with Dundee United, an experience that lent him a sense of perspective not always seen in the modern game. 'People are always on about pressure in football, but it's the wrong word. People who have pressure are those who live in poverty, or people with incurable illnesses,' he once reflected. After injury cut short his playing days, he spent time as a coach at Tannadice with his former club as well as at various levels in the Scotland set-up, before joining Souness as assistant manager at Ibrox in 1986. On finally stepping up to become the boss, Smith appeared to wallow in the history and traditions of the club he had long supported, and, hoping for inspiration, he hung the eight oil paintings of his predecessors at Ibrox, which had been scattered in various locations around the ground, together in his oak-panelled office at the top of the marble staircase.

Explaining his thinking, the new Rangers manager reflected, 'Every single thing that happens at the club is related to something that happened here before. There is always someone around the place who will remind you of that. Or there will be someone who says, "Old Bill [Struth] wouldn't have done that," or "Deedle [Willie Waddell] would have done it this way." And you listen to that. I know there are those people who say that you cannot operate on history or live in the past, but that is not a view I agree with. When you have a club with a rich tradition, then you examine that tradition and take from it what can still remain important to the club in any era. It is something which is almost tangible when you walk into the foyer at Ibrox, and you live with these feelings every day of your life.' The manager also later acknowledged that, as part of the club's much-lauded tradition, a 'Protestant superiority syndrome' still existed at Ibrox during the period of his tenure as manager, which, even in the 1990s, Rangers were still unable or unwilling to move on from.

Regardless, it clearly wasn't taking long for the new Ibrox manager to warm to his task and his elevated status at the club. Craig Brown, another of Smith's former colleagues with the Scotland set-up, remembered, 'I recall meeting him a few weeks after he had been appointed Rangers boss, and he was bristling with purpose, and he looked as if he couldn't wait to get down to business with his team, his methods.' Rangers, already a transformed and successful outfit from Souness's time in charge, were about to go from strength to strength on the Scottish domestic scene under their new boss.

It would be a very different story in Europe, however.

4.

If You Build It,
They Will Come

FERGUS McCann wasted little time in surveying his new surroundings in the east end of Glasgow before getting down to work once the formalities of his takeover of Celtic had been completed. 'I am delighted to be joining the board,' he told reporters in the aftermath of his coup. 'Thankfully we have been able to resolve the critical short-term financing of Celtic and shortly we will be able to discuss a long-term package.' His acquisition of the club had, he claimed, been a 'total victory' for the rebels and a vindication of his strategy in playing the long game with the old board, whose incompetence and unpopularity he always believed would eventually catch up with them. The ousted directors retired to lick their wounds and consider their futures, with few of them ever heard of in connection with Celtic again. The exception was Michael Kelly, who continued to write defensive and self-justifying newspaper articles for several months after his resignation from the club and, in October 1994, he appeared on Radio Scotland's *Sportsound* programme claiming that the campaign to remove him from the Parkhead board was orchestrated by 'a determined group of people that was prepared to damage Celtic in order to obtain their ends'.

The radio interview formed part of a publicity campaign for Kelly's book on the subject of his exit from Celtic, *Paradise Lost: The Struggle for Celtic's Soul*, published around the same time, which in many ways offered an insightful and interesting view of events, but was also bitter and, with the benefit of hindsight, inaccurate in its predictions for the club's future under McCann. 'He [McCann] overestimates the commercial value of the Celtic brand; in short I think he will lose his money,' wrote Kelly, perhaps demonstrating his failure to appreciate the importance of the club to its community of supporters, something McCann had a first-hand grasp of from his pre-emigration days. 'I'm sure that the fans won't be daft enough to take up more than a small fraction of the currently proposed issue of voteless preference shares,' Kelly continued, with another contention that, in time, turned out to be wide of the mark.

Pride of place, however, must be given to Kelly's less than prophetic assertion concerning McCann's plan to convert Celtic Park into a 60,000-capacity all-seater stadium: 'Having studied the physical and financial challenges involved in this, I am prepared to state categorically that it will never be finished,' he emphasised. With foresight like this, it's perhaps no surprise that Kelly failed to predict the club's looming insolvency or anticipate the approaching hour when the Bank of Scotland would finally turn against the directors and step in to recover its money. Even 20 years later, Kelly was still unhappy with the board's treatment by the bank, telling *The Herald* in March 2014, 'It is no surprise, looking back, that the bank Celtic had used for 106 years behaved in such an immoral and cowardly fashion. A few years later, they raped the whole of the British economy in the same way.' Here, at least, Kelly may have had a point, after the role played by the merged Halifax/Bank of Scotland in the global financial crisis and the 'credit crunch' of 2008.

Quickly getting down to business, McCann's first act, once Kelly and co. had departed into the sunset and the Canadian was confirmed in his role as the club's new managing director, was to send in the accountants to survey and catalogue every aspect of Celtic's commercial activities. The team from the firm Pannell Kerr Forster pored over every invoice and examined every statement on the club's books in minute detail, from the players' wages to the catering contracts, until they had completed a thorough audit and recorded the full extent of Celtic's financial position. The subsequent report, running to hundreds of pages, painted a gloomy picture of mismanagement and debt, worse even than had been expected, with the club's dire predicament underestimated in the old regime's internal management accounts. The club's method of servicing the overdraft was also revealed in an agreement with the bank to reduce the debt by half of all income received from transfer fees, including the recent sales of Stuart Slater and Gerry Creaney, an arrangement that seemed to vindicate new company secretary Dominic Keane's allegation at the EGM in November 1993 that a process of asset stripping had been taking place at Celtic.

In addition, the club had overestimated its income from media rights deals and was selling itself short with poorly negotiated sponsorship and advertising agreements, while the commercial department was yielding a low return from matchday catering and the club's shops, bringing in only a fraction of what Rangers were making from similar activity. Finally, season ticket sales had earned the club a mere £1.5m from a total number of 7,000 hardy supporters, with the board having placed minimal emphasis on promoting the idea of season tickets, believing that few fans could afford them. By the time McCann left the club at the end of his five-year turnaround assignment, the number of supporters who were prepared to commit their money to the club through the purchase of a season ticket had risen to 53,000 and the resulting revenue had become the foundation of Celtic's entire financial model.

Armed with this expensively procured information, the next step in the McCann revolution was for the new chief executive to hold an EGM so that he could invest his money and recapitalise the club through a share issue. This was still potentially problematic, however, as the club's largest individual shareholder was now Gerald Weisfeld, who for some time had been buying up shares from, among others, Brian Dempsey, in order to facilitate his own plans for a takeover at Parkhead. The two rival camps now had to come together and reach a deal, because with Weisfeld set to see his percentage diluted in the share issue, his opposition to McCann's proposal could still have seen the Parkhead club put into receivership. If McCann, by now Celtic's largest unsecured creditor after taking on the debt to the bank, had subsequently called in his loan, he would then have been obliged to buy the club back from the insolvency practitioners and Celtic, as a viable business, would have had to start again from scratch.

In such circumstances, the club's debts, including the money still owed to Stoke City in compensation for their manager Lou Macari and his backroom staff, would have effectively been cancelled or at least drastically reduced, a scenario that might have represented the cheaper option from McCann's point of view. It would also have caused the club great embarrassment, however, and the fans, in raptures following his takeover, would have immediately been plunged back into despair and may, in all probability, have lost their faith in the Canadian's entire mission at Celtic. On Tuesday, 26 April, the two sides met in a lawyer's office on St Vincent Street, where after a lengthy period of horse-trading and negotiations that continued through the night and into the next day, a deal was agreed that satisfied all parties. Later in the week, the EGM went ahead, where the plans for a share issue and McCann's investment of capital were approved unanimously. Unlike the club's previous recent experiences with EGMs, this time there was no infighting or arguing and the meeting had lasted just over an hour.

With the prospect of £21m being invested into the club through the share issue, McCann was now ready to deal with the outstanding question over the club's stadium. The old board had spent nearly £500,000 on consultancy fees over the Cambuslang scheme, and while McCann initially vowed that all options would remain on the table, it quickly became clear that the project was a non-starter and, with the deadline for compliance with the requirements of the Taylor Report just a few months away, the decision to go ahead with the redevelopment of Celtic Park was given the green light. The stadium was currently furnished with almost 13,000 seats, including 5,000 in the North Stand that had been installed the previous summer in an attempted short-term fix by the old board. In common with so many other pre-Hillsborough grounds around Britain, the move had finally spelled the end of Celtic Park's most iconic stand, the famous 'Jungle' terrace, which had witnessed the most boisterous and, often, the most humorous backing of the team over many decades. Under the new plans, however, almost the whole stadium would be rebuilt, and at the end of the season the bulldozers were sent in and the North Stand, as well as the Celtic End to the west and the Rangers End to the east, were all flattened. In their place would emerge a new, fully compliant, all-seater arena, which when completed would turn out to be one of the finest modern football stadiums in Britain.

In the meantime, as the Parkhead side played out another dismal season on the field, the club continued to fulfil the remainder of its fixtures at the current ground. After McCann's takeover had been greeted the following day by a 1-0 win over St Johnstone in Perth, when the new owner's appearance in the directors' box was cheered almost as loudly by the travelling fans as the early strike from Paul Byrne that settled the match, Celtic had to wait a further three weeks before their first home fixture under the new regime. With an expectant crowd, which had swelled to over 36,000 – an almost fourfold increase on the last home match, the boycotted game against Kilmarnock – anticipating the dawn of a new era, the fans were left to consider that there was still a long way to go and that any transformation in the club's fortunes would be a slow and gradual process, as the Parkhead men succumbed to a 1-0 defeat at the hands of Motherwell.

The setback seemed to confirm the caveat issued by Brian Dempsey in the days immediately following the takeover, when the former director warned supporters that there was no magic wand and that it would be a while before the club could sustain a credible assault on the league championship. Nevertheless, just four days later, on 30 March, the team won their first game under McCann at Celtic Park, a 2-1 victory over Raith Rovers, but this proved to be the club's last home win of the season, as the Parkhead side's campaign eventually tailed off with a series of draws, culminating in a lowly fourth-place finish and failure to qualify for European football.

The summer saw the rebuilding process at Parkhead begin in earnest as McCann dispensed with the services of the club's manager Lou Macari. The former Scotland international had been appointed by the old board in October 1993, but it quickly became clear that his methods were grating on his squad of players, with Scotland international John Collins insisting that the new manager's unsophisticated approach was 'chalk and cheese' in comparison to the more mellifluous style of football that they had been encouraged to play under Liam Brady. Collins certainly wasn't the only member of the Celtic playing staff to voice his concerns at Macari's techniques, as several of the midfielder's team-mates also derided the manager's coaching and motivational skills, including Frank McAvennie, who was forced to endure a second spell working under Macari at Parkhead following the manager's short stewardship of West Ham United. The blond striker later described Macari as 'the worst manager with whom I ever worked', lambasting in particular the team's style of play under the diminutive Scot, which he described as 'head tennis'.

If Macari's rapport with his players was frosty, it quickly became clear that the relationship between manager and chairman at Parkhead, traditionally regarded as one of the most important aspects of a properly functioning football club, was a veritable cold war of silence and mistrust, with Macari repeatedly disappearing for long spells back to his home in Stoke and declining all requests from McCann to move his family up from the English Midlands, a refusal that was later cited as grounds for dismissal by the new owner. To be fair, Macari had scant resources at his disposal to mould and shape his team during his short spell in charge at Parkhead, with his remit under the old board, if anything, aimed more at reducing costs and getting some of the club's better paid players off the wage bill. While few Celtic fans lamented the departures of strikers Andy Payton and Gerry Creaney, for their replacements Macari was forced to trawl for bargain basement signings and rely on his knowledge of the English lower leagues, resulting in the likes of Wayne Biggins, Carl Muggleton and Willie Falconer arriving at the club.

Biggins, described by the manager, unflatteringly, as a 'target man', made ten appearances for Celtic without, in cricketing parlance, troubling the scorers. Meanwhile, Falconer, a popular figure, played his part, indirectly at least, in the demise of the old board; when his former club Sheffield United called in the first tranche of the £350,000 fee they were due for the player on 3 March, the Bank of Scotland refused to pay out, a move that quickly consolidated the determination of Rowland Mitchell and his colleagues at the bank to unload Celtic's debt. With criticism of his style of play, his coaching methods and his relationship with his staff all adding up, it seemed that the writing was on the wall for Macari when, on 14 June 1994, after just eight months in the job, the manager was informed of his dismissal as he was about to go on holiday with his family to America, where he planned to take in the sights and the razzmatazz of the 1994 World Cup.

McCann pondered for some time over a potential replacement for the departed Macari, with serious consideration being given to offering the Dutchman Guus Hiddink the manager's role at Parkhead, while the former England manager Bobby Robson turned the club down. In the end, the chairman settled on fans' favourite Tommy Burns, who had been working wonders on a shoestring budget as player-manager of Kilmarnock since his departure from Celtic in 1989. With 14 years' service to the Parkhead club's cause as a player, McCann knew that the supporters, starved of glory and impatient for success, would at least afford Burns some time in his quest to bring honours to Celtic, in what was unquestionably a difficult transitional period for the club.

Burns was officially unveiled as the club's new manager on 12 July, but his arrival at Parkhead became mired in controversy when McCann was accused of 'tapping up' the former Kilmarnock boss, along with his assistant Billy Stark, and of making an illegal approach to secure the services of the two ex-Celtic players. While there was never any doubt, as long as Celtic's interest in the pair was genuine, that Burns and Stark would leave Kilmarnock, McCann appeared to have jumped the gun by meeting and discussing the vacancy with Burns at a Manchester hotel after the Ayrshire club had initially refused Celtic permission to speak to their manager. In August, Celtic were fined £100,000 by the Scottish League for the illegal move for Burns, an amount that was felt by many connected to the Parkhead club to be excessive and even vindictive. Most people in the game believed that the alleged transgression was common practice in modern football, with one journalist subsequently admitting that an unnamed colleague had at one time or another, while acting as a middleman between football clubs and prospective employees, 'tapped more players and managers than a shipyard worker has rivets'.

McCann subsequently cited the previous record fine for such an offence, the £5,000 figure imposed on Rangers for an illegal approach to Dundee United striker Duncan Ferguson, as evidence of the harshness of the sanction against his club, although the apparent anomaly was later explained, at least in part, by League secretary Peter Donald, who stated only that the Burns case was 'more complicated'. The League's decision was later ratified as 'final and binding' by the SFA's chief executive, Jim Farry, after McCann appealed the verdict and the severity of the fine, and Celtic were also later ordered to pay £200,000 in compensation to Kilmarnock for the loss of their management team.

McCann had maintained all along that Burns had applied for the vacant position at Celtic and was entitled, with a £150,000 per year salary on offer at Parkhead, to advance his career, but coming so soon after his arrival from the very different culture of North American business, McCann was noticeably still showing signs of naïvety in regard to the unquestionably arcane methods of Scottish football administration. He may also have underestimated the apparently gleeful way in which his misjudgement would be seized upon by the game's bureaucrats and the press, who for the most part were scathing in their criticism of McCann's handling of the affair throughout. Alan Davidson seemed to sum up the general mood with a piece for the *Evening Times* in which he claimed, 'Celtic, and McCann in particular, should be having a right good look in the mirror ... Why McCann felt it necessary to personally sound out Burns beggars belief ... he must recognise the rules of the game were not established to be so blatantly disregarded by a man who knows virtually nothing of the structure of Scottish football.' McCann's honeymoon period, it seemed, was well and truly over and the first shots had been fired in a conflict that would continue between McCann and large sections of the media in Glasgow over the next five years and beyond.

Also over the close season, in addition to the new football management team, the restructured boardroom at Parkhead began to take shape, with the departure of all four remaining directors from the old regime – Jack McGinn, Tom Grant, James Farrell, who held on until September before bowing to the inevitable, and Kevin Kelly – finally being confirmed over the summer, although the role of the former chairman Kelly in assisting McCann's bid for the club was acknowledged as he retained the title of Chairman Emeritus and President of Celtic Boys Club. They were replaced by Eric Riley, the new financial director, John Keane, an Edinburgh-based builder who had previously helped the club out of a financial hole, and the duo from the Weisfeld-led consortium, Michael MacDonald, who brought his experience of public relations and marketing from his time with Weisfeld's chain of shops, and Willie Haughey, a prominent Glasgow businessman.

Brian Dempsey, however, refused the offer of a directorship, perhaps after it became apparent that McCann had no clearly defined role for him other than as a popular figurehead who would keep the media and the fans onside. The relationship between the two former allies turned sour relatively quickly after the takeover, and Dempsey, having been previously ousted from the club's boardroom by Kelly and co. a few years earlier, clearly didn't want to suffer the embarrassment of having to leave the club once again in similar circumstances. Instead, with revenge over those who had expelled him finally accomplished after the pivotal part he played in McCann's coup, he took to criticising the new regime from the sidelines, at one point complaining to Archie Macpherson that, 'Fergus McCann took away the heart and soul of Celtic and replaced it with a cash register.'

Dempsey was unhappy in particular that McCann had surrounded himself with outside advisers, mainly lawyers and accountants with no emotional attachment to Celtic, and after withdrawing his offer to invest £1m in the club, he departed the scene. Others, meanwhile, described McCann's control of the club in the early stages of his time in charge at Parkhead as an 'autocracy' and there was a feeling among many, including a few former rebels, that Celtic had merely lurched from one form of dictatorship to another following the removal of the old board. In McCann's defence, however, some of his critics were perhaps forgetting that the Canadian had invested more than two thirds of his entire fortune in Celtic and, with so much at stake for him personally, he was understandably reluctant to allow other people's interests and agendas to intrude on the clearly defined, long-term path that he was plotting for the club.

It was certainly evident from the start, however, that McCann hadn't arrived in Glasgow purely for the purpose of philanthropy, a white knight motivated only by his love for Celtic, as he was honest enough to admit shortly after the takeover. 'I'm not Santa Claus. I'm an investor and I expect to get my money back eventually. This is not a donation. I think Celtic can be made into not only a successful football team but also a successful business,' he stated. McCann's single-mindedness can perhaps be seen and explained in a letter to Dempsey as early as December 1990 as the pair were still plotting a takeover strategy, when he explained the personal risks and problems he foresaw with the plans he hoped to implement: 'My exposure with £7m in equity locked into a difficult business, plus five years in a tough job at a low salary, then a personal guarantee of a £5m bank loan, ending with an obligation to sell at a price and date I cannot change is more than you could expect from any investor.'

McCann's detractors were quick off the mark, and as the volume of criticism rose over the course of his five-year tenure at Celtic Park, from the media and elsewhere, the Canadian might have had cause to reflect how he could have benefited from Dempsey's gregarious presence around the club to deflect and absorb the mounting negativity that was being aimed at his Parkhead regime. Regrettably, however, it quickly became obvious that the two men had irreconcilably different personalities and were very far from being bosom brothers, so it was almost inevitable in the end, and perhaps even in their mutual best interests, that the pair never formally worked together at the club.

With his new board now in place, McCann was finally in a position by the end of the year to launch the long-awaited public share issue, which allowed willing supporters to invest their money in exchange for a stake in the ownership of the club. Opening on 20 December 1994, the offer gave fans the opportunity to spend a minimum of £620 for a block, or 'unit', of ten shares, with McCann promising that the subsequent recapitalisation of the club would allow him to proceed with the reconstruction of the stadium and provide the manager with funds to strengthen his squad of players. At first the uptake appeared to be slow following the EGM to launch the initial flotation, which took place just before Christmas, when ordinary fans clearly had other financial priorities, but as the deadline approached on 24 January, Celtic supporters responded in astonishing numbers, much to McCann's relief. Fans on the day were queuing out the door of the stadium and up the stairs to the Jock Stein Lounge in order to complete the paperwork in time and put their money into the club. The signing of Pierre van Hooijdonk for £1.2m from NAC Breda at the start of the new year also gave the flotation a boost, with £178,000 worth of shares being sold on the day that the Dutchman concluded his transfer to Parkhead. A series of open days at Celtic Park also had the desired effect, as the club had to take on more staff and print extra copies of the share prospectus in order to cope with the increased demand.

The initial overall target of £5m to be raised from ordinary supporters was soon adjusted to £9.4m, with Parkhead PR manager Peter McLean admitting, 'The interest has now gone through the roof ... we have been overwhelmed by the demand ... everyone at the club is delighted at how incredibly successful the operation has been.' In the end, the recalibrated target was also oversubscribed by £4.4m, requiring an additional, subsidiary issue to be hastily put together, and the fans, even at a time when there appeared to be no end in sight to their suffering, following a painful defeat to Raith Rovers in the League Cup Final at Ibrox in late November, had raised more cash than any other share flotation in the history of British football, an outcome that left even experienced investment analysts impressed and not a little surprised. For McCann, who initially had sounded like a worried man after the launch of the flotation, it was a pivotal moment and a turning point in his stewardship of the club. The new owner was overjoyed with the eventual response, subsequently claiming with the benefit of hindsight that it was the moment when he realised that his hopes for the future of the club would be realised. 'I felt a great heavy burden. People had put their cash down. I learned at that moment that I was right and the supporters were going to be there,' he later recalled.

As well as the ordinary Celtic fans, there were also other notable investors, including the Irish businessman, Dermot Desmond, who after meeting with McCann over lunch at the Dorchester Hotel in London to discuss the new owner's plans for the club, agreed to put in an initial £4m through his financial services company, QFS, a sum that was eventually matched collectively by the existing directors. He also agreed to underwrite £4m more, although in the end this insurance was rendered superfluous by the remarkable uptake from the fans. The following year, Desmond joined the board at Parkhead as a non-executive director in what would be the start of a long and productive association with Celtic, as the Irishman later went on to succeed McCann as the club's largest individual shareholder.

In the meantime, following the share issue, Celtic had become a plc, and as part of the restructuring of the business side of the club, the old 'Celtic Football and Athletic Company', which had been incorporated in 1897, became a subsidiary of the re-registered company, with a role to manage and promote the club on a day-to-day basis and deal with supporters' issues under the guidance of its own separate board of directors. In the end, McCann himself invested £9.4m in Celtic, roughly 70 per cent of his entire worth, to take a 51 per cent stake in the newly calibrated total share capital of Celtic plc. This allowed him overall control of the company for his self-appointed period of five years, but the public flotation also ensured that no individual or group of vested interests, from either the football or the corporate world, could claim absolute authority over Celtic again. The club's ownership base was now spread among roughly 10,000 individual supporters who had subscribed to the flotation and paid, on average, over £1,000 each to buy shares.

The total investment in Celtic plc, from a combination of ordinary fans, McCann, corporate investors such as Desmond, as well as the club's directors and many of the playing staff, had left the former debt-ridden club with well over £20m in its bank account. Even the media, who had initially been sceptical, were impressed with the scale of the eventual response, with the *Daily Record* carrying reaction from well-known Scottish comedian, 'Celtic daft' Tony Roper, one half of the famous *Only an Excuse* double act with Jonathan Watson, who had invested an undisclosed sum in the Parkhead club. Commenting on the size of the uptake of shares, which even at a time when the club's stadium was being demolished and the team were struggling badly on the park had surpassed the amount raised by Manchester United at their public flotation a few years earlier, funny man Tony remarked, 'We must be the most loyal fans ever. We've been, to say the least, disappointed over the last five or six years. Yet when we were called on to do our bit for Celtic, we were all willing to show our loyalty … At least we can say we've beaten the English in this case – even if there isn't a cup involved.'

The Herald, meanwhile, called it a 'staggering response' from the club's fans, a change of tune from the paper, which had been issuing only prophecies of doom in the run-up to the launch, when its apparently forensic analysis of the figures involved had seemed to indicate that McCann's sums didn't add up. Now, despite underestimating the scale of investment at £7m from 7,000 subscribers, the paper's reporter Iain Wilson claimed, 'Manager Tommy Burns was already due to receive £4m to boost the squad before the target figure was surpassed. That spending power is likely to increase even further under a promise from managing director Fergus McCann that Burns will receive "the lion's share" from the share issue.'

There was, however, a curious coda to the euphoria following the fans' remarkable level of investment in the club; in order to pay for their block of shares, McCann had offered supporters financial assistance in the form of a low-interest loan from the Co-operative Bank, with staggered repayments that amounted to just £7.77 per week, a sum which, as McCann pointed out at the time, came to less than the price of a matchday ticket. By now it seemed that the relationship, stretching back over 100 years, between the Bank of Scotland and Celtic had broken down in the aftermath of McCann's takeover at Parkhead. In the run-up to the share issue, when the club had been seeking additional finance, the bank had offered Celtic's new owner a loan facility of just £2.5m, insisting even for this small amount that the line of credit should be fully secured against the club's assets. McCann immediately took his business elsewhere, thanking the bank for their courtesies publicly and expressing regret that 'the level of support required by Celtic was not obtainable at this time'. Privately, however, the Canadian was fuming, as he later admitted: 'The Bank of Scotland, having been completely taken off the hook for £5.25m, unrecoverable in 1994 … offered only a £2.5m loan, fully secured, which was not much more than an insult. The club had no difficulty going to another bank; in this case it was the Co-op Bank, a comparatively small bank in Manchester, which provided a £10m line of credit, unsecured, at a very reasonable rate of interest.'

The treatment of Celtic, and in particular of McCann, by the Bank of Scotland seemed puzzling; this was the same institution that in the years ahead went on to lend an estimated £120m to other Scottish football clubs, including tens of millions to David Murray and Rangers, almost all of which, certainly by the time of the global financial crisis in 2008, it had been unable to recover. McCann, it seemed, having arrived from the business community of North America, was now gaining a first-hand insight into the altogether different world of Scottish football.

With the media, the game's administrators and now the banking community in Scotland proving a thorn in his side, the Parkhead supremo was perhaps entitled to think that there were people out there who, for whatever reason, were less than enamoured with what he was trying to achieve at Celtic.

The transitional nature of the first full season under the partnership of Burns and McCann was perhaps best illustrated by the club's need to find a temporary home for the entire duration of the on-field campaign. With Celtic Park undergoing a facelift to meet the requirements of the Taylor Report, a ground-sharing arrangement with Queen's Park FC was put in place for the 1994/95 season that allowed Celtic to play their home games at the national stadium, which was itself in the process of being transformed into a 50,000-capacity all-seater arena. However, unlike at Celtic Park, the reconstruction work at Hampden was already well down the road to completion.

Queen's Park, the oldest football club in Scotland, whose history as the Victorian pioneers of the amateur Scottish game stretched back to 1867, were curiously difficult to deal with over the potentially lucrative ground-sharing agreement, with solicitors for the amateur side, who finished eighth in Scottish football's fourth tier that season, insisting that as part of any deal with McCann's club, no foreign flag should be allowed to fly over the stadium during the period of Celtic's lease. This was clearly a reference to the Irish Tricolour, which, along with several other flags, had flown over the old Celtic Park for decades, with Queen's Park maintaining that failure to agree to the banning order clause being inserted into the £500,000 agreement between the two Glasgow clubs was a potential deal-breaker. McCann, though somewhat taken aback at the unnecessary stipulation, simply shrugged his shoulders and acquiesced.

At Hampden, the Celtic team were obliged under new regulations to wear numbers on the backs of their jerseys for the first time, replacing the tradition, peculiar to Celtic, of the figures being displayed on the players' shorts. On the whole, the club's fans were slow to embrace the temporary move to the south side of Glasgow, although a record 18,500 bought season tickets for the campaign, which would be fought in exile. The national stadium appeared to lack atmosphere during the club's tenancy, however, despite McCann's efforts to spice up the half-time entertainment with Rod Stewart impersonators and other such gimmicks. At a game against Kilmarnock on 17 September 1994, a look-a-like performer belted out a few of rock star Stewart's old classics for the Celtic fans during the interval, before moving round towards the away end of the stadium and, in response to the 'Judas Burns' banners that were on display, a reference to the Ayrshire side's erstwhile manager, the hirsute artiste then proceeded to taunt the travelling fans, cavorting and gesturing in front of them like an on-stage Stewart himself in his heyday, much to the amusement of the rest of the sparse Hampden crowd. Despite these bookings, which brought a touch of showbusiness to the club's generally unhappy sabbatical from Celtic Park, results at the national stadium were poor for Celtic, with a succession of drawn matches, 18 out of 36 in total, in a season that saw the introduction of three points for a win in Scotland, effectively ruling out a title challenge by Burns's side from the very early stages.

The supporters' misery was further compounded when, after reaching the final of the Coca-Cola (League) Cup, played at Ibrox on 27 November, Celtic failed to overcome Raith Rovers, a team the Parkhead men had fared well against, despite their struggles, when the sides had met during the course of the previous season, at the end of which the Fife club had been relegated. On this occasion, Celtic lost a tortuous penalty shoot-out after a 2-2 draw, a result that afforded the First Division side the first major domestic honour in their history as well as qualifying them for a place in Europe's UEFA Cup. In the aftermath, the overreaction was as predictable as it was merciless, with *The Scotsman* describing the giant-killing upset as 'a defeat too far' for the Parkhead side, while another newspaper claimed that Celtic's loss in the final represented 'the blackest day in the club's history'.

In truth, the whole club at this time seemed to be wallowing in despondency, from the manager, the players, through to the fans, as the team, after a bright opening to the campaign, which included a convincing 2-0 victory over Rangers at Ibrox in late August, completed a winless streak of 12 consecutive matches, a miserable run that started at the end of September and persisted through until the turn of the year. Only Fergus McCann seemed to be keeping his head while all around him were losing theirs, with the owner pointing out after the Raith Rovers debacle that: 'There were 38 other clubs who did not even make it to Sunday's Coca-Cola Cup Final. We need to make changes but we are not in crisis,' although it's perhaps hardly surprising, in such circumstances, that McCann seriously considered aborting his plans to go ahead with the upcoming share issue.

Redemption eventually arrived, after another lowly fourth-place finish in the league for the Parkhead club, when all eyes turned to Hampden, as Burns's side reached the final of the Scottish Cup where they once again faced lower league opposition in the shape of Airdrieonians, the Lanarkshire outfit managed by former Rangers midfielder Alex MacDonald. It was another tense game, with the Parkhead men once again appearing nervous and uneasy throughout the contest, despite effectively playing on home soil after a full season as temporary residents at the national stadium. The only goal of the game was fashioned and scored by two of Burns's new recruits, with Tosh McKinlay, signed from Hearts in November, crossing for Van Hooijdonk to head home in the ninth minute, the Dutchman's strike eventually ending a six-year drought without a trophy for the Parkhead club.

The relief on the face of club captain Paul McStay was there for all to see as he lifted the trophy and celebrated with the fans at the end of the match. It was, after all, McStay's missed penalty that had cost his team at Ibrox in the League Cup Final the previous November, after which the long-serving Celtic man admitted: 'My whole world caved in. I felt responsible for everything and it didn't matter how much people tried to console me. I couldn't be calmed.' Now, by contrast, a chisel would not have removed the smile from McStay's face, as Celtic claimed the cup for a record 30th time, prompting one commentator to observe subsequently of the club's long-awaited triumph that 'Celtic were back in the land of the living'. It was the first step in the long road to recovery for McCann's club.

By the start of the 1995/96 season, the Parkhead men, with a trophy in the cabinet for the first time since the end of the previous decade, were able to return to their spiritual home at the partially rebuilt Celtic Park, which was officially reopened during pre-season in a ceremony led by comedian and Celtic fan Billy Connolly. The main stand had remained, a recognisable remnant of the old arena, but otherwise the ground was totally transformed with a new, two-tiered and fully seated North Stand able to hold 26,000 fans now towering over the pitch where the Jungle had once stood. The east and west ends of the ground, meanwhile, remained a work in progress behind the two goals, limiting the capacity of the functioning stadium to around 34,000 at the time of reopening.

Before the new season got under way, however, the relationship between the manager and the chairman at Celtic Park appeared to be coming under strain. Perhaps using his position of relative strength after the cup final victory, Burns took the opportunity to criticise McCann publicly over the course of the week following the win against Airdrie at Hampden, in particular chastising the chairman for treating his squad like 'second class citizens' during a warm weather training session in Milan before the final. McCann was accused by the manager of keeping too tight a hand on the purse strings at the club and not allowing the players some spending money, an outburst for which he was later obliged to issue a public apology. Burns was often guilty of making sarcastic or vexatious remarks to the media, centred primarily on McCann's perceived thrift, which may have been intended to express his genuine exasperation in a humorous or light-hearted manner. However, his comments, unsurprisingly, were seized upon by the press, who by this time had apparently identified McCann as some sort of pantomime villain character in charge of Celtic. In the end the pair made a conscious effort to patch up their differences before the start of the season, issuing a joint statement after clear-the-air talks, which, although sounding rather forced, commended their 'good professional relationship' and their common long-term goal, namely 'the prosperity of Celtic'.

Burns may have been placated to an extent by the eventual arrival over the summer of German international forward Andreas Thom, who was signed from Bayer Leverkusen for £2.2m, adding to the squad enhanced by the purchases of

McKinlay, Van Hooijdonk and midfielder Phil O'Donnell over the course of the previous campaign. In addition, £1m was spent on John Hughes and Jackie McNamara, who were joined before the end of the year by Morten Wieghorst from Dundee, as Burns began to reshape the squad he had inherited. The club, however, missed out on forwards Marc Degryse and Dimitri Radchenko, after Burns had taken the unusual step of publicly confirming his transfer targets, as well as defender Gordan Petrić, who joined Rangers, while French winger David Ginola later admitted that he had used the contract negotiations with Celtic as a vehicle to speed up his efforts to secure a transfer to Barcelona. Instead, the out-of-contract Paris Saint-Germain (PSG) winger ended up at Newcastle United, and was roundly booed by the Parkhead crowd when the Geordies came to Glasgow for a pre-season friendly, in the game that marked the formal reopening of the new ground.

Burns's Celtic, over the course of the unfolding campaign, played some of the best and most fluent football seen in the Scottish game for many years, much to the delight of their supporters, including 30,000 season ticket holders housed in the rising new stadium. The team had very evidently made giant strides forward after the pain and purgatory of the hapless season at Hampden, and with a title challenge seemingly in the offing, McCann gave his approval to plans for the construction of a temporary stand, accommodating 3,500 additional spectators, complete with cagoules in case it rained on the uncovered seating, which opened to the west, where the Jock Stein stand would eventually be constructed. On 25 November the increased crowd of over 34,000, including thousands of schoolchildren from Ireland in the new seating area, witnessed a John Collins hat-trick, as the home side consigned Hearts to a 3-1 defeat.

Hopes were still high among supporters of a credible bid for the championship, but once again the fatal mistake, particularly in the new three points for a win environment, of drawing too many matches cost the club, who lost only one league match over the course of the entire league season yet still finished in second place behind Walter Smith's Rangers. The Ibrox side had, quite correctly, identified their city rivals as a rejuvenated threat and they stepped up their game accordingly, after winning the league almost by default over the previous few seasons. That solitary defeat for the Parkhead side had come at Celtic Park on 30 September, when Smith's side showed once again that they were capable of absorbing relentless Celtic pressure and still coming out on top in the end. Despite infuriating their manager with an apparent inability to wrestle control of the game from their hosts, Rangers full-back Alex Cleland headed his side into the lead towards the end of the first half before Gascoigne sealed the 2-0 win for the Ibrox men with a late counter-attacking strike. Rangers also managed to defeat Burns's men in the two cup competitions, after the other league games between the teams ended in draws, thereby managing to remain unbeaten over the season in six matches against Celtic at a time of the Parkhead club's resurgence. The Ibrox side, much to Burns's frustration, seemed to have successfully developed the useful attribute of being able to get the better of their main challengers without ever consistently dominating the play in the fixture.

For the Parkhead side to be really taken to school, however, it would take the slick French outfit PSG to present the viewing public with an altogether superior level of football, which the Celtic fans were gracious enough to appreciate. The Parisians travelled to Glasgow and won 3-0, on the back of a 1-0 victory in the first leg in France, to see off Burns's men in the early rounds of the Cup Winners' Cup. Elimination provided a timely reminder to the Parkhead men that, on top of their efforts to catch up with and overtake Rangers, there was still a considerable gap to be bridged if they were ever to return to the upper echelons of elite European football. To his credit, in the wake of the Cup Winners' Cup defeat to PSG, who subsequently went on to lift the trophy, Burns set about revitalising the coaching structure at the Parkhead club, visiting Ajax's renowned academy in Amsterdam, which had just helped to produce a Champions League-winning team, and remodelling Celtic's training sessions along more technical lines.

The tension and personality differences between the manager and the owner remained just below the surface throughout Burns's spell in charge of the club, however, and another bone of contention between the pair developed over the 'Bhoys Against Bigotry' campaign, which was launched by McCann in the *Celtic View* in January 1996. There was much that was commendable about the initiative, including a pledge to support the Northern Ireland Children's Hospital Scheme, which promoted integration among youngsters from deprived and segregated communities in the divided province, and a commitment on the club's part to draft a new mission statement and social charter, which would lay out clearly the club's opposition to discrimination and bigotry in all its forms. Announcing the new project, McCann confirmed, 'The club's role as a major social institution carries with it a responsibility to work against groups or individuals who use football, and particularly Celtic matches, as a medium for promoting their extreme and/or political views. Celtic has a greatly diversified supporter profile in terms of age, sex, religion and political background and it is the club's responsibility to aim to create a positive and acceptable environment for all supporters.'

Burns, initially at least, appeared to support the scheme, although he declined to get involved in any talk that referred to the traditional forms of discrimination and sectarianism usually found in the west of Scotland between Catholics and Protestants. The manager stated, 'No one at Celtic wants to be associated with bigotry – not the players, the management, the directors or the staff. I am a proud Christian and that is my personal right. However, I have strong respect for other religions and other people's rights to stand for what they believe in. Let's show that respect to everyone who comes to Celtic Park.' It later emerged, however, that Burns's support for the project was half-hearted at best, with the manager subsequently confiding to close colleagues that he felt the scheme was little more than a publicity stunt on behalf of McCann and that there was scant evidence for bigotry or religious discrimination being a recognisable phenomenon at Parkhead.

Shortly before he died of melanoma skin cancer in May 2008 at the age of just 51, Burns wrote an essay, published posthumously the following year in the anthology *Celtic Minded 3*, when he admitted, 'Celtic did have, and always has had players and supporters who were Protestant or of no faith, but we have always been a club where Catholics were not inhibited in the way they might have been elsewhere. The Catholic faith was something people here were comfortable with and no one felt a need to hide or disguise it. This is one of the reasons why I had a lot of difficulty with Fergus McCann's Boys [sic] Against Bigotry campaign. I had been here a long time and as far as I was concerned our club had no problem with bigotry … I never sensed anything untoward against people at our club or elsewhere who were not from the Catholic faith.' Burns wasn't naïve enough to believe that in any large group of people, such as the numbers who made up the fanbase of a popular club like Celtic, there would not be a substantial number of 'idiots' as he called them, and the Parkhead club were certainly no exception in that regard, but Burns was nevertheless left unconvinced by the scheme's merits. 'I always felt that the Boys [sic] Against Bigotry campaign was not really addressing these people and a whole lot of other things were being thrown in or invented,' he wrote.

Despite the manager concealing his scepticism at the time, the club's supporters were quick to register their opposition to the initiative, when it became clear that McCann was targeting the singing of Irish political and historical songs by sections of the Celtic Park crowd as part of his efforts to make the club appear more corporate friendly to his new customer base. The particular song that's often cited in such circumstances as an example of the unwanted intrusion of Irish political interests into the Celtic Park matchday experience is 'Boys of the Old Brigade', a lively number that refers to Michael Collins's revolutionary, self-trained battalions taking on the forces of the crown during the Irish War of Independence in the immediate aftermath of the First World War. Collins's IRA volunteers were ultimately instrumental in obtaining a version of home rule for Ireland with the foundation in 1922 of the Irish Free State, which later evolved into the modern Republic of Ireland.

Outside of the west of Scotland, this wasn't seen as a taboo or even a particularly controversial subject, with Collins himself being given the Hollywood treatment with a proclaimed film, *Michael Collins*, starring Liam Neeson, also released in 1996. In addition, disdain for 'Boys of the Old Brigade' from within the

Scottish establishment appeared hypocritical and unjustified, particularly when the song was compared with the remarkably similar 'Flower of Scotland', which the country had taken to its heart and, in recent years, had even adopted as its surrogate national anthem. Critics appeared to have no answer to the charge of double standards when the corresponding lyrics of the two songs were compared: 'they fought and died that Ireland might be free' for example, expressing almost exactly the same sentiment, and in a strikingly similar fashion, as 'fought and died for your wee bit hill and glen', with the only obvious difference being on the timescale of centuries to which the events of the songs referred.

The fans also believed that McCann's new scheme and his blanket ban on songs that were unfashionable with the establishment only added to the broadly perceived impression, particularly outside of Glasgow, that the two duelling Old Firm clubs were little more than, in the vernacular of football fans, two sides of the same coin when it came to their involvement in religious-based bigotry. Celtic fans felt that their club occupied the moral high ground over this issue because, while Rangers had been flagrantly operating an exclusionary employment policy at Ibrox for most of the 20th century, Celtic had always been a club open to all, and that while it may have been acceptable to congratulate the club over its long-held position, mission statements and other pledges aimed at reminding people of these well-known facts were unnecessary.

Others disagreed; because of the nature of the footballing rivalry in Glasgow, which had been divided along quasi-religious lines for many years, there were some Catholics and Celtic supporters who believed that, even if 90 per cent of the bigotry in Scottish society had historically been directed towards them, there had always been the other ten per cent going back in the opposite direction, if only, in an age before such modern-day concepts as political correctness, by means of retaliation. They therefore felt able to welcome McCann's initiative as an important first step on the road to some form of mutual reconciliation. Nevertheless, such disagreements only highlighted that McCann had waded into a complicated issue, which was never realistically going to be solved in a satisfactory manner by a campaign based on a three-word slogan.

A 1-0 victory for Rangers at Celtic Park on 19 September, with the only goal of the game scored by the prolific Ally McCoist, had allowed the Ibrox men to reach the semi-final of the League Cup at the expense of Burns's side. However, the second of the two cup successes for Rangers in the derby fixture that season, achieved in the Scottish Cup semi-final the following April, became mired in controversy, after the SFA failed to implement the transfer of Portuguese striker Jorge Cadete to Celtic in an apposite and timely fashion. Cadete had agreed a deal with the Parkhead club and was introduced to the Celtic Park crowd before a match against Partick Thistle on 24 February, but it wasn't until 1 April, after an inexplicably long delay in processing the player's registration, that the forward finally made his debut for Celtic, when he came off the bench and scored in a 5-0 rout of Aberdeen at Celtic Park. In the interim, the Parkhead side had dropped points and looked decidedly short of striking options in games against Rangers, 1-1 at Ibrox, and Motherwell, 0-0 at Fir Park, before on 7 April, Celtic met the Ibrox side at Hampden in the cup semi-final and lost 2-1. Once again, however, despite making his long-awaited debut the previous week, Cadete was absent from the Celtic line-up from the potentially season-defining match because, according to the rules of the competition, the paperwork on the player's registration hadn't been completed by the deadline of 23 March.

As far as McCann was concerned, responsibility for the unexplained oversight rested unequivocally with the SFA and its officious chief executive, Jim Farry, the most senior administrator of the game in Scotland. It was Farry who was ultimately responsible for ensuring that the SFA's procedures and processes ran smoothly and that the whole organisation was a properly functioning bureaucracy, but clearly, for whatever reason, the governing body had failed to adequately look after Celtic's interests on this occasion. In his book, *Walk On: Celtic Since McCann*, club historian David Potter posits three possible explanations for Farry's conduct over the delayed registration of Cadete, which led to the period of frustrating inactivity on the part of the Portuguese striker: bigotry-based malicious intent towards Celtic in the tradition of some of Farry's predecessors at the SFA; incompetence, again a long-standing attribute of previous SFA administrators; and third, what the author refers to as 'Farry's legalistic and pettifogging mind'. In the end, Potter comes down on the side of the third option, but others at the time begged to differ and it was certainly right that the other two possibilities were aired and considered by the respected author because there were unquestionably many among the Celtic support who believed that the alternative choices were at least equally feasible.

When the governing body, after conducting two internal investigations into the affair, subsequently cleared Farry of any wrongdoing, McCann threatened to take the organisation to court, and the matter was finally decided at an independent tribunal in March 1999, three years after the original offence and just weeks before the Canadian left Celtic and Scotland for good. It was only then that McCann finally won his case, leading to Farry initially being suspended and then fired for gross misconduct, with the former milkman and window cleaner and self-proclaimed 'one of the best football administrators in Europe' effectively found guilty of corruption at the Parkhead club's expense. The SFA councillors, after listening to their doomed CEO for several hours under cross-examination from Celtic's lawyers, had thrown in the towel in order to spare the poorly performing Farry from any further humiliation.

McCann's club subsequently received compensation and a letter of apology, but as journalist and author Kevin McCarra later pointed out, 'It is hard to come up with another example anywhere of it being proven that a football association has acted improperly towards a member club. The SFA had been humiliated by this demonstration that it could not be trusted.' Composer Sir James MacMillan, meanwhile, noted of the affair, 'The snarling jibes about Catholic paranoia were for once brought to a sudden, gob-smacked silence.' It was apparently the case that, for all the money and modernisation sweeping into the game at this time, Scottish football in many aspects was still in the dark ages in the 1990s. If, however, by the middle of the decade, McCann was becoming increasingly frustrated with the apparent culture clash between his accustomed business methods, honed in North America, and the wacky world of Scottish football, he was about to see before too much longer how things could become a whole lot stranger.

5.

A Double-Edged Sword

WALTER Smith's first spell in charge of Rangers in the 1990s was characterised by a frustrating and perplexing dichotomy. For while Smith's side continued to dominate the domestic and often parochial landscape of Scottish football in a relatively untroubled manner, albeit at times against feeble and waning opposition, they consistently came up short when faced with the challenge posed by the top sides in Europe, a criterion by which the management of the Ibrox organisation insisted that they should be judged. 'I'll buy the league,' was a bold Murray assertion that seemed to demonstrate the power of the chairman's wealth and self-assurance, and led to a promise fulfilled. 'Judge me on Europe' was another claim by the Rangers owner, which, over several years of successive and worsening disappointments on the Continent, echoed only of hollow overconfidence.

Smith used the summer of 1991 to begin the process of rebuilding and reshaping the Rangers squad that he had inherited from his predecessor, as 'foreign' players not affiliated to Scotland, such as Woods, Walters and Steven all departed the scene at Ibrox, with the 'native' Goram, McCall and Robertson among the club's new recruits, alongside Alexei Mikhailichenko, the talented Ukrainian midfielder who arrived from Sampdoria. At first, the signs seemed very promising indeed for the new manager following the transition from the volatile regime of Souness to the more becalmed and circumspect stewardship of his successor, as Smith's first full season in charge at Ibrox saw the club retain the league championship, Rangers taking the title for the fourth season in a row. In addition, although the League Cup was surrendered on the back of a shock semi-final defeat to Hibernian, the Ibrox side finally won the Scottish Cup, a trophy that had eluded Souness, after a dramatic, rearguard action semi-final victory over Liam Brady's Celtic was followed by a 2-1 win against Airdrie in the Hampden final.

The decisive match had been the last-four encounter with a Celtic team, which despite the self-immolation that the Parkhead club was inflicting on itself behind the scenes by this stage, pummelled a Rangers side reduced to ten men on the night following an early red card for defender David Robertson, but still contrived to lose 1-0. New signing Stuart McCall later hailed the defensive resolve shown by Rangers that night as the making of Walter Smith's team, telling *The Herald*, 'We had that bit of luck. Celtic should have had a stonewall penalty, McStay hit the bar and Goram was what he always was – inspired. You can look back through the history of games for little defining moments. And Walter might look back at that one. Once we managed to win with ten men for 85 minutes the belief in each other really grew.'

The club's European campaign, however, failed to get off the ground after a narrow, away goals defeat to Sparta Prague in the first round of the European Cup. Rangers performed poorly in Prague, losing the first leg 1-0, but looked to have retrieved the situation at Ibrox when two goals from McCall put the home side within reach of the second round, only for an unfortunate injury-time blunder by new goalkeeper Goram, which contributed to a Scott Nisbet own goal for the Czechoslovakian champions, to send Rangers spinning out of the competition at the earliest possible stage.

Despite UEFA's implementation of its controversial 'three plus two' foreigner rule at the start of the 1991/92 season, Smith's team made amends for their European frustrations the following season with an extraordinary run in the newly formatted Champions League, which took the Ibrox side to within one game of reaching the final, as Rangers enjoyed their best series of results in Europe for over 20 years. After a straightforward victory over Lyngby of Denmark, Rangers saw off the challenge from Leeds United in the final qualifier, winning 2-1 in both legs of the contest, inevitably dubbed the 'Battle of Britain' by the press on both sides of the border, to qualify for the round-robin mini-league phase of the competition. In the aftermath of victory over the English champions, forward Mark Hateley emphasised Rangers' ambitions and appeared to leave no one in any doubt about how the Ibrox club now viewed itself, when he told reporters, 'We regard ourselves as one of the biggest, if not the biggest club in Britain, and one of the biggest in Europe. I would rank us among the top five clubs in Europe,' the big striker maintained, revealing Rangers' inflated perception of their own status in the game at this time. He was also perhaps delivering an oblique rebuke to his countrymen, and in particular to the English media, the majority of whom had casually written off his team's chances in the build-up to the tie.

Rangers' opponents for the incipient group stages of the tournament would be Marseille, CSKA Moscow and Bruges, and again the Ibrox club enjoyed considerable success, managing to complete the campaign undefeated, which coming on the back of a domestic Treble for Smith's side, saw the Ibrox men chalk up a remarkable 44-game unbeaten run in all competitions. A draw in the Stade Velodrome against Marseille in the penultimate match, when victory was required, followed by a goalless stalemate at Ibrox against CSKA, ultimately put paid to Rangers' chances of topping the group and qualifying for the final, but despite losing out to the French champions, soon to be disgraced when a domestic bribery scandal engulfed the club, hopes were raised that European glory was now a realistic target for the Ibrox side, an ambition that everyone at the club, from the chairman down, was now openly acknowledging.

Early in the new season, and still with a relatively new manager at the helm, who by now appeared to be fulfilling his remit, Murray reflected on the club's best season on the Continent in decades. 'Rangers are the biggest club in Britain, people better realise that,' the chairman affirmed. 'We used to think we were a big club; we are the biggest club now. We made our mark in Europe, unfortunately we didn't get the position in the seedings, which was a big disappointment, but our ambitions hold no bounds. We've said it for years, we've nearly spent all the money on the ground and more and more money will become available. This will be a regular feature at Rangers. Our ambition is to go all the way.' At times, particularly in the afterglow of Rangers' successive on-field triumphs, it was almost as if Murray couldn't help himself in terms of the sustained truculence and volume of his proclamations, but unfortunately, despite what the chairman was promising, Rangers' European achievements in season 1992/93 proved to be a flash in the pan for the club. The following year the heartache returned after another narrow defeat on away goals in the first round, with Smith's side on this occasion coming up short against Bulgarian champions Levski Sofia.

While it could certainly be argued that Rangers had been unlucky in certain aspects and had contributed to their own downfall in the ties with Sparta Prague two years earlier and now against Levski, these former Eastern bloc clubs were hardly considered to be European powerhouses and Rangers' inability to brush aside such opponents represented a chastening rebuke to their claims to be considered among the Continent's elite sides. In addition, although Murray's club had once again reigned supreme in the domestic league, taking their sixth title in a row, their season had limped to a curiously unconvincing conclusion, with Smith's side failing to win any of their last five league games and finishing the season with 19 points fewer than in the previous, all-conquering campaign. Then, with the prospect of securing unprecedented back-to-back Trebles to spur them on, the Ibrox men lost the Scottish Cup Final to Dundee United, by now under the stewardship of the enigmatic Serb Ivan Golac following the recent retirement of long-serving club guru Jim McLean, with the Taysiders capturing the old trophy for the first time in their history after a 1-0 victory over Smith's side at Hampden.

The following year Rangers bounced back strongly, making amends for the cup final setback and taking the league championship by fully 15 points from Alex McLeish's second-placed Motherwell. Celtic were still struggling through a first full, transitional season at Hampden following new owner Fergus McCann's takeover, while the two 'New Firm' sides, Aberdeen and Dundee United, finished in the league's bottom two positions. By the mid-1990s, the alarming decline in the standards and reputation of Scottish football was beginning to hit home, as the Tayside club, UEFA Cup finalists just a few years earlier, were relegated in 1995, while Aberdeen, still the only Scottish side to have won two European trophies after their Cup Winners' Cup victory over Real Madrid in 1983 was followed later in the same year by a Super Cup win against European champions Hamburg, avoided a similar fate only after escaping from a two-legged play-off with Dunfermline Athletic.

A few years later, in 2000, the Dons were again fortunate to be reprieved from relegation, on this occasion as a consequence of league reconstruction, after the Pittodrie side finished bottom of the ten-team Premier Division. Aberdeen's failure at this time was made all the more dismal and incomprehensible by the club's policy of maintaining high levels of spending in an attempt to keep up with the top sides, a strategy that included the £1m purchase of Paul Bernard from Oldham Athletic in September 1995. The Pittodrie club's board, led by local businessmen Ian Donald and Stuart Milne, had sanctioned the outlay of a club record fee for the Scots-born midfielder, a transfer that still to this day represents the only instance of a team in Scotland outwith the Glasgow duopoly paying a seven-figure sum for a player.

It wasn't just Aberdeen and Dundee United, however; at the time, Scottish football generally seemed to have entered a period of steep decline, and while there were many theories and arguments being put forward for the causes of this evident regression, it seemed undoubtedly the case that there was an obvious link to the changing social and political landscape of the day. Ever since the 1980s, the roots and traditions of British football had come under attack from Conservative Prime Minister Margaret Thatcher's ideological undermining of working-class people and institutions, and it appeared that the ensuing transformation of British society as a result of her government's policies was having a deleterious effect on the game in Scotland.

The romantic rise of the New Firm sides, who had toppled the Glasgow-based hegemony of the domestic game and challenged the best teams in Europe during the 1980s, had very evidently peaked and was now going into rapid decline, while the general standard and style of play in Scottish football was becoming ugly and over-physical, at times often nasty and unpleasant, with aggressive, even violent defenders complemented by Jack-the-Lad, in-your-face-type forwards, epitomised at Rangers by the triumvirate of McCoist, Cooper and Durrant, or across the city at Celtic successively in strikers Nicholas, Johnston and McAvennie. While many of these players had their apologists and admirers, it seemed clear that the self-seeking approach was now becoming more widespread, and without realising why, this new type of footballer was gradually replacing the 'men of the people' heroes of yesteryear, such as Jim Baxter at Rangers and Celtic's Jimmy Johnstone, or the honest as the day is long, genuine hard men like Billy McNeill and John Greig, or going back further, Rangers' famous – some would say notorious – 'Iron Curtain' defensive line of the 1950s.

Footballers, it seemed by the late 1980s and early 1990s, could no longer be considered simply as fans who had got lucky, and while it would be wrong to pin the blame for the decline of Scottish football on just a few individuals, who for the most part would have been unaware or unconcerned with how the world was changing around them, this new breed of players, despite their media profiles and their cult status with some, can be seen as part of a trend that was eroding one of the enduring strengths of the Scottish game, namely its link with working people and their communities. Their emergence also came at a time when the steady flow of talent, which had fed and enriched Scottish football since the Victorian era, appeared to be drying up, as fewer young players were being successfully integrated into the major clubs' first teams.

These problems certainly were not unique to Scotland, but they affected the country particularly badly, where watching and playing football had been the single most important recreational activity in the lives of the urban, industrial working-class for 100 years and more. Perhaps most importantly, while in England floods of cash from various previously untapped sources were replacing the old methodology and reshaping how the game was being seen and regarded, by contrast, north of the border the cupboard was bare in financial terms. Clubs in Scotland were forced to accept no more than crumbs from the English banquet when seeking television rights deals and other sources of income, a development that seemed to undermine the historical balance between the two nations, as the traditional strengths of the Scottish game were swept along on a tide of avarice.

It seemed futile, particularly for a small, politically dormant country like Scotland, with no accountable government of its own in the 1990s, to resist the changes that were taking place in football at this time; the game was evolving, the times were changing and nobody wanted to be stuck in the past forever. Far better, it seemed, to try to manage the new developments effectively and keep tabs on the direction that the modern game appeared to be taking, with a watchful eye on the impact on standards as well as on the wider trends and consequences. With men such as David Murray on hand during this period, however, to take advantage of the shift in football's vulnerable status and role in society, the sport was gradually transformed from the working-man's game into the plaything of rich, well-connected and narcissistic businessmen. Football supporters, meanwhile, in return for relinquishing their previously unchallenged position as the lifeblood and focus of the sport, were instead now being asked to pay through the nose for something that they had once considered as almost sacrosanct, namely their right to habitually attend football matches as an affordable part of their fortnightly routine.

At the same time, during this period of steady and seemingly irreversible deterioration, both in the Scottish game and among the other have-nots of British football, the sense of ownership of the game passed from the fans, where it had always resided, to football's new paymasters, namely big media, who, completing the vicious circle rather neatly it seemed, were also largely supportive of the Thatcher government's radical agenda for societal reform. This new ethos put unregulated free enterprise ahead of what essentially had been the fabric of society, namely the solidarity and strength derived by working people from a shared sense of community and identity, of which football had always been an important part.

Although Rangers were at the vanguard of the new developments that were affecting Scottish football, following the changes in ownership and strategy at the club in the 1980s, the reversal in the fortunes of the domestic game in Scotland appeared to coincide with the team's ongoing disappointments in Europe around this time, as Walter Smith's side, playing a curiously old-fashioned brand of archetypal British football, fell flat on their faces once again at the start of the 1994/95 season. The Ibrox men lost home and away to a decent, but hardly exceptional AEK Athens side and consequently suffered another early elimination from the Champions League at the hands of the Greek champions, meaning that Rangers had now been knocked out of the competition in the first-round qualifiers in three of the last four seasons. Moreover, Smith's side had been defeated by such mid-ranking European teams as Sparta Prague and Levski Sofia, and now, with expensive new recruits including Basile Boli, Brian Laudrup and Duncan Ferguson recently added to their squad, another lesser light of European football in AEK had also claimed the scalp of the underperforming Scottish champions.

On this latest occasion, however, there was no lament over self-inflicted wounds or regret for what might have been, as Rangers had been thoroughly outclassed by the low-profile Greek outfit, a reality that seemed to irk Smith as his side's early dismissal from the competition led to a caustic exchange between the Rangers manager and BBC reporter Chick Young in the tunnel at Ibrox the following morning. The result was a notorious interview, which these days can be seen all over social media and the streaming service YouTube, in which Young questions whether the players brought to the club over the summer, in particular Boli and Laudrup, the imperious Dane who had arrived from Fiorentina, were good enough to play at the top level in Europe. Smith responded angrily, and the exchange proceeded as follows:

Smith: 'How can you say that? I mean, they've just come to the place. You've got to give everybody a chance to settle in … Boli's won a European Cup winners' medal for fuck's sake. You cannae say he's no' a good enough player to play in Europe. That's fucking stupid, isn't it? You cannae say that Boli and Laudrup cannae fucking play. Laudrup played seven out of ten games [on loan] for AC Milan last year, and Boli played in a team that's won the European Cup, and the only reason he didn't play last year was because they [Marseille] were banned. For fuck's sake ... Have you been up all night working that out? ... That was your fucking words to me, that they two couldnae play in Europe. Archie, come here and hear this fucking interview ... He's coming out with worse shite than ever.'

Smith's assistant Archie Knox walks past, with a thinly disguised glare of contempt in his eyes, saying, 'I'd have him out of here on his fucking arse if it was up to me.'

Smith, resuming: 'You can't be fucking serious wi' that.'

Young: 'All right, I'll do it again,' and clears his throat, before continuing, 'The Rangers fans are demanding ...'

Smith, interrupting: 'Your questions to the chairman last week were fucking shite an aw, right, and this week's exactly the fucking same. If we had a bad night last night, then you're having a fucking horrendous morning the now.'

Young: 'You did have a bad night last night.'

Smith: 'Aye, that's what I said to you.'

Young: 'Do you not agree with me that the two of them didnae play well last night?'

Smith: 'Aye, but that doesnae mean they aren't good enough to play in Europe. Surely they have fucking proved on many occasions before that they are good enough. It's just fucking silly to be talking about this ... that'll go down well at the Christmas fucking party, won't it!'

Clearly, the tension was starting to mount at Ibrox, as Rangers lost 2-0 at home to Celtic a few days later and then followed up the derby reverse with a third defeat at Ibrox in a week, after Smith's side suffered an early exit from the League Cup at the hands of newly promoted Falkirk. It was the first time that Rangers had chalked up three successive home losses since April 1972. As the dust settled on another European failure at Ibrox, however, it was gradually becoming clear that there was another target potentially distracting the Ibrox men from their European ambitions, much to chairman Murray's chagrin, namely Celtic's record of nine consecutive league titles, achieved by Jock Stein's great Parkhead side of the late 60s and early 70s. As their goal approached, Ibrox defender John Brown recollected how early the squad had their objective in mind as well as their confidence that they would ultimately be able to achieve it: 'From our second or third title in a row we really believed that we were strong enough and good enough to make it to nine-in-a-row. Celtic were in a bit of a state and our main challengers were Aberdeen, although Motherwell and Hearts also pushed us at times. Aberdeen came closest but the good thing was that whenever we needed to push on the manager was able to go out and buy more quality, thanks to the full backing of the chairman.'

Brown's reference to the power of the chairman's money re-emphasised the reliance that Rangers were placing on the spending policy that was in force at Ibrox, thanks largely to Murray's seemingly limitless credit line with the bank. The chairman was frequently heard bragging about his club's financial muscle and how he intended for the strategy of chequebook management to continue at Rangers, regardless of the extent of the liabilities that the club was accumulating. The rising debt question in Scottish football was an issue that was occasionally starting to be mentioned in the media, as other clubs sought to emulate the practices that were being successfully implemented at Ibrox and buy their way to more modest, but still largely unattainable levels of achievement. The pertinent issue of where all the money was coming from, however, was rarely, if ever, addressed, as many Scottish football clubs, with vanguard Rangers the particular focus, were allowed to effectively bankrupt themselves over the years ahead. At the same time, while Murray's ambitions for the club continued to grow, the chairman's promises and declarations about where he wanted to take the club were sounding ever more reckless and increasingly detached from reality with every passing season.

This was all a long way from Rangers' traditional approach to handling the club's finances; by way of contrast to the outlay on spending that was being greenlighted by Murray, back in 1965 Rangers had previously been described by former striker Ralph Brand as 'totally stingy' in regards to players' wages and transfer fees. In the 1970s, the club's financial affairs had been looked after with a miserly diligence, in the tradition of true Presbyterian thrift, by general manager Willie Waddell, while in the early 1980s the upper limit on wages at Ibrox, for the club's top performers, was restricted to just £350 per week. It was the old, floundering Celtic directors who had often been reprimanded and ridiculed for their overzealous economising, which had latterly led them to be saddled with the label of the 'biscuit tin' board, a reference to where they were alleged to have kept the club's money, but in truth Rangers had been no different in the decades prior to the arrival of Souness and Holmes at Ibrox, and Murray's policies were completely out of step with the club's customary way of doing business.

Murray had always relied on his ability to persuade other people to put up money for his projects and to back his vision for the future success of his businesses, even since his early days in charge of his private firm, Murray International Holdings. In 1981, with his fledging operation now growing to maturity, Murray sold off a 9 per cent stake in his company, putting away the proceeds as a 'nest egg' for his two sons, David and Keith, and their future children. Around the same time, the young businessman struck up a close relationship with Gavin Masterton, a senior executive at the Bank of Scotland, who later became the bank's treasurer and managing director. Very quickly, Murray managed to catch the eye of Masterton, who proved to be a useful ally in the years ahead, lending money to the industrialist's growing portfolio of companies from almost the moment the pair first became acquainted. It was Masterton's bank that provided the cash for Murray's original purchase of Rangers, when it was said that the incoming chairman was able to secure the £6m in finance he required to complete the transaction with a single phone call to his friend in Edinburgh.

As time went on and the chairman's ambitions grew, this relationship would become a key aspect of Rangers' success, with the bank's indulgent attitude towards Murray's requirements for his club fuelling the spending strategy at Ibrox and allowing Rangers to run up enormous and, in a Scottish football context, unprecedented levels of debt. Journalist Ian Fraser, the respected financial commentator who some years later wrote the book on Rangers supporter Fred Goodwin's disastrous time at the head of the Royal Bank of Scotland in the period leading up to the 2008 financial crisis, observed of Masterton's policy towards Murray and Rangers over this period, 'It almost reached the stage where the bank seemed to believe that David Murray could walk on water … they would lend money for almost anything that he seemed to want it for.' Despite the liabilities in the balance sheet, however, there appeared to be no risk of an insolvency event at Ibrox at this time because, unlike the situation at rivals Celtic, the company's assets had a comparatively high net worth, most notably Ibrox stadium and the Albion training facility, which were valued at roughly £35m in the mid-1990s.

Masterton was a lifelong fan of Dunfermline Athletic, the Fife club, which after a sustained period of success in the 1960s, seemed to operate a kind of yo-yo existence from the late 1980s, bobbing up and down between the Premier League and the lower divisions without ever quite managing to establish themselves as a permanent feature of the country's top flight. The exception came in the early part of the new century when, under the management of Jimmy Calderwood and his assistant Jimmy Nicholl, the Pars enjoyed a brief period in the limelight. It later transpired, however, that Murray and Masterton's clubs had a tacit understanding regarding Calderwood, whereby the former Birmingham City player, who had returned to his native Scotland after a spell coaching in the Netherlands, was being groomed at Dunfermline to eventually take over as manager of Rangers, the team he had long supported. In the end, the move never transpired, but Calderwood's candid revelations over the proposed arrangement, disclosed years later, only re-emphasised the close personal and working relationship that existed between the owners of the two clubs.

Meanwhile, Rangers' form had been patchy towards the end of the 1994/95 season, particularly after the departure of Dutch winger Peter Huistra, who joined Japanese side Sanfrecce Hiroshima in January and whose loss upset the balance of Smith's team. Things improved the following year, however, in response to Celtic's overdue renaissance, as over the summer the talented but flawed Paul Gascoigne joined the club in a £4.5m deal from Lazio, ending the mercurial Geordie's injury-checked sojourn in Italy. Switching to a back three defensive formation, Smith's men held off the renewed threat from the

Parkhead club, who lost only one league game over the course of the season, a 2-0 loss to Rangers at Celtic Park in September. The Parkhead men were also frustrated by their rivals in both the League Cup, although Rangers later were eliminated from the competition by Aberdeen, and the Scottish Cup, following a controversial semi-final encounter between the Glasgow sides, which Celtic were obliged to play without new signing Jorge Cadete. Rangers subsequently completed a notable Double with a resounding 5-1 victory over Hearts in the Hampden final.

In Europe, Scottish football's reduced status of latter years obliged the Ibrox club to continue to play qualifiers for the Champions League, and in August 1995 Smith's men found themselves paired in the preliminary round, so often the stumbling block in recent seasons, with Cypriot champions Anorthosis Famagusta. After a tense 1-0 aggregate victory over their unheralded opponents, Rangers progressed to a tricky-looking section featuring Steaua Bucharest, Juventus and Borussia Dortmund, where the Ibrox side eventually stumbled to an embarrassing fourth-place finish, ending the group with a minus-eight goal differential after failing to win any of their six matches.

Europe at this time was beginning to look not so much like a foreign country, but more of an alternate reality for Smith's inveterate side, as a matter of days before Rangers were soundly beaten 4-1 by Juventus in Turin, goalkeeper Andy Goram was arrested for drink-driving, while another member of the Ibrox squad, defender David Robertson, was also in trouble with the police around the same time after he was alleged to have vandalised the car of a member of staff in a bar where he and his team-mates had been drinking. There were numerous other such incidents involving this group of Rangers players and the unfortunate combination of alcohol and arrest, including a charge of breach of the peace that was incurred by McCoist and Durrant following an incident in an East Kilbride chip shop. The apparent indiscipline within the squad was beginning to irritate and confound a large section of the club's supporters, a frustration that was particularly in evidence after the team's repeated failures in Europe.

Writing in *Rangers: The Complete Record*, club historians Bob Ferrier and Robert McElroy opined of the club's disciplinary problems at this time, 'Many Rangers fans were disquieted by all these incidents and in particular, following the Goram affair, felt that a true disciplinarian in the manager's chair would have put Goram on the transfer list immediately, making it clear to him that he had burned his boats and that there would be no way back for him … It was surely the time for the club to make a once and for all example, with immediate and beneficial effect on club discipline.' In fact Goram was indeed later threatened with expulsion from the club, after going on an unsanctioned drinking spree in Tenerife, but in the end the errant goalkeeper was reprieved due to a lack of formal interest in the player from other clubs.

The attitude of the Juventus players, meanwhile, was summed up by striker Fabrizio Ravanelli who, when asked if he drank, replied, 'Yes, of course – mineral water.' The drinking culture at Ibrox during Smith's spell in charge seemed to be a step back from the days of his predecessor Souness, who had introduced a new diet of pasta and fresh fruit to the club when he took charge of Rangers a decade earlier, an outlook that he had acquired during his own playing days in Italy. Smith's approach, however, for the most part seemed to involve turning a blind eye to all the drinking, with some sessions going on for days, as the manager allowed his players to 'let off steam' in accordance with the traditional, but by now increasingly old-fashioned, attitude among British sides.

Another theory that was aired at the time to explain the club's repeated failures on the Continent held that a better standard of refereeing in European matches hindered Rangers, particularly when set against the more easily swayed officials in Scotland, where just about every team in the land, it seemed, had occasion to feel hard done by in games against the Ibrox side around this period. In particular, Scottish officials were accused of an apparent reluctance to take action against the wayward Gascoigne, who, as well as displaying intermittent signs of his innate genius, was often at the centre of controversy, both on and off the field. During one game at Ibrox against Aberdeen, there were claims that the English midfielder should have been ordered off on four separate occasions, with no less a figure than Bob Crampsey, Scottish football's broadcasting guru, describing the referee's persistent failure to take action against Gascoigne's repeated head-butts and flailing elbows as 'a dereliction of duty'.

Rangers' Continental misadventures continued the following year, as Smith's team again finished bottom of the table in their Champions League group after successfully negotiating their way past Alania Vladikavkaz of Russia in the qualifiers following an extraordinary pair of matches between the sides, which eventually saw the Ibrox men notch up a 10-3 aggregate victory. Rangers subsequently failed to make an impression on the group, however, winning only one and losing five games in a section that, unlike the previous year, seemed to be comprised of far less menacing opposition in Auxerre, Ajax and Grasshoppers Zürich. A last-place finish saw perhaps the dawning of a new realism about Rangers' status as a European side, with new signing Joachim Björklund subsequently conceding that his team simply weren't good enough to compete at this level of competition, despite all the bravado that had accompanied previous campaigns.

The Swede later reflected on his first season at the club, admitting, 'Maybe we thought we were better than we actually were. I think maybe we should have been a bit cleverer. Look at the Champions League draw we got that season. It was Ajax, Auxerre and Grasshoppers … Maybe we were overconfident and in the end that was our undoing.' Elimination, however, allowed Rangers to concentrate on what had become clear to everyone was their main target for the season, namely matching Celtic's 23-year-old record of winning nine consecutive league titles. The previous year, the two rivals had gone head to head, with Rangers taking the title by virtue of their ability to grind out wins even when not at their best. Celtic by contrast had chalked up 11 draws over the season to Rangers' six and, with little between the sides in the derby matches, which saw the spoils being shared in three out of the four games, the ten-point differential proved crucial in determining the outcome of the title race.

For the nine-in-a-row campaign, however, it was the matches between the sides that proved crucial; all four were feisty and often controversial affairs, which turned on decisive moments, but in the end, when the dust had settled, Rangers had emerged with victories in all four encounters, the first time that such a feat had been achieved by either side in the Premier League era, although Celtic managed a meagre consolation in March after eliminating their rivals from the Scottish Cup. The first game between the sides was played at Ibrox on 28 September when second-half goals from Gough, with a towering set piece header, and Gascoigne, finishing off a counter-attacking move seconds after Celtic's John Hughes had hit the crossbar with a late header, sealed victory for the home side and consigned the Parkhead men to their first league defeat in a year. Rangers captain Gough was lucky to be on the field, after dragging down Di Canio in the penalty box, but the Italian had sprung up from the ground in an attempt to finish off the attack and, after the ball was cleared from the goal line, referee Willie Young opted to allow play to continue without penalising the Rangers skipper. Celtic's grievances increased shortly before the interval when Tosh McKinlay was ordered off for a second yellow card offence, leaving the visitors to fight a rearguard action for most of the second half.

The battle then moved to Celtic Park and another tense affair between the teams in November was settled by a Brian Laudrup strike just before half-time, after the Dane took advantage of a slip by Brian O'Neil in the Celtic defence. Remarkably, this proved to be the only goal of the game, as both sides missed penalties over the course of the 90 minutes and Rangers' Dutch striker Peter van Vossen squandered an even easier opportunity, somehow managing to skew the ball over the crossbar in front of an open goal after rounding the goalkeeper. Both sides passed up numerous other opportunities, but in the end the win saw Rangers leapfrog their rivals at the top of the table, a position that, as the campaign unfolded, they were not to relinquish.

These derby matches were frantic, incident-packed affairs, but unquestionably the most eventful and controversial tussle between the sides came in the third encounter of the season, played at Ibrox on 2 January 1997. Rangers took the lead with a blistering free kick from German midfielder Jorg Albertz, the former captain of Bundesliga stalwarts Hamburg, who had cost the Ibrox club £4m over the summer, but Celtic fought back and earned a deserved equaliser in the second half through Di Canio. By now it was the visitors who were pushing for a winner against a Rangers side missing Laudrup and Gough, but following an injury to Stubbs, a mix-up between McNamara and O'Neil in Celtic's makeshift defence allowed substitute Erik Bo Andersen, a Danish forward who later admitted that his short spell at Ibrox was troubled and unhappy after he was bullied by Paul Gascoigne, to nip in and restore Rangers' lead.

The match was then decided over a few contentious minutes following what looked like a second equalising goal for Celtic by the Portuguese forward Cadete, a strike that was wrongly ruled out for offside by the stand-side linesman. It was a decision that was still proving to be a source of controversy many years later, with Cadete telling *The Sun* in December 2016, 'I still can't believe the decision. The goal should have stood 100 per cent. There was nothing wrong with it. It would have been a very important goal for us. Looking back, that Old Firm win gave the title to Rangers. There was no way back for us after that.' Expanding on the episode, Cadete claimed, 'I remember that incident so clearly, even after all this time. I knew I was onside when I controlled the ball and scored. When I saw the linesman put his flag up I couldn't believe it. I was stunned. [Rangers defender Gordan] Petrić was behind me. I knew there was no way I could be offside. It wasn't possible. I ran to the referee but he accepted the linesman's decision ... We had so many chances that night at Ibrox. We controlled the game, we had all the possession and the best chances. We deserved to win or at least draw. Instead we lost.'

In the days following the consequential match, it was claimed in the tabloids that the linesman in question, Gordon

McBride, was a former Rangers season ticket holder who was, even at the time of the game, still on the Ibrox club's mailing list. Coming on top of Celtic's high-profile public issues with the SFA over this period, it was very much a case of the Parkhead club and its supporters suspecting that ulterior motives had been involved over the decision, particularly after it was also claimed that McBride had recently worn a Rangers strip while playing in a charity match. Responding to the allegations, the SFA's then head of refereeing development, George Cumming, confirmed that the rumours were indeed true, but backed his under-fire official, telling the *Daily Record*, 'There is some truth in the claims but they have no effect on his refereeing duties ... Yes, Gordon wore a Rangers strip in a charity match but that is not a hanging offence.'

The allegations of impropriety lingered on, however, as stories later circulated that McBride's brother Jim, also a referee, would on occasion be heard bragging to colleagues in his office at the *Sunday Post* newspaper of how his younger sibling had 'done his bit' for nine-in-a-row. Whatever the case, even by the standards of the wacky world of Scottish football, never short of paranoia or conspiracy theories, the incident remains one of the most controversial decisions by an official in a major Scottish match in recent years. Just to make matters worse for Celtic on the night, shortly after they were denied a legitimate equaliser, Rangers raced up the field on the counter-attack and made it 3-1, with another strike from Andersen sealing the match.

The fourth and final league fixture between the sides was the least engrossing match of the quartet, an ugly, spiteful game lacking in quality, which was once again settled by a lone strike from Brian Laudrup, who latched on to Durrant's lob just before half-time to capitalise on a mistake in the Celtic defence. The scratchiness of the match was epitomised by red cards for Mark Hateley, returning to Rangers on a short-term loan deal from QPR, and Celtic's Malky Mackay, while there was also a mêlée at the end of the game, with Di Canio taking exception to allegedly being called an 'Italian bastard' by Ian Ferguson, who had earlier upset the home fans by firing the ball into the Celtic Park crowd at point-blank range. The behaviour of some of the celebrating Rangers players, lapping up the victory by mocking Celtic's pre-match huddle, a move planned in advance by Ferguson and Goram, also added to the general mayhem at the end of the match.

With an eight-point gap opening up between the sides following their victory at Celtic Park, it seemed that Rangers were almost home and dry in their pursuit of the club's long-established target of matching Celtic's fabled nine-in-a-row record. However, closing in on their goal, Smith's side wobbled precariously, losing at home to both Kilmarnock and Motherwell, before the title was claimed at Tannadice with a 1-0 win over Dundee United, at which point the Ibrox club almost fell on top of itself with relief. In addition to the championship, Rangers also managed to secure the League Cup after a thrilling 4-3 victory over Hearts in the final at Celtic Park in November, although after the match Smith bemoaned the apparent apathy among the club's supporters, stating his belief that Rangers had become victims of their own success and that the winning of domestic trophies, in contrast to the club's travails in Europe, was now being taken for granted by some fans.

With all the talk of matching nine-in-a-row, which had been escalating within the Ibrox dressing room for several years by the time it was finally accomplished, Rangers seemed to have overlooked the possibility that they could in fact surpass Celtic's achievement and set their own new record by winning a tenth consecutive title the following year. Over the summer, the Ibrox club embarked on another enormous spending spree, bringing a raft of players from Italy's Serie A, still the best and most cash-rich league in the world in the late 90s, but the core of Smith's Scottish contingent was also retained, largely for sentimental reasons, to allow the nine-in-a-row stalwarts to have a crack at the tenth title. The resulting, bloated Ibrox squad turned out to be a particularly strange brew, and Rangers never seemed to really get going in the new, potentially record-breaking campaign until, in fact, the season was almost over.

A particularly egregious example of the problems within the squad at this time was narrated by new signing Lorenzo Amoruso in his autobiography, *L. A. Confidential*, published in 2002 and ghost-written by a couple of Scottish tabloid journalists. The Italian narrates how, after a 2-1 defeat to Motherwell as the season approached its climax, Walter Smith gave Paul Gascoigne such a row, accusing him of not being sober enough to train for the previous two weeks, that the Geordie midfielder wet himself in the changing room in front of all his team-mates. Gascoigne never started a game for Rangers again and, within days, was shipped out of the club to Middlesbrough, while Amoruso himself was injured and unable to compete for almost the whole of his first year in Glasgow. It seemed clear that the chemistry and the unity of purpose between the old and the new Rangers players was lacking in the wake of the nine-in-a-row triumph, and in the end Celtic held off their rivals, finally taking the championship on the last day of the season.

By this time, Smith had already announced his intention to step down as Rangers manager, following another twin-pronged catastrophe in Europe earlier in the season. UEFA's new rules allowed teams eliminated from the Champions League qualifiers to have another go in the subsidiary UEFA Cup, and Rangers became one of the first teams in history to be knocked out of Europe twice in the same season, after an aggregate defeat to Gothenburg in the main event was followed immediately by another loss, to Strasbourg, in the back-up tournament.

Clearly, Smith had failed in his task of guiding Rangers towards chairman David Murray's initial primary objective of establishing the Ibrox side as a credible force in Europe, and indeed of staking a claim to the Continent's most coveted prize of all, the Champions League, before the focus on nine-in-a-row distorted everything else that was going on at the club. Following his initial appointment, however, it was unarguable that Smith had taken Rangers forward at a time when it was felt by many that the loss of Souness would prove to be a setback from which the club would struggle to recover. Instead, Smith had shown that he was a much shrewder operator than his predecessor, with Souness readily admitting in hindsight that Smith turned out to be a far better man-manager than he had ever been.

A useful illustration of the difference in the approaches of the two managers was provided by Smith's treatment of goalkeeper Andy Goram, whom the new boss had staked a great deal on early in his tenure when he brought the player to the club from Hibernian in a ruthless, but calculated move that saw the dependable Chris Woods replaced and effectively discarded by Rangers, as the club tried to adapt to UEFA's recently introduced 'three foreigners' rule. The Scotland-affiliated Goram initially found things difficult following his transfer to Ibrox, conceding soft goals in his first few games for his new club, including the blunder that ultimately led to the elimination of Smith's side from the European Cup on away goals to Sparta Prague in October 1991. Under Souness's shouty-shouty regime, the new goalkeeper's performances would in all likelihood have led to an out-and-out bollocking, probably in addition to a dressing-room scolding in front of his team-mates, accompanied by an order to shape up or the revolving door at Ibrox would once again soon be in full swing. Instead, after a chat with the player, Smith agreed to bring in Goram's mentor, the goalkeeping coach Alan Hodgkinson, on a part-time basis. It was a plan that paid dividends in the end, as Goram, after a shaky first season, went on to become a key player for Rangers in their quest to equal nine-in-a-row.

Ultimately, European failure had cost Smith his job, however, and after Celtic took the title for the first time in ten years in 1998, chairman David Murray recalibrated his ambitions and adopted a new strategy at Ibrox, placing his faith for the first time in the club's history in the fresh ideas and disciplined methods of a highly regarded foreign coach. In other aspects, though, as McCann's reinvigorated club threatened to flex their own financial muscles for the first time, Rangers' new direction bore all the familiar hallmarks of Murray, as the chairman announced, 'For every five pounds Celtic spend, we will spend ten.'

6.

One in a Row

IN lieu of any tangible reward, Tommy Burns's Celtic had been forced to settle for a clear case of progress being made on the field at the end of the 1995/96 season, the club's first since their return to the new, all-seater Celtic Park, which was at last now in full compliance with the recommendations of the Taylor Report. The following year, however, after the disappointment of losing the league to Rangers for the ninth season in a row, Fergus McCann again took the decision, just as he had in the summer of 1994, to dispense with the services of the club's head coach. While Celtic's deep desire to finally wrest the title from their rivals was understandable, Burns's side had at times played with an edge of desperation to their game during the nine-in-a-row campaign. This failure was particularly manifest in the matches against Rangers, at a time when it should have been, and on occasion quite evidently was, the Ibrox side who appeared nervous and frantically keen to get over the line in their bid for the record-equalling championship.

At the start of what proved to be Burns's last season in charge, and in response to the challenge of defending the record held by Jock Stein's celebrated side, the Parkhead club had brought in centre-back Alan Stubbs for a club record £3.5m from Bolton Wanderers and the talented but unpredictable Italian winger Paolo Di Canio from AC Milan for a reported £1m. Both players were put on serious wages, estimated to be around £8,000 per week in Di Canio's case, while the signing of Stubbs, announced initially to the Stock Exchange following Celtic's recent listing on the Alternative Investment Market, appeared to send out a message that the Parkhead club were now prepared to compete with the top sides from south of the border for the best English talent, with Stubbs ranking among the most coveted of the country's young defenders. 'We pay top dollar,' McCann announced around the time of the transfers. 'I hope that people will get the message that Celtic are very serious about competing with the highest order here and on the Continent,' the Canadian proclaimed, before sounding a very modern note of caution. 'No one here is expected to play entirely for the jersey,' he added pointedly.

The club, however, proved unable to hold on to midfielder John Collins, who became one of the first players to take advantage of the Bosman ruling, recently handed down by the European Court of Justice, when he joined AS Monaco on a free transfer during the summer, although McCann's lawyers would have a field day over the next few months arguing that, despite Monaco competing in the French league, the tiny principality itself wasn't in the European Union, where the new regulations governing freedom of contract were now in effect. Nevertheless, Celtic's forward line now contained the notable talents of Di Canio, Van Hooijdonk, Cadete and Thom, although on the only occasion when all four appeared in the starting line-up together, against Hamburg at Celtic Park in the UEFA Cup, the result was a 2-0 defeat.

The problem with these players appeared to lie not in their ability, which was undisputed and regularly in evidence, but in their temperament, with three of the quartet at times very obviously distracted by various off-field issues, as Celtic, even in an era when boyhood devotees of the club such as Peter Grant and Paul McStay were still an important part of the playing squad, were obliged for the first time perhaps to confront and effectively deal with the more mercenary mind-set of foreign imports. The exception was Andreas Thom, who displayed typical levels of German professionalism throughout his spell in Glasgow but was unfortunately all too often hampered by injury.

With 50,000 fans at their back, following the completion of the Lisbon Lions stand in the east end of the ground over the summer, Celtic enjoyed an almost perfect home record over the course of the 1996/97 season – except for the matches against Rangers, who beat them 1-0 on both occasions when they visited the impressive new stadium. The sense of frustration was exacerbated when, on top of the four defeats in the league to the Ibrox men, Celtic failed to capitalise on their only win over Walter Smith's side, a 2-0 victory at Celtic Park on 6 March in the quarter-final of the Scottish Cup, as the subsequent semi-final, played at Ibrox in poor weather conditions, was lost to second-tier outfit Falkirk, 1-0 after a replay, in what proved to be Tommy Burns's last game in charge of the Parkhead side.

It was another deflating defeat for Celtic, the second loss in two and a half years to lower league opposition in the domestic cup competitions, with *The Scotsman* reporting on events at Ibrox: 'Last night, Burns' side got a bite from an underdog which could not have been cured by a tetanus injection.' Burns himself pointed the finger at his demoralised and deflated squad after the game, claiming, 'We have too many players who can't take the strain … We have been hanging on to Paolo Di Canio's coat-tails and need someone to help him shoulder responsibility. There was a desperate lack of leadership against Falkirk. It was disappointing and embarrassing.'

Ultimately, however, responsibility for results rested with the manager, much loved by the support due to the heroics of his playing days and his admirable devotion to the Celtic cause, but in truth Burns's team had failed to live up to expectations over the course of his final season in charge at Celtic Park and the Parkhead men had been unable to build on the good work of the previous campaign. In addition to the squandered opportunity in the Scottish Cup semi-final, Celtic had also been knocked out of the League Cup in September, when they suffered a 1-0 extra-time defeat at Tynecastle against a Hearts team who were missing a quartet of key players through suspension, after four of the Edinburgh side's men had been sent off against Rangers the previous weekend. The club had also failed to impress in Europe, making heavy weather of their efforts to eliminate Slovakians FC Košice, Cadete's lone strike eventually settling the tie minutes from the end of the second leg, before Burns's side, somewhat predictably, came up short against Hamburg, losing both games 2-0 against decent, but hardly elite opponents.

Burns and McCann had by now been at loggerheads for some time, and as the minutes of board meetings from this period reveal, the directors had more or less reached a decision to replace the manager as early as the previous Christmas, since when they had been deliberating only over the timing of his dismissal. There was therefore a sense of inevitability to Burns's eventual departure from the club and the axe finally fell on Friday, 2 May, with the diehard Celtic man, in a last act of defiance, ignoring the instructions of his now former employer and exiting the stadium for the final time as the club's manager by the main doors, where roughly 1,500 fans had gathered in anticipation of the news, instead of using the side exit on Janefield Street where McCann had directed him.

The media loved that gesture on Burns's part, immediately taking the opportunity to heap further criticism on McCann for the way he had treated the popular manager. Amid talk of broken promises and hidden agendas on the owner's part, the *Sunday Mail* accused the club of 'dumping in their own nest' over the way the dismissal was handled, while McCann's reputation, three years after saving the club, was now, according to the paper, 'down the toilet'. In the same week that directors Willie Haughey, who was accused of leaking information to the press, and Dominic Keane, who resigned in support of his colleague, left the club's board, the *Sunday Mail*'s sister publication, the *Daily Record*, appeared to encapsulate the withering attitude of the media towards McCann and his club at this time, when one of the tabloid's columnists observed simply, 'Trust Celtic – if you want a PR disaster then you know where to call.'

After three years in the job, Burns turned out to be the longest-serving of the seven Celtic managers who held the position at the club over the course of the 1990s, a remarkable change for an organisation that had seen only six men employed in the role over the previous 100 years. Burns, who turned down an offer to take over as the club's new head of youth development following his sacking, was unlucky in certain aspects, most notably in that he found himself coming up against a Rangers team of considerable quality, managed by the astute and relentless Smith and financed by the reckless and ultimately unsustainable borrowing of chairman David Murray. In addition, his task of catching and overtaking the Ibrox men, at a time when they were nose-down in pursuit of the fabled nine-in-a-row, was made all the more daunting by the context of Celtic's own predicament, which saw the Parkhead side caught up in a period of laborious transition, as the club was uprooted from its traditional home and forced to spend a largely unhappy sabbatical year at Hampden Park. Burns's side then returned to a half-built stadium in the east end of Glasgow, shorn of its full potential to arouse the kind of atmosphere, both intimidating to opponents and inspiring to the home team, that the Jungle had elicited in a previous era and that the full-capacity, 60,000-seat ground would eventually reprise when it was completed.

The enforced modernisation at Celtic also meant that Burns, a dyed-in-the-wool supporter of the club, had to deal with a troupe of emotionally unstable foreign players in Van Hooijdonk, Cadete and Di Canio, known as, in a phrase reportedly coined by McCann, the 'three amigos'. While man management and ensuring that players were kept feeling happy and valued was always an important part of any football boss's job, Burns was faced with a particular problem in being required to deal with issues pertaining to the motivation and professionalism of three lavishly remunerated footballers, which would have been largely unknown to his predecessors.

In answer to this defence, however, and notwithstanding the issues and events that may well have been beyond his control, it was notable that the captivating form and free-flowing football of the previous season hadn't been maintained or improved upon in Burns's final year at the club, despite a number of expensive acquisitions to the squad. In the end, Player of the Year Di Canio may have hampered the team's progress, as Campbell and Woods noted of Celtic's 1996/97 campaign in *Dreams, and Songs to Sing*: 'The exceptional teamwork and brilliant passing game of the previous year was frequently abandoned, and Celtic's main tactic was to give Di Canio the ball and hope for developments. Too many Celtic players had their initiative eroded as the Italian ran a "one-man show".'

It seems that many of their opponents, and Rangers in particular, had to a certain extent worked Celtic out by this point, with Burns's reliance on attacking football not sufficiently well backed up by a more comprehensive tactical system, a glaring oversight that allowed defensive-minded opponents, when they regained possession, to play on the counter-attack and exploit Celtic's often alarming vulnerability at the back. Additionally, in their desperation to stop nine-in-a-row, Burns's side had acquired a poor disciplinary record, with more than a dozen red cards notched up in all competitions during the course of the campaign, and overall, at a time when the club was looking to push on, with average attendances at Celtic Park growing year on year in the gradually expanding arena, the season represented a period of stagnation. It was clear, therefore, in a results-driven business such as modern professional football, that Burns had come up short and it was the correct decision to let him go, with the manager's eventual departure in the first week of May coinciding with the landslide general election victory of Tony Blair's New Labour Party, which finally brought down the curtain on 18 years of divisive and, by the end, corrupt Tory rule.

It seemed that change was very much in the air, and over the summer McCann took the decision to modernise the structure of the club behind the scenes, dividing the manager's traditional duties between the two newly created positions of general manager and head coach, in accordance with the practice widely used on the Continent or, as McCann described it, 'the

Arsenal model'. The general manager would be responsible for staffing and budgetary issues, including the identification and appointment of the new head coach, whose remit, McCann was keen to emphasise, now extended no further than strictly football matters. Reporting to the general manager, the new head coach would be free to focus his attention and efforts solely on team affairs.

McCann had been left aghast in September 1994, not long after Burns was appointed, when he discovered that his manager had negotiated the terms of the transfer of midfielder Phil O'Donnell from Motherwell more or less entirely on his own initiative, with the Celtic owner's role in the agreement between the two clubs effectively reduced to not much more than putting his final seal of approval on the deal. The alternative, belatedly interfering in the details of the transaction, could have seen McCann undermine his new manager and put at risk a potential signing that had already been widely reported as being imminent. Celtic in the end paid a club record £1.75m for the services of the midfielder, 'twice the price' as the owner subsequently lamented, and still, over a quarter of a century later, the highest fee received by the Lanarkshire club for one of their players.

McCann believed strongly that allowing the team manager, a football man, to negotiate the terms of multimillion-pound transfer deals was every bit as preposterous an idea as a chairman or chief executive interfering in strictly football matters, such as team selection or the scouting and recruitment of players. As Graham McColl noted in *The Official Biography of Celtic*, 'McCann's deep dislike of the traditional system of British team management, whereby the manager would have a say in how the money was spent, on transfers, wages and such like, and the type of wastage that he believed it produced, stemmed to a large degree from his desire, and from a deep sense of responsibility, to see the supporters' money spent wisely, prudently and well.'

This caution and thoroughness on McCann's part, however, was already attracting increasing amounts of criticism, and the Celtic owner was starting to gain a reputation for excessive thrift, an impression that was only compounded when compared to the extravagance on display on the other side of the city. Offering an explanation for his perceived parsimony, McCann later observed, 'You had to think of the dangers of going out to buy a star player and getting it wrong because you wanted to make yourself a hero, which is the David Murray approach.' In fact, McCann's modus operandi, in contrast to that of his rival on the other side of the city, could be best summed up in his simple and often expressed mantra of 'Don't do bad deals', an outlook that in the end came to define his five-year term in control of the club.

Following the decision to put in place a new managerial structure at Celtic, and with the new season set to get under way in a matter of weeks, McCann quickly embarked on a long and meticulous recruitment process aimed at identifying candidates for the two newly created and vacant positions at the club of general manager and head coach. The first of the posts to be filled was the more senior and administrative role, with McCann's three-week selection process eventually resulting in the appointment of Jock Brown, the former STV and current BBC Scotland commentator and the brother of Scotland national team manager Craig Brown.

Brown was also a practising lawyer, who had previously represented athletes and coaches in the often complex negotiations involved in sports contracts, including acting on behalf of Davie Hay when he was sacked from the Parkhead dugout in 1987 and Murdo MacLeod when he was named manager of Partick Thistle, so he seemed to tick a lot of boxes from McCann's point of view. The reaction of the club's supporters to the news, however, was mixed, with some accusing the former broadcaster of allegiances towards Rangers and of failing to conceal his supposed favouritism in his match commentaries, a charge that was trumped up by the media even on the day of Brown's appointment.

In anticipation of the press conference that saw Brown unveiled in his new role at the club on 23 June, the *Daily Record* had reported, under the back page headline 'JOKE BROWN', that the Celtic Supporters Association was being 'inundated with protests' and threats to hand back season tickets, although by the next day the mood among the fans appeared to have brightened, with the paper's 'Hotline' dominated by messages of support for the new man. Nobody had any illusions about Brown coming from a Celtic-supporting background – or being 'Celtic Minded' as he later described it in the title of a book on his spell with the Parkhead club – it was widely known at the time that another of Jock's brothers was a Church of Scotland minister, while Scotland coach Craig was later accused in the tabloids of singing sectarian, anti-Catholic songs on his lover's answerphone.

Brown in fact had no allegiances towards either of the big Glasgow teams and expressed only a preference for his home town club Hamilton Academicals. He later recalled the story of how his father, a professional football player, took an equally adversarial position towards both of the Old Firm sides, due to their large supporter base and the perceived favouritism on the part of match officials towards the bigger clubs, so he would bring home sweets and other treats for his sons on the rare occasions when both Celtic and Rangers lost. The media had successfully played on the perceived paranoia of Celtic supporters, finding and giving voice to a few disgruntled fans, as Parkhead PR executive Peter McLean indicated to Brown in reference to the negative headlines, and in particular to the 'Joke Brown' story, which appeared even before his first official day in the job: 'There you are. For 51 years you have been subjected to generally favourable media comment and your image has not been in question. Now you have joined Celtic. You haven't done anything, you haven't made a decision, but you are now portrayed as a joke. Welcome to the club!'

'I'm not interested in any of that,' was McCann's response to Brown's cautious warning during the selection process that there might be some opposition to the appointment to a senior position at Celtic of someone who demonstrably had no previous association with the club, an emphatic retort on the owner's part that left the interviewee feeling pleased and relieved. 'He actually looked shocked and offended that I had raised the matter,' was Brown's recollection of McCann's response to his tentative inquiry, and despite the initial scepticism of some, most Celtic fans concurred, as the news of Brown's arrival at Parkhead was largely welcomed across the fanbase, with many believing that the owner had engineered something of a coup in luring such a recognisable and well-known figure to the club.

McCann was only interested in Brown's capability to perform in the job, but what the Canadian had probably not foreseen, or had perhaps underestimated, was the media's reaction to Brown joining the club. Part of the new general manager's job description involved dealing with the press on a regular basis, with McCann insisting that the position should incorporate the duties of frontman in order to remove the burden of responsibilities from the head coach, who would only be expected to fulfil his obligations to the media in pre- and post-match interviews. Brown hinted to McCann that he wasn't entirely comfortable with this aspect of the role and that he suspected the policy might be a mistake, but the owner remained adamant and Brown became the first point of contact between the club and the press.

It was to prove a difficult and fractious relationship throughout the former broadcaster's spell at Celtic Park, as many in the newspaper and broadcasting industry continued to appear flabbergasted by the appointment of their former colleague to such a role at Parkhead, with a thinly disguised 'we thought he was one of us' attitude characterising how he was largely treated by a sizeable section of the media during his time at the club. Celtic historian David Potter appeared to hit the nail on the head when he observed, 'Journalists, always jealous of one of their own who has done better than they, lost no opportunity to do him down, even in circumstances in which no blame could reasonably been laid at his door.' Brown himself suggested a 'poacher turning gamekeeper' hypothesis behind the media's immediate hostility towards him, hinting in his book, *Celtic-Minded: 510 Days in Paradise*, at a plausible explanation for the attitude of some of his former colleagues: 'I was going to become privy to information which would be gold dust in the hands of a journalist. I would have the inside track on what was happening about the appointment of a head coach. I would know what transfer deals were brewing. It would be regarded by the media as intolerable if I were to keep such information to myself.'

No one should have been surprised, therefore, when the press's frustration with Brown quickly became apparent following the general manager's failure to offer any insight into the identity of Tommy Burns's successor at the club, whose arrival in Glasgow was expected imminently. Forgetting perhaps that Brown's loyalties now lay with Celtic, and not his former buddies in the fourth estate, the media soon went into typical bunfight mode in their quest to reveal the club's new head coach, with a pantheon of bigger and more high-profile figures in the game, including Bobby Robson, Terry Venables, John Toshack and Kevin Keegan being linked with the job on an almost daily basis. McCann, however, had insisted all along that the new man should be non-British and, in the end, with the list of famous names growing seemingly endless, many in the media were left wrong-footed and not to say a little underwhelmed when confirmation came of the appointment of the Dutchman Wim Jansen to the position on 3 July 1997.

Jansen was a former World Cup finalist, having played in the tournaments in West Germany in 1974 and Argentina in 1978, when the Dutch lost out in the final on each occasion to the host nation. He had earned 65 caps for the Netherlands during the era of the greatest international side in his country's history, although from a Scottish perspective he was perhaps best remembered trailing in the wake of Archie Gemmill as the diminutive midfielder famously waltzed through the Dutch defence to score a memorable goal and put Ally MacLeod's men within touching distance of an unlikely qualification for the second phase of the World Cup in Argentina. In addition to his international exploits with the Netherlands, Jansen had won the European Cup with Feyenoord in 1970, after the underrated Rotterdam outfit defeated Celtic in the final in Milan, 2-1 after extra time.

With such a stellar playing career behind him, Jansen's coaching credentials by contrast appeared relatively modest, after spells as assistant trainer, head coach and then technical director of Feyenoord were followed by a three-year stint in Japan as boss of Sanfrecce Hiroshima. He had been credited with the revival of Feyenoord, however, taking his home town club to the title in the Netherlands and the semi-final of the Cup Winners' Cup, in the process restoring the fortunes of one of European football's great names, an achievement that Brown and McCann doubtlessly believed he could reproduce at Celtic. Importantly, Jansen was entirely comfortable with the Parkhead club's new managerial set-up and harboured no desire to potentially involve himself in the club's administrative or financial affairs, but instead was happy to concentrate on drilling his squad of players in how to perform in his somewhat rigid tactical system.

This ability to convince his team to operate within a framework and maintain a disciplined adherence to the game plan, while playing fluent, technical football, was seen as being among Jansen's key assets, with the Dutchman also reported to be keen to develop and promote the club's young players, rather than rely almost exclusively on imported talent. Joining Jansen at Parkhead as his assistant was the former Celtic and Scotland midfielder Murdo MacLeod, who would provide the new man with valuable insight into the Scottish domestic scene, while two more former players completed the reorganised line-up behind the scenes at the club, with Davie Hay named Jock Brown's assistant and Willie McStay installed as the new head of youth development, a position that had earlier been offered to but declined by Tommy Burns following his dismissal as the club's manager.

The response of the press, almost inevitably, was unenthusiastic, with the *Daily Record*, in a manner that was entirely typical of the media's reaction to Jansen's appointment, reflecting that 'Celtic have taken the biggest gamble in the club's history by appointing a foreign coach unknown to most of their fans'. In addition, columnist James Traynor spoke of the 'bemused, maybe stunned silence' that greeted the news of the Dutchman's arrival in Glasgow, adding, 'Celtic say he comes highly recommended and no one can argue with that. After all, the manager of your local amateur side could be recommended in glowing terms depending on which of his friends you approach for information.' Jansen's friends in this instance included Johan Cruyff, his former team-mate with the Dutch national team and one of the game's leading lights. He immediately offered his own endorsement, congratulating the Parkhead club on their choice of head coach and intimating that Jansen's deep understanding and knowledge of the game meant that the new man in charge of Celtic's first team was, according to the Dutch master, one of only four men in the world whom it was worth having a discussion with about football.

'It is a massive statement of Celtic's ambition and I have no doubt that he will be a huge success because he is a top-class coach,' Cruyff announced, conferring his seal of approval on the appointment. Nevertheless, Jansen was described in one less-than-esteemed journal, after a sticky start to his spell in charge of the club and following his three-year sojourn in Japan, as 'the second worst thing to hit Hiroshima', while other, less tasteless publications were quick to point out that the new head coach's first task would be to win over the doubters and convince the considerable number who were sceptical as to his suitability for the post that he was the man to bring to Celtic the level of success that the club was longing for.

The reporting of Jansen's appointment seemed to provide another illustration of the extent to which the relationship between Celtic and the media in the west of Scotland, which for a long time had quite conspicuously been based on a mutual sense of antipathy and mistrust, had deteriorated further during the McCann years and seemed to be at an all-time low by the time of the Dutchman's recruitment. This suspicion and antagonism between the club and sections of the press appeared in microcosm in the reporting of one Hugh Keevins of *The Scotsman*, who turned out to be one of the earliest casualties of the shake-up at Celtic Park, after he wrongly announced on the day of Jansen's arrival at Parkhead that McCann's club were instead on the verge of engaging the services of the Portuguese Artur Jorge in the position of the team's new manager.

It was suggested in Keevins's less than prophetic piece that Jorge, the current boss of his country's national team, who had previously led Porto to the European Cup in 1987 and, less memorably, Switzerland to Euro 96 in England, would be announced as the new head coach at Parkhead, possibly as early as that very afternoon, with McCann and Brown reported to be in London, ironing out the last-minute details of the deal. 'Jorge is under contract to them [Portugal] until October, but Celtic are willing to go that extra mile to get the man they want,' the article alleged. 'The club have already agreed to pay Jorge the kind of money necessary to persuade him to walk out on his own country and start a fresh career in a new country,' Keevins continued, before brandishing around figures such as a £750,000 per year salary as well as a multimillion-pound transfer budget.

After getting the story so spectacularly wrong, Keevins's reaction the following day, once Jansen had been unveiled, was one of almost unrestrained disgust, with the journalist slaughtering the Dutchman's standing in the game and his previous track record as a coach, remarking that the new man in charge of the first team at Parkhead would be working 'to disprove the theory that he was the last resort, and not the first option that Celtic had in mind'. Keevins also then claimed that the club's supporters had been left distinctly underwhelmed by the news of Jansen's appointment, because they were – as if Artur Jorge and his notable moustache were somehow being regularly analysed around dinner tables the length and breadth of the country – 'expecting a household name'.

Having condemned the new man in the dugout, Keevins then vented his fury on the club itself, declaring, 'In spite of having tens of thousands of season ticket holders and a stadium that's the equal of any in Europe, Celtic have become the club who have everything and nothing. Only one trophy, the Scottish Cup, has been won in the last eight years.' It was left to general manager Jock Brown to make the salient point in response to the wave of scepticism and negativity that followed the Dutchman's appointment: 'If there is speculation about someone taking over at Celtic Park and it fails to materialise, the person concerned is said to have snubbed this club. The reality is different … He [Jansen] has improved every club he has been with in Holland, Belgium and Japan, and in particular it was Wim who revived Feyenoord and made them a big club once again,' the general manager explained, batting away allegations that Jansen had been one of the last names on the club's original shortlist.

Subsequent speculation centred on Keevins and how such a well-known figure among the community of sports journalists in Scotland could have been hoaxed into making such a public fool of himself in this manner. Celtic had, in all probability, at least considered Jorge for the vacant post and completed their due diligence on a prospective candidate, but had someone from within the club taken it upon themselves to leak that information, perhaps along with interview notes and a 'fact file', which subsequently appeared in Keevins's piece, as a false indication of his imminent appointment? Or was it just simply a case of downright bad journalism on Keevins's part? If it was the former, then who was responsible? Was it a lone individual within Celtic Park, who had, for reasons of his own, decided that he had had enough of Keevins's remorselessly egotistical self-aggrandisement in his reporting, which appeared to come so often at the Parkhead club's expense? Had McCann himself been involved or approved the release of Jorge's name as some sort of revenge mission against a hostile press, and Keevins in particular? It seemed unlikely, but regardless, Keevins's stay at *The Scotsman* thereafter was brief and it wasn't long before he joined the tabloid *Sunday Mail*, and later its sister publication the *Daily Record*, where his perceived anti-Celtic and anti-McCann outbursts continued intermittently right up to the point of the Canadian's departure from Scotland and beyond.

One of Jansen and MacLeod's first priorities, once they had taken up their positions in the dugout at Celtic Park, was to deal with the loss of club captain Paul McStay, after the player, at the age of just 32, took the difficult decision to retire over the summer due to a persistent ankle injury, which had left him sidelined for most of the previous campaign. Known as 'The Maestro', McStay had made his debut for Celtic as a 17-year-old in 1982 and went on to make 677 appearances for the club, spending his entire career at Celtic Park, during which time he often seemed to be carrying the misfiring Parkhead side on his own, with the player having had the misfortune to reach his peak while the club seemed to be imploding. Coming from a Celtic-supporting and a footballing family, which also saw brothers Willie and Ray progress through the ranks of the

Parkhead side, McStay in addition had two great uncles who wore the famous hooped jerseys, with one, Jimmy, becoming only the second man in Celtic's history to manage the club after he was elevated to the post in 1940 following the retirement of Willie Maley. One of the most gifted midfielders ever to appear for the club, McStay earned 76 caps for Scotland and won three league championships and four Scottish Cup medals during his playing days at Celtic Park.

In addition, vice-captain Peter Grant also left Parkhead over the summer, joining Norwich City. Grant, while nowhere near as talented as McStay, was noted for his unswerving commitment to the Celtic cause, which led Tommy Burns on one occasion to remark, with no apparent sense of irony, that he wished he had 11 Peter Grants in his team. A relic perhaps from a bygone age, the almost simultaneous departures of Grant, along with McStay and Burns, finally severed the link to a previous, simpler era in the history of Celtic and indeed of British football, when footballers were said to play for the jersey, an admittedly quaint concept by the late 1990s, but one for which the departing trio needed no encouragement.

Their loyalty to the cause was in noted contrast perhaps to the more mercenary approach witnessed by such as Pierre van Hooijdonk, who joined Nottingham Forest in March 1997 after Celtic finally lost patience with the player and his financial demands, which had seen the striker repeatedly stalling on the offer of a new contract. Players had left Celtic for financial reasons in the past, in the days of the parsimonious old board, often professed lovers of the club, but it was harder to take when footballers were earning fortunes at Parkhead, and Van Hooijdonk's remark, attributed to him at the time, that he considered a weekly wage of £7,000 to be enough for a homeless person but not for a striker of his quality did the Dutchman no favours at all personally, while his outlook seemed to sum up the direction that the modern game appeared to be taking.

Following the negative fall-out from the appointment of Jansen, the media were given further ammunition with which to attack the club after Jock Brown insisted that the want-away duo of Paolo Di Canio and Jorge Cadete would not be allowed to leave Celtic, before the general manager promptly performed an about-turn and allowed the pair to be sold. Coming so soon after Van Hooijdonk's undignified departure earlier in the year, it quickly became apparent that Di Canio and Cadete also wished to further their careers away from the club, after both players failed to return to Scotland for pre-season training on the stipulated date at the start of July. Di Canio had initially claimed that he was unfit, while Cadete had informed the club by fax that he was suffering from a mystery illness, with speculation centring on the liver complaint hepatitis A as well as the state of the striker's mental health. When Celtic subsequently asked to see a medical certificate, detailing the Portuguese forward's condition, the reply they received contained only a transfer request.

Brown recollects the efforts that were made to convince Cadete to remain with the Parkhead side, as he and club doctor Jack Mulhearn, who had a strong relationship with the striker, travelled to Portugal in an attempt to entice the player to return to Glasgow. The Celtic party was well received at Cadete's Lisbon home, where they met with the player and his agents for over two and a half hours, during which time a new deal was put to the forward, which, following protracted negotiations, eventually met with the approval of the Portuguese camp and was verbally accepted. Brown later wrote that he remembered two strange aspects of his time in Cadete's house, however; the first was that a video of the striker's career goals was playing on a loop throughout the duration of the meeting, while the other bemusing element of the visit featured Cadete's wife, who didn't introduce herself or become directly involved in the discussions, but instead remained outside by the swimming pool, clad only in a bikini, from where she was overheard intermittently shouting instructions at her distracted husband.

Nevertheless, Brown returned to the UK believing that Cadete would soon be joining him back at Celtic Park under the improved terms of a new agreement, but instead the player left messages on the general manager's mobile phone, letting him know that he had changed his mind, apologising and insisting regretfully that his wife had vetoed their new arrangement and that the player would not therefore be coming back to Scotland. A disappointed Brown was reluctantly forced to give up on Cadete, whom he later described as a very nice man but 'younger than his years', and the striker was eventually sold to Celta Vigo for £3m, where his career subsequently went downhill so rapidly that just a few years later, accompanied by a new Mrs Cadete, he returned to Glasgow to play for Partick Thistle.

The case of Di Canio was similar in that the Italian winger believed, like Cadete, that he had been made a verbal promise by McCann on the offer of a new contract, which after a full season in Glasgow was to be renegotiated on more lucrative terms over the summer of 1997, a reputed undertaking that the Celtic owner denied had ever been given. The Italian was also upset over the departure of Tommy Burns, who at times he had played his heart out for, but with the popular manager now gone, and with his expected salary increase failing to materialise, Di Canio effectively withdrew his labour and refused to join up with his team-mates, who were heading to the Netherlands for a pre-season training camp just days after Jansen's appointment. Despite the Italian's errant behaviour, however, the new head coach was insisting that he wanted the player to be part of his squad for the new season, but Di Canio had burned his bridges with the club's management, after Jock Brown accused him of a lack of professionalism over his refusal to show up on time and attend pre-season training, an allegation that provoked an outburst of the Italian's notoriously fiery temper.

After finally joining up with the Celtic party, briefly, for a summer tournament in Ireland, Di Canio took himself off to Rome, announcing his intention never to return to the club. The result was an uneasy stand-off that presented Brown with a potentially tricky problem. Jansen wanted the player on his roster, no matter what, and he asked the general manager to put his pride aside and go back and offer the Italian the money he was looking for. Brown ultimately refused, however, maintaining that it would potentially set a dangerous precedent if a wayward player was allowed to break the terms of his contract with impunity by going on strike until the club was forced to cave in and accede to his wishes. Instead, the general manager threatened to play hardball with the absent winger and force him to train with the reserves, insisting all the while that the Italian would not be sold. In the end, however, faced with the prospect of having an unhappy and potentially disruptive player on their hands, Brown eventually relented and, on 6 August, Di Canio was allowed to join Sheffield Wednesday.

To explain the about-face, Brown claimed, somewhat unconvincingly, that the Italian had in fact been 'traded', not sold, with Regi Blinker, a former protégé of Jansen's at Feyenoord, moving to Celtic from the South Yorkshire club in exchange for the Italian and a fee of around £2m. In the end, the deal for a player who had cost around £1m 12 months earlier represented a good piece of business for the Parkhead club, but the media's reaction to Brown's 'traded' explanation was one of almost uncontrolled ridicule. The general manager may have been technically correct about Di Canio being involved in a cash plus player exchange rather than a straight sale, a point that doubtless seemed perfectly reasonable to Brown's legally trained mind, but only the most neurotic pedant could have argued, especially given his already fractious relationship with the press, that he hadn't made a rod for his own back in such circumstances. In his defence, Brown claimed that he had amended his previous statements over the club's refusal to sell Di Canio, and as negotiations with manager David Pleat and owner Dave Richards at Sheffield Wednesday continued, he had indicated a softening of his stance on the Italian's position at Parkhead by informing the press that 'the situation would remain constantly under review', and as the transfer agreement neared its conclusion, that the circumstances were being 'updated by the hour'.

The press, however, were having none of this. In his book, Brown took the opportunity to explain how the media generally operate in such situations, and how they can choose to effectively pursue as hostile an agenda as possible against an individual, if the newspapers collectively decide that they have a shared grievance or wish to collaborate on an agreed angle of attack against someone: 'After a press conference is concluded, many of the journalists, but not all, go into a huddle to decide how they will present the material they have obtained. Whatever then appears the next morning appears largely across the board and if a spin or twist is put on the material by one, the same spin or twist is employed by all those in the huddle ... So forget all about ... the changing circumstances ... *En masse* the huddle members portrayed me as a liar and as someone who had deliberately deceived them over di Canio.'

Brown, it has to be said, hadn't helped his cause by previously misleading the press about Jansen being the club's only target for the head coach vacancy. In fact, there were other candidates considered, with both Brown and McCann flying off to Cyprus and the USA to interview applicants, neither of whom was Jansen, even before Brown's appointment had been publicly confirmed. What the general manager was trying to reassure people about was that Celtic hadn't been rejected by a bigger name, after he promised the media that the club's new boss would be on the shortlist of the biggest clubs in Europe if they had been recruiting a head coach at that time. Instead, Brown, who had previously been employed by the media and clearly knew how they operated, had made a foolish error of judgement, a mistake that he now compounded by presenting his antagonists with a clear open goal over the Di Canio affair, and the press, inevitably, went on to have a field day at his, as well as at Celtic's, expense.

It seemed to be a calamitous time for the club, at the start of a campaign that everyone associated with the Parkhead side assumed would represent a pivotal period in their history, as the spectre of ten-in-a-row loomed large, with even the Celtic players of Jock Stein's day, such as Billy McNeill and Davie Hay, admitting that there was no way they wanted to see their cherished record surpassed by the team from the other side of the city. Celtic had also lost, and been obliged to replace at short notice, a host of key figures at the club, including both Burns and Billy Stark, the manager's assistant who had resigned at the end of the season, the club captain and his deputy, McStay and Grant, and their three best attacking forwards in Van Hooijdonk, Di Canio and Cadete. In addition, the structure of the club had been radically reorganised, meaning that McCann had been required to recruit two newcomers to the club in the shape of a rookie general manager and an untested head coach, both of whom, when they were eventually appointed, were pilloried by a hostile and agenda-driven press.

The scepticism at least, if not the ridicule, in many ways appeared justified after Celtic made a slow start to the new league campaign, losing both their opening fixtures, as a 2-1 loss to Hibernian at Easter Road was followed two weeks later by an excruciating home defeat to Dunfermline by the same scoreline. The Hibernian result was particularly awkward, after new signing Henrik Larsson, who had been pursued by Jansen for some time, was introduced from the bench with the scores level at 1-1 and promptly gave the ball away on the edge of his own box, allowing Chic Charnley, a self-confessed Celtic fanatic, to fire home the winner for the Edinburgh side. Larsson was another of the new Celtic boss's former players, after the striker had made the move to Feyenoord from Swedish side Helsingborg in 1993, but not long afterwards Jansen was replaced as head coach of the Rotterdam club by Arie Haan, the former Dutch international midfielder famous for blasting in a couple of sumptuous long-range shots at the 1978 World Cup, and Larsson subsequently found himself being played out of position and regularly substituted.

Celtic eventually signed the unhappy Swede towards the end of July after the player had been involved in a lengthy legal dispute over a clause in his contract with the Dutch club, the outcome of which eventually allowed Larsson to join the

Parkhead side for a bargain £650,000. Despite his inauspicious start against Hibernian, the dreadlocked striker would go on to become one of the club's greatest-ever servants, eventually finding a place alongside Kenny Dalglish and members of the 'Lisbon Lions' in the Parkhead side's all-time greatest XI, as voted by the club's fans in 2002. Larsson would ultimately spend seven years at Celtic, during which time he netted a total of 242 goals for the Glasgow side, the majority of which, when scored at Parkhead, were accompanied by the theme tune from the movie *The Magnificent Seven*, in recognition of Larsson's shirt number and his iconic status at the club. In addition, the Swede won the European Golden Shoe in 2001 and claimed four Scottish Premier League titles, before joining Barcelona in 2004, with whom he won the Champions League in 2006.

Larsson and Blinker were joined at Parkhead by forward Darren Jackson, who arrived from Hibernian, French full-back Stéphane Mahé from Rennes, Jonathan Gould, signed as a third-choice goalkeeper from Bradford City but who eventually played 70 consecutive games for Celtic, Marc Rieper, a sturdy Danish centre-half purchased at a cost of £1.5m from West Ham, and Scotland international Craig Burley, who had been used sparingly as a right-back for Chelsea over the past eight years, but who would now take up an important role for Jansen's side in his preferred position in the centre of midfield, while the out-of-contract defensive duo of Tosh McKinlay and Malky Mackay were given new deals at the club.

Things gradually began to improve for the misfiring Parkhead side, with the team's inauspicious start under their new head coach blamed, in part at least, on a misunderstanding of Jansen's instructions, which were wrongly interpreted as a directive to play the ball forward as quickly as possible and rely on a vertical, long-ball game. With the language barrier eventually overcome, Celtic belatedly won their first serious competitive game of the season with a narrow extra-time victory over St Johnstone in the League Cup, a result that was repeated four days later when the teams met again on league business, as Jansen's side notched up their first win of the title campaign, finally lifting themselves off the bottom of the table, after strikes from Larsson, with a diving header, and Jackson gave the Parkhead men a 2-0 win at McDiarmid Park. More impressively, Celtic then went on to capture the first available trophy of the season, lifting the League Cup after a convincing 3-0 victory over Dundee United in the final at Ibrox in November, with the goals coming from the club's new signings Rieper, Larsson and Burley. It was only Celtic's second piece of silverware in over eight years, so it was particularly enjoyed by the club's supporters, who were now starting to believe, especially with Rangers showing signs of tiredness and inconsistency following the announcement in October that Walter Smith would be leaving Ibrox in the summer after another poor showing in Europe, that a realistic title challenge under their new manager may at last be on the cards.

In the meantime, however, Jansen's side had suffered another setback after losing 1-0 away to Rangers in early November, with the winning goal coming from Ibrox skipper Richard Gough, who, after scoring with his head, held up both hands, with fingers splayed, to indicate the tenth title triumph that he believed his team was on course for. It was an outcome that the Ibrox side may well have felt even more confident about had not a last-minute equaliser from Alan Stubbs rescued a 1-1 draw for Celtic in the return fixture, played just 11 days later at Celtic Park in a match held over from the start of the season following the untimely death of Princess Diana.

The Parkhead side, however, managed to restore a degree of credibility in Europe, and in the process impress a UK-wide audience, following two tight games against Liverpool in the first round of the UEFA Cup. Earlier in the campaign, Celtic had negotiated their way through two qualifying rounds, when a routine 8-0 aggregate victory over Welsh minnows Inter Cable-Tel was followed by a tricky-looking tie against the Austrian side Tirol Innsbruck. In the first leg, Jansen's side suffered a 2-1 away defeat, the result of an unconvincing performance, with Celtic's goal coming from the boot of defender Alan Stubbs, who only rescued an acceptable result for the Parkhead men with a late, powerfully struck but deflected free kick, after the home side had scored twice in the first half.

The return leg at Celtic Park was a match of high drama and, in the end, nine goals, as Celtic twice took the lead in the first half before being pegged back, with Larsson scoring an unfortunate own goal just before the interval to give the visitors a narrow half-time advantage. After the break, the Swedish striker, in imperious form, won a penalty that was converted by Donnelly, and following a deflected shot from Burley, the 4-2 scoreline seemed to put Celtic in charge of the tie. Once again, however, the Austrians edged back in front on aggregate through a late header from substitute Krinner, and as the clock ticked down, it looked as if the visitors would progress on the away goals rule, only for Jansen's side to secure qualification with two decisive late strikes. A neat finish from Wieghorst was followed quickly by the clincher from Burley, who polished off a fine run from Larsson in the fifth minute of injury time to send Celtic Park into raptures.

The club's reward was a tie against Liverpool, when the inspirational atmosphere of Celtic Park was again in evidence in the match against the high-flying Merseysiders, with a nerve-jangling rendition by the two sets of fans of 'You'll Never Walk Alone', an anthem of both clubs, greeting the teams and astonishing a TV audience of millions as the players took to the field for the first leg in Glasgow. In the initial stages, it was the home side who appeared perhaps overawed by the occasion, as Liverpool's 17-year-old striker, Michael Owen, was allowed to steal in behind the Celtic defence and score the game's opening goal. The Parkhead men eventually rallied, however, and second-half efforts from McNamara and Donnelly, the latter from the spot, turned the game on its head, before a late counter-attacking strike from McManaman against a retreating Celtic side, who had been pushing forward in search of a potentially crucial third goal, levelled the scores at 2-2 on the night to leave the tie finely balanced.

The second leg at Anfield two weeks later was a more cagey affair, by the end of which, despite the 0-0 scoreline that proved enough to see Liverpool through to the next round on away goals, TV pundit and former Reds defender Alan Hansen was forced to admit, 'I thought Celtic were the better team.' In spite of their eventual elimination, the tie with Liverpool had earned Jansen's side the respect of viewers on both sides of the border, and the outcome seemed to galvanise the squad, who had been performing inconsistently under their new manager, into producing the kind of form that was eventually to deliver trophies.

Returning to their domestic duties, the autumn proved to be an eventful period for Celtic, both on and off the park, as the victory over Dundee United in the League Cup Final at the end of November was preceded by some bizarre events behind the scenes at the club earlier in the month. Just days before the opening Glasgow derby of the season, defender Tosh McKinlay was involved in a training ground bust-up with star striker Henrik Larsson, after the full-back head-butted the Swede in an apparent unprovoked assault at the club's Barrowfield training facility. McKinlay was subsequently put on gardening leave by Jock Brown while the incident was investigated, but that didn't stop the press from having a field day over the episode, including Hugh Keevins in the *Sunday Mail*, who wrongly reported that McKinlay had been sanctioned following the altercation by being effectively suspended without pay and put on the transfer list by the club, with rumours already starting to circulate that Celtic were attempting to offload the player to Mark McGhee's Wolves.

Keevins and Brown were old colleagues, and when the journalist left *The Scotsman* to join the Sunday tabloid in the wake of the Artur Jorge fiasco, Keevins assured the Parkhead general manager that he would be working and acting in the capacity of a 'Captain Sensible'-style figure in his new sphere, and that he would not allow himself to be drawn into any of the tabloids' more lurid techniques, with the reporter maintaining that he was determined to eschew the muck-raking sensationalism so common at that end of the newspaper market. Lamenting the changes that he believed had taken place in the sports journalism industry over the 30 years that they had known each other, Brown subsequently observed of Keevins's assurances over his probity, 'I listened and indicated I would give him six weeks before he fell into line to satisfy his masters. I take no pleasure whatsoever in having been proved correct.' In the aftermath of the training ground confrontation between the two players, McKinlay accepted full liability for his actions and was fined by the club, but his opportunities in the Celtic first team would be limited from that point onwards.

Around the same time, assistant general manager Davie Hay left his post at Celtic after his contract was terminated following a dispute between himself and the board over the nature of his responsibilities at the club, and the remuneration he was receiving for performing them. Hay had been operating as the club's chief scout for the previous four years, but now he believed that he was being asked to take on a more senior role at the club without the benefits of a substantial pay rise. The subsequent disagreement over the structure of his salary led to a breakdown in relations between Hay and Brown, who had known each other for some time, with the pair initially appearing to have formed a strong behind-the-scenes partnership at the club. Over the summer, Hay had been acting as general manager on an interim basis and seemed to be in contention for the permanent position, but following Brown's appointment, he was kept on as assistant general manager, combining his duties in Brown's office with his continuing role heading up the club's scouting department.

By the end of October, however, it had become clear that the arrangements that had been put in place were unsatisfactory and, from Hay's point of view, very obviously not working, leading to tension between the football and administrative departments of the club. Eventually, following protracted negotiations, which failed to provide Hay with the kind of substantial salary increase he was seeking, the former Parkhead full-back and manager was relieved of his duties on 3 November. Jansen and MacLeod, who had formed a close connection with Hay, and as a trio were essentially running the football operations at the club, sided with their colleague in his dispute with the general manager, and with both the head coach and his assistant clearly dismayed at the final outcome, they made their feelings on the matter very clear to Brown.

The case eventually ended up in court, although Hay later admitted that this could have been avoided if his stubbornness hadn't got the better of him, after he refused the offer of a pre-tribunal compensation package from the club. It was a decision that Hay subsequently came to regret when the final judgement in the case went against him. As Brown later admitted of the failed friendship and partnership: 'David Hay really broke my heart,' while Hay himself remarked of the events that led to his departure from Parkhead: 'It was a bit of a tragedy and one of the lowest points of my football career.'

Despite these distractions behind the scenes at the club, the supporters were provided with some positive news when, early in November, the Parkhead squad was boosted by the arrival from Borussia Dortmund of Scottish international midfielder Paul Lambert, who signed a three-and-a-half-year contract at the club. Lambert had won the Scottish Cup as a 17-year-old with St Mirren in 1987, but the highlight of his career was becoming the first British player to win the European Cup with a foreign club, after he played a key role in overseeing his German side's victory over Juventus in the Champions League Final in May. With a sick baby son and an unsettled wife hampering his ambitions on the Continent, Lambert was keen to return to Scotland, and the player had been identified as a key transfer target by both Davie Hay and Wim Jansen.

The fly in the ointment appeared to be Jock Brown and his alleged opinion of Lambert as a player, because if Brown didn't rate him, as the midfielder later contended in his autobiography, there would be an understandable reluctance on Lambert's part to leave a team where he had become a legend after his exploits in the Champions League for a club where the hierarchy were less than enamoured with his footballing abilities. Brown, meanwhile, denied any suggestion that he harboured a low opinion of Lambert and he put the misunderstanding down to a conversation between his assistant Davie Hay and the player's former agent Jim Melrose. In the end, a deal was struck, and despite a last-minute effort by Dortmund to convince the player to remain in Germany, Lambert arrived in Glasgow on 5 November following a £1.7m transfer and quickly became a key member of Jansen's evolving side, with the head coach describing the acquisition as: 'The most important part of the jigsaw … Paul brought the perfect balance to the team. He was also my coach on the pitch.'

With Lambert gradually being integrated into the team, Celtic went on to claim the League Cup with a 3-0 defeat of Dundee United in the Ibrox final, the club's first victory in the competition for 15 years. The result lifted the team's spirits at the end of a troubled month, with the Parkhead side's fortunes subsequently taking a marked turn for the better. However, if the ultimate prize of the league championship was to be achieved, Celtic would have to overcome their recent dreadful record against Rangers, which included a winless run in the league over the Ibrox men stretching back all the way to an effectively meaningless end-of-season victory in May 1995, when the club were still leasing out Hampden. A potentially decisive encounter between the sides came in the New Year fixture at Celtic Park, played on 2 January 1998, when second-half strikes from midfielders Burley and Lambert, who latched on to a clearance and fired in a spectacular, long-range shot to score his first goal for the club, gave Celtic a deserved 2-0 win over their rivals.

The club's victory in the traditional turn-of-the-year derby fixture, always a seemingly crucial encounter in determining the ultimate outcome of the title race, went a long way to setting the tone for the next few months, as Rangers soon surrendered their position at the top of the league. The Ibrox men endured an extraordinary spell of mediocrity and ineffectiveness over the next few weeks, with only one game in six between the end of January and the middle of March resulting in a victory for Walter Smith's side, a sequence that allowed both Celtic and Hearts to surge ahead of the Christmas league leaders, as the Edinburgh club, managed by the experienced taskmaster Jim Jeffries, put in a realistic and credible title challenge for the first time in many years.

Meanwhile, following their defeat of Rangers, Jansen's side dropped points to Motherwell in their next fixture, with Lambert firing home another eye-catching, long-range effort to secure a 1-1 draw against Alex McLeish's side. This result was followed by a fortuitous 2-1 victory over Dundee United at Tannadice, when Burley's late shot was deflected into the net for a barely deserved winner. Once again, however, before the end of the month, the club had to deal with off-field issues, as details of the fallout between Davie Hay and Jock Brown, which had resulted in the assistant general manager's departure from Parkhead in November, became public, with Hay selling his side of the story to the *Sunday Mail* and Brown issuing a riposte in the club's own *Celtic View*. The press, it seemed, were very much on the club's case once again, but despite these distractions, after Celtic beat Aberdeen in a game held over for television purposes on Monday, 2 February, all three title challengers found themselves locked together at the top of the league on the same number of points.

With the title race approaching its climax, Celtic and Hearts twice recorded draws against one another, as a late equaliser from José Quitongo, which robbed Celtic of a merited victory at Tynecastle, was followed by a scoreless encounter between the pair in Glasgow at the end of March. The latter result allowed struggling Rangers, who seemed to have dropped out of contention as winter gave way to spring, to gather their resources for a final assault on the title, and after defeating Celtic 2-0 at Ibrox in April, a week after knocking Jansen's men out of the Scottish Cup in a semi-final played at the designated neutral Celtic Park, the two teams were once again locked together on 66 points, with Smith's side now edging ahead on goal difference. Rangers, however, lost ground once again after a 1-0 defeat to Aberdeen at Pittodrie in a game that saw Italian defender Lorenzo Amoruso ordered off, and the Ibrox title charge appeared over as the defending champions stumbled once again in the penultimate fixture of the season, losing 1-0 at home to Kilmarnock following a late strike from Ally Mitchell.

This was the game that had been controversially awarded to referee Bobby Tait as a retirement present, another official who was accused of barely disguised Ibrox allegiances and of habitually wearing his Rangers kit in public. With time running out in the goalless match, Celtic fans tuning in on the radio were left cursing the SFA once again, as Tait allowed the contest to continue well beyond the 90-minute mark. The anxiety of the Parkhead fans turned to elation, however, as Mitchell made a late run into the box to finish off a counter-attacking move from the Ayrshire side and score the game's only goal with almost the last kick of the match. The result meant that Celtic could win the league the following day and stop the dreaded ten-in-a-row with victory over struggling Dunfermline at East End Park.

Jansen's side started the match in Fife strongly, appearing focused and determined, and with Donnelly's strike in the fifth minute giving them the lead, Celtic went into the half-time interval deservedly ahead and on the brink of finally securing the long-awaited championship. The second half initially developed along similar lines, but as the match wore on with the visitors failing to add to their lead, anxiety began to creep into Celtic's play, as the Parkhead men made the mistake, perhaps understandably in the circumstances, of starting to watch the clock rather than maintaining their focus on the match itself. In the 83rd minute, with the Celtic defence retreating too deep towards their own goal line, Dunfermline equalised from a set piece, as a long free kick into the box was met by the head of substitute Craig Faulconbridge, a beanpole striker on loan to the Pars from Coventry City, and the ball looped agonisingly past Jonathan Gould into the Celtic net. It would be a long week for the Parkhead club's supporters, as the race for the title went down to the final match of the season.

Nerves were clearly beginning to fray, and sensing a final opportunity, which they originally assumed had been squandered after the defeat at home to Kilmarnock, the Rangers management, and in particular owner David Murray, began to make preparations for the celebrations that would greet the capture of a tenth consecutive title, with news leaking out in the press – no accident to be sure – about a helicopter being put on stand-by to take Walter Smith's squad back to Ibrox if the title should be won in the club's last fixture of the season against Dundee United at Tannadice. To prevent such a scenario, Jansen's side were required to secure a home win over St Johnstone, as any other result would allow Rangers the opportunity to finish in top spot with victory on Tayside. On Saturday, 9 May, the final fixtures of the season kicked off simultaneously at 3pm, and within 90 seconds the nervous tension inside Celtic Park was eased by Swedish striker Henrik Larsson's dipping shot from the edge of the box, which beat Saints keeper Alan Main to give Celtic an early lead, as the Parkhead ground, in the words of one writer at the time, 'exploded in what can only be described as a volcanic eruption of happiness'.

With the early goal, however, the edge began to come off Celtic's play, and after opportunities to add to their lead were wasted, St Johnstone missed arguably the best chance of the half as the interval approached, when striker George O'Boyle headed over the bar from just outside the six-yard box. The anxiety was starting to ripple around the stadium once more, with the experience of East End Park still fresh in the memory, and particularly after news of Rangers' two-goal lead at Tannadice began to filter through. Celtic historian David Potter, recalling the mood among the supporters as the second half progressed and the Parkhead side fought to cling on to their narrow advantage, wrote: 'One goal from St Johnstone would kill all Celtic hopes and plunge us into the sort of Stygian melancholy that would be unimaginable in its ferocity, intensity and permanence,' before comparing what happened next to Armistice Day, 1918 in terms of the sheer, bloody relief that it was all over.

In the 72nd minute, Norwegian forward Harald Brattbakk, who had appeared as a substitute for Donnelly on the hour mark, accelerated into the box and, latching on to a perfectly weighted pass from McNamara, calmly placed his shot past Main to extend Celtic's lead. It was the clincher, and supporters inside Celtic Park, as well as fans of the club listening around the world, were at last able to celebrate and savour the occasion, as the club finally claimed its first league title in ten long years.

It had been a period during which supporters had witnessed their club plumb new depths of often self-inflicted hardship at a time when, conversely, their rivals had ascended to a period of unrelenting dominance of the Scottish domestic game, and the celebrations and street parties around Glasgow continued long into the night and for many days thereafter.

'This has got to be one of the highlights of my career as a coach and something I will always remember,' Jansen, who became the first foreign coach to lead a team to the Scottish league championship, announced at the end of the match, even as the celebrations continued in the background, but the Dutchman, when asked, refused to be drawn on his future in the aftermath of the victory. Paul Lambert, meanwhile, along with his team-mates wearing a pre-printed T-shirt which read '1Ø in a row', compared the feeling of satisfaction at finally reclaiming the title from Rangers to winning the Champions League with Borussia Dortmund the previous season, and joked that he was now considering retirement. Meanwhile, owner Fergus McCann, despite his joy, shunned the hysteria inside the stadium, claiming that he 'had to be back because of the babysitter'. Speaking in all seriousness, McCann later elaborated on his memory of the occasion and his desire to retain a low profile, even at such a moment. 'The other thing was that I didn't want to get involved in the on-field celebrations. The players would have been chasing me and so forth. It was something for the players and fans and it's not really my thing, he admitted.

It had unquestionably been a struggle at times, after Jansen's side initially lost their first two matches, and with the team understandably affected by nerves as the campaign approached its dramatic conclusion, Celtic's aggregate points total, which saw the Parkhead side finish in first position with 22 wins and eight draws from their 36 fixtures, was lower than had been accumulated by champions in previous seasons, even when adjusted for the introduction of three points for a win two years earlier. All three title challengers, Rangers, Hearts and Celtic, had on occasion shown a high degree of inconsistency over the course of the season, but Celtic were the team, despite being dogged by off-field issues and bearing the heavy burden of their supporters' expectations, who had won the war of attrition and for that reason they were deserved champions, as their rivals ultimately had the grace to acknowledge. Midfielder Craig Burley later summed up the pressure and the demands from supporters that he and his team-mates had been subjected to during the campaign, telling *FourFourTwo* in February 2020, 'They [the fans] were besotted with stopping Rangers and would remind us it was the most important fucking season in the history of the club. If you couldn't handle the pressure then it wasn't a place for you. Luckily, we had players who thrived on it.'

In the end though, amid the delirium, there would be a sting in the tail for Celtic, as long before the denouement, Jansen had made up his mind to quit the club at the end of the campaign, exercising a get-out clause in his three-year contract and taking the decision to leave Glasgow after only one season in charge at Parkhead. It had become clear that a rift had developed between Jansen, along with his assistant Murdo MacLeod, and the club's brash general manager Jock Brown, which had left Brown convinced by as early as December that Jansen would not be remaining at Celtic beyond the summer of 1998. On 4 February, Brown admitted in the *Celtic View* that the two men were not the best of pals, but he maintained that the working relationship between the pair was strong and that the team was unaffected by any clash of personalities.

Things became more problematic, however, towards the end of March when the press, on the eve of a crucial home game against Hearts, finally got wind of Jansen's contractual situation and reported that the head coach would be considering his position at the end of the season. Hugh Keevins of the *Sunday Mail*, flailing about in the dark, wrongly pinned the blame for the Dutchman's apparent disillusionment with life at Celtic on the club's owner, Fergus McCann, whose parsimonious approach was alleged to be at the root of the problem, specifically in relation to the terms of the manager's contract, which McCann, it was claimed, was refusing to renegotiate. In fact, Jansen's decision had nothing to do with his salary, but had been taken on the basis of his reluctance to continue working under the supervision of the media's other favourite target, Jock Brown.

At first, Celtic supporters appeared unsure how to react to this new information, with many initially believing that the reports of seemingly irreconcilable differences behind the scenes at the club were no more than further evidence of anti-Celtic hostility on the part of an antagonistic section of the press, which had become public, somewhat predictably it seemed, at an important stage of the season. Brown himself later observed, 'It was always felt within the club that just before a crunch match … some story would appear in the press to destabilise the camp. It got to the stage where I used to joke about this so that it did not come as any surprise when the disruptive story broke. That strategy worked, because it was always a source of some amusement within Celtic Park when the negative story appeared right on cue.'

In this instance, however, Jansen had given an interview to a website and admitted on television that the get-out clause existed, although he refused to confirm whether he was thinking of using it. The revelations of the Dutchman's potentially imminent departure from the club might have had catastrophic consequences for Celtic's bid to claim their first title in ten years, and indeed, in the aftermath, the Parkhead side won only three of their remaining eight fixtures, a run which included back-to-back defeats to Rangers in April, as the Ibrox men regained their position at the top of the league and eliminated their rivals at the semi-final stage of the Scottish Cup.

In the end, Celtic fell over the line and took the title on the last day of the season, but on Monday, 11 May, just two days after the Parkhead celebrations had begun in earnest, Jansen resigned from his position as the club's head coach. At the time, the squad were in Lisbon preparing for a friendly match against Sporting, which had been organised as part of the deal that had brought striker Jorge Cadete to Glasgow two years earlier. Jansen first broke the news to his players, and then, at a press conference arranged to confirm his departure, the Dutchman didn't hold back, berating Brown over the sale of Cadete and Paolo Di Canio at the start of the season and blaming him also over the departure of Davie Hay. 'In the last few months I couldn't even speak to Jock Brown. In fact, I wanted to resign two or three weeks after I took the job, but they wouldn't let me do that,' Jansen claimed.

Brown, a lawyer by trade, mounted a passionate and unquestionably skilled defence of his role in the affair in his book *Celtic-Minded: 510 Days in Paradise*, published a short time after his own resignation and departure from Celtic Park later in the year. In the book, Brown maintained that Jansen was a surly character, whom he found very difficult to deal with almost from the start of their working relationship. The head coach was alleged to have meticulously restricted himself to first-team affairs, and while this was always an important part of the remit that the club had been keen to impose on their new coach following the dismissal of Tommy Burns, Jansen had apparently pursued the policy to an almost neurotic degree, refusing to interact with the other developmental coaches at the club and overlooking the interests of players on the fringes of his first XI. It was this perceived disregard for the concerns and wellbeing of other players and staff at the club, Brown claimed, which was the root cause of the evident friction within the squad and provided the context for the training ground incident in November between Tosh McKinlay, who had been replaced at left-back in Jansen's team by Stéphane Mahé earlier in the season, and star striker Henrik Larsson.

Another bone of contention for the club's board and management concerned Jansen's refusal to travel to Norway to watch the targeted forward Harald Brattbakk in action for his team Rosenborg before the player eventually joined up with the Parkhead squad in December. Brattbakk had been scoring at a rate of almost one goal per game in Norwegian football, but Celtic's company policy at the time stipulated that the head coach was required to observe any potential new signing in action first hand if the fee involved was more that £2m. Even after the club had chartered a plane to fly the manager to Trondheim, however, Jansen rejected the request, player recruitment presumably from Jansen's point of view not being part of the head coach's job description. The Dutchman later admitted that he had indeed refused to go to watch Brattbakk in the flesh, but the coach also pointed out in his own defence, 'Well, I didn't see Jonathan Gould, Marc Rieper, Craig Burley or Stéphane Mahé. I also wanted to sign Karl-Heinz Riedle, but the club didn't even make a phone call to see if he was available. Two weeks later, he signed for Liverpool.'

A further allegation pursued by Brown was that Jansen had been unwilling to provide any detailed information going forward on the squad's strengths and weaknesses, and that it therefore became almost impossible for the club to plan for the season ahead in terms of budget and player recruitment. Once again, Jansen countered the accusation by claiming that the board had refused to let him know how much money was going to be available for salaries and transfer fees, and that consequently he was always dealing with hypotheticals. With hindsight, this reluctance on Jansen's part to go into detail about the second season was understandable, and it must have been an awkward conversation indeed between the two men, given that any future planning would have been hindered by the coach's already arrived at decision not to remain at the club beyond the end of the current campaign and Brown, as he claimed, having already worked out that the Dutchman was intending to leave!

Having fallen out with the coach at a very early stage in their relationship, Brown also claimed in his book that he reluctantly took the decision to pursue a policy of 'appeasement' in relation to Jansen's behaviour, to treat the head coach with kid gloves and, in the interests of the pursuit of the vital league championship, to refrain from confronting or exercising his authority over a subordinate employee in a manner that might have been expected, although he conceded that adopting such a stance was so difficult at times that it 'almost killed me'. Brown, it seems clear, would have been glad to see the back of Jansen, although there was understandable trepidation on the part of the general manager about the ensuing fall-out in the media from the Dutchman's departure, which turned out to be predictably vicious, as the club's supporters experienced the anticlimax of losing their championship-winning figurehead just days after the longed-for title was finally won.

Brown was, however, able to count on the support of the Celtic board following his dispute with the club's coach and in particular on owner Fergus McCann, who was sounding sanguine about the long-term effect of losing the Dutchman when the club subsequently released a statement in McCann's name, which read: 'The decision Wim has taken is one that the board also believes is the best for the club … The nature of football now sees players and coaches changing club more frequently than in the past. We must all accept and embrace change as an exciting challenge and ensure that it also results in progress … Individuals will always come and go but the legend that is Celtic continues.'

It was an announcement that produced another excoriating response from Jim Traynor in the *Daily Record*, a paper that had already wheeled out a number of disgruntled former employees of the club, such as Brian Dempsey, Michael Kelly and former finance director Dominic Keane to prey on and compound Celtic's embarrassment at losing their head coach in such circumstances. 'The responsibility for this latest disgrace should be laid at the doors of McCann and Brown,' Traynor castigated the management of the recently crowned champions. 'The people will not forget their seemingly arrogant and intransigent behaviour which brought a club crashing [down] from the heights of ecstasy. The next manager, if there is still anyone out there willing to work under such a regime, had better be prepared … This is now a job for a corporate strategist. A penchant for bullshitting might also help.'

In the end, the circumstances surrounding the coach's departure from Celtic were unsatisfactory for everyone concerned at the club, and Jansen's sudden resignation took the gloss off a historic achievement by the Parkhead side. It was a situation in which neither party had been devoid of blame, but it also appeared to be the case that, rather than the responsibility for what had occurred being restricted to the individuals involved, it was the structural changes at the club, implemented only a year earlier, which had been at the heart of the problem. The idea of a head coach reporting to a non-footballing general manager had proved unsuccessful, with Brown seemingly, and with the benefit of hindsight, too authoritarian a figure to sit easily within the corridors of power of a club like Celtic. It's likely that, probably quite unintentionally, his remoteness and inflexibility just rubbed too many people up the wrong way, although as far as Brown himself was concerned, he was simply doing his job and fulfilling the remit that had been handed to him. Similarly, Jansen had concentrated his efforts almost exclusively on his first XI in accordance with the instructions he had been given on his appointment. Responsibility for the new structure, introduced following the departure of Tommy Burns the previous year, rested with McCann and, perhaps realising his mistake and the issues that his reorganisation of the club had thrown up, it wasn't long before a change was made.

When Brown eventually left the club the following season on the morning of Saturday, 7 November 1998, the team responded later that day, after an initially slow start to the defence of their title, by thrashing Dundee 6-1 at Celtic Park and then, in their next home match, even more impressively by engineering a comprehensive 5-1 win over Rangers. It almost seemed to have gone unnoticed, but over the next few months the position of general manager at Celtic Park was quietly made redundant, with a chief executive instead assuming overall responsibility for the company's affairs. It was a modification that perhaps in the end provided something of a belated vindication for Jansen, the departed Dutch coach, whose stay in Glasgow was ultimately short, but who nevertheless managed to attain, thanks to his achievements on the field, a legendary status among the club's supporters, as the man who stopped ten-in-a-row and began the long process of the Parkhead club's redemption.

7.

Distortion

DAVID Murray's fury at losing the league to Celtic in 1998 was perhaps understandable – it was, after all, the first time his club had failed to secure the championship since the chairman's involvement at Ibrox, but his subsequent reaction set Rangers on a path to ruin. With the liabilities in the balance sheet continuing to grow, over the next few months the Bank of Scotland, which had previously indulged Murray's every appetite, moved to acquire a 7 per cent stake in The Rangers Football Club plc as part of a process of 'corporate restructuring' at the club's parent company MIH. At the same time, the bank also secured a floating charge over the company's assets, including Ibrox Park and the Albion training ground, just as they had with Celtic under the old board earlier in the decade, meaning that, in the case of an insolvency event at Rangers, the bank would be at the head of the queue of the club's creditors.

Any concerns being expressed around this time, however, over the condition of the finances at Ibrox or the direction in which the chairman seemed to be taking the club, proved to be a warning that Murray showed no signs of heeding, as by any standards, the spending spree that Rangers embarked on over the summer of 1998 was as enormous as it was reckless. The wholesale restructuring of the playing department after the team had failed to secure a trophy during the previous campaign was overseen by the new managerial partnership of the experienced Dutch duo, Dick Advocaat and his assistant Bert van Lingen. Their outlay on expensive foreign imports – players of considerable pedigree with a proven track record in the game – was funded to a very large extent at this time by a business deal secured with ENIC, the sports and media investment arm of the Tavistock Group, owned by the Bahamas-based businessman Joe Lewis. In late 1996, Murray had persuaded Lewis to add Rangers to his company's growing portfolio of football clubs around Europe, which included Slavia Prague, AEK Athens, Vicenza and Tottenham Hotspur, in a deal that brought a headline-grabbing £40m into the coffers at Ibrox. This revenue had immediately been deployed by the chairman as part of his spending strategy for the club, with Rangers matching and surpassing the wages on offer in Serie A to bring, among many others, top Italian players such as Lorenzo Amoruso, Marco Negri, Sergio Porrini and Rino Gattuso to Glasgow at the start of Walter Smith's final season in charge at Ibrox.

ENIC were effectively playing with loose change, but having taken their money, Murray subsequently treated his business partners with contempt once the funds were safely secured. The group had initially believed, presumably as a consequence of the chairman's unctuous solicitations, that their investment in Rangers would quickly yield a profitable return, but they soon found themselves out of the loop at Ibrox, despite the presence of company man Daniel Levy on the club's board. Crucially, unlike at many of the other sporting institutions in which they had become involved, ENIC's purchase of shares in Rangers had seen them take only a 25 per cent stake in the company, meaning that they were still a minority interest, unable to directly influence policy at Ibrox. With Murray effectively still in sole control of the club's affairs, Levy and the other directors were powerless to limit his profligacy, and the chairman certainly didn't sound as if he was about to be deflected from his ambitions in October 2000, by which time the group's original investment had been written down to £15m, when he dismissed their concerns over the way he was running the club, stating, 'They might not agree with the way we've done it, but I've been at Rangers 12 years and we've won 11 championships and 20 trophies ... So I must be doing something right.'

Murray's negotiating skills and his powers of persuasion were becoming legendary, as other deals brought further revenue and investment into the club, including a one-for-three share issue in spring 2000 that allowed South African-based businessman, Dave King, to put £20m into Rangers through his Ben Nevis Holdings, all of which was subsequently lost. It couldn't have been easy to dupe such hard-nosed wealth accumulators – Lewis at the time was estimated to be the eighth-richest man in Britain – but nevertheless these outside investors, succumbing to Murray's talent for relieving other parties of their cash, were now replacing the indulgent bank loans that had fuelled the club's spending earlier in the decade. As often as not, it seemed, it was other people's money that Murray was flashing around so ostentatiously, and the chairman's ability to bring others into his camp, naturally, included a pliant local press, who at times appeared to be vying to outdo one another in terms of the sycophancy and approbation they were affording the Rangers chairman in their coverage of his questionable business methods at Ibrox.

One particularly egregious example of the kind of brown-nosing servility that Murray was able to induce from certain sections of the media at this time, backing his ambitious and extravagant plans for the club, accompanied the share issue in March 2000, when James Traynor, under the headline 'Out of Sight', reported in the *Daily Record*, 'Rangers are about to embark on a money-spinning strategy which will leave Scottish football stunned. The Ibrox club are close to announcing fresh investment which business analysts describe as "enormous". The amounts involved will easily top the £40m received from Joe Lewis almost three years ago and a large slice of the cash will be used to add the final touches to Dick Advocaat's European team ... The business community are convinced Murray is about to take his club into the big league by pulling off another coup like the Lewis deal which staggered football at the time. They say this next one will have an even greater impact.'

Such promises of almost unlimited wealth being poured into the club's coffers and being weaponised by the chairman in his quest to bring domestic and European glory to Ibrox must have sounded incredibly enticing to the club's fans – and equally worrying for their rivals. Without the considerable benefit of hindsight or the analysis offered by the development in more recent years of citizen journalism through social media platforms, the reader of the day had little choice but to accept Traynor's quivering proclamations of another gold rush at Ibrox at face value, especially as the message was being delivered across all platforms, with a parallel, even more gushing report appearing in the broadsheet *The Herald* a few days later.

These and many other similar articles, which were being published in a diverse range of newspaper titles around this period, favourably profiling Murray and his contribution to

Rangers, regardless of the obvious lack of concern being displayed by the chairman for the club's future financial security, appeared to come at a curious time for the media sector generally. The 1990s and early 2000s, it seemed, represented a strange era of power games across the communications industry where, in an expanding information age, certain megalomaniac tendencies encouraged media executives and owners to believe that their organisations could control the flow and supply of news and information, and could therefore affect events, including, of course, sporting events. If *The Sun*, as the newspaper had claimed, could sway the result of the 1992 UK general election in one party's favour, then it seemed reasonable to assume that the distorting lens of large mass media conglomerates could similarly bring their influence to bear on the outcome of a minor footballing competition in a small, unimportant semi-state in the north-west corner of Europe.

There is plenty of evidence to suggest that Murray believed he could harness this media influence and wield it effectively in his determination to ensure that, after losing the league to Celtic in Walter Smith's final season at Ibrox, his club regained control of the domestic game and returned to a position of dominance in Scotland once more. In November 1998, Murray celebrated ten years as chairman of Rangers by inviting a select group of journalists for dinner at his offshore retreat in the Channel Islands, and it subsequently came as no surprise when the eulogies accompanying the anniversary started to appear in the national press. James Traynor – him again – marked the occasion with an infamous article in the *Daily Record*, in which he introduced the world of Scottish football to the now familiar concept of 'succulent lamb' journalism. 'To hear him [Murray] speak,' Traynor declaimed in his now notorious piece, 'was to listen to a man who believes himself to be charged with some kind of great and mighty mission ... He was about to take in another mouthful of the most succulent lamb – anyone who knows Murray shouldn't be surprised to learn that he is a full-blooded, unashamed red meat eater – when he put down his knife and fork ...' At last, fans of the game in Scotland had a name for the kind of reporting that had been directed towards Murray and Rangers down the years, and 'succulent lamb' subsequently passed into the vernacular and became a byword for the kind of obsequiousness and flattery that Traynor was evincing and that Murray was regularly able to elicit from his friends in the press throughout his spell in charge of Rangers, and even beyond.

Traynor wasn't done there, however, and the ingratiating tone in the piece continued with the reporter quoting Murray at some length on his plans for the future. 'It was like a statement of intent and looking directly across the table to make sure I hadn't yet succumbed to the wine, he said: "Bring on the next ten years, there's more to come from Rangers. Understand that I care passionately about what I'm doing with Rangers and believe that in ten years' time we will still be setting the pace. Too many of us have put too much into this club and we won't let someone come along and take it all away. What I'm saying here is that no matter who buys Celtic from Fergus they will need to have the deepest of pockets imaginable ... In the past, Celtic's people maybe just haven't fancied trying to take Rangers on financially, but if I have to go in deeper to keep my club up there then I will. I have done it too many times to be frightened now."'

What Traynor had failed to appreciate, however, was that Murray, in his conceit and as hindsight was later to reveal, was sowing the seeds of his club's destruction with his 'bring them on at all costs' bravado. A more serious sports writer, Graham Spiers, later observed of all this hoopla, 'Such credulous journalism had been Murray's staple in Scotland, leading to much lampooning of reporters by more accurate football observers who know the dangers the world over of big, colourful sports magnates toying with local journalists like glove puppets. Suffice to say that Rangers, far from entering the elite of Europe, were soon in the financial grubber and about to experience a trophy famine due to the very policy that the reporters had so extolled.'

The chairman, in his folly, had also displayed an immature attitude towards losing the league to Celtic the previous season, failing to understand that defeat is a necessary and universal part of professional sport, and that how a competitor, whether on the field or in the boardroom, deals with and reacts to the setbacks, when they inevitably occur, can say much about their character as well as their ability to bounce back and achieve success once again over the longer period. Murray, in admitting that he had been contorted with anguish over the loss of the league title to Celtic, and in vowing to his clique of journalists that he never wanted to taste defeat ever again, was betraying a fundamental flaw in his style of leadership and management, which was particularly consequential in a volatile business such as football. Traynor, meanwhile, later took up a position at Ibrox as head of the club's PR department, a role that many felt he had been operating in unpaid for several years.

Another illustration of this kind of pseudo-journalism, which is worth mentioning, in respect to the status and profile that Murray, together with his club, was able to command from the would-be opinion formers of the west of Scotland at this time, appeared in late 1996 when the chairman tried to recruit former Celtic idol Kenny Dalglish to a scouting role at Ibrox.

In early November of that year, *The Record* ran a story about a supposed Rangers 'dream team' being put together, with players of the calibre of Paolo Maldini and Jurgen Klinsmann reportedly on their way to Ibrox, along with a galaxy of other stars of the footballing firmament. The article also named, among others, Overmars, Cantona, Fowler and Petit, as well as somebody called Sean Dundee, as potential targets. Dalglish was described as 'the Franz Beckenbauer of Rangers' and a 'roving spy' with £80m at his disposal to attract the likes of Kluivert and Ronaldo, the original Brazilian version, who, it was suggested, would only be required to offer his services to Rangers while on Champions League duty. The rest of the Ibrox *galacticos* presumably would be able to take care of Rangers' more mundane task of maintaining the club's dominance of the Scottish domestic scene on their own.

Regarding the enormous cost of potentially luring these superstars to Ibrox, the article reported that Dalglish would be afforded, thanks to his 'brilliant record' as a manager in England, 'an open chequebook to make sure the big names are made an offer they can't refuse'. This was the stuff of fantasy of course, almost entirely fictitious, but it shifted newspapers. Dalglish, out of work after leaving his director of football role at Blackburn Rovers, would later describe his putative role at Ibrox, with characteristically minimalist rhetoric, as nothing more than, 'If David Murray wanted me to go and have a look at a player, then I was happy to do that.'

Perhaps the strangest aspect of this whole cult surrounding Murray at the time was that it wasn't always like this in Scotland; yes, Rangers had enjoyed favourable and discreet coverage in the past over many decades, but the mutually beneficial, almost symbiotic relationship between sections of the media and

Murray's Ibrox regime, where broadcasters and newspapers no longer seemed to care if they were seen as biased, or lacking objectivity and balance, was a relatively recent phenomenon. In September 1987, just over a year before Murray's purchase of the club, *The Herald*, then still Glasgow's respected broadsheet newspaper, had called Rangers out in the wake of manager Graham Souness's latest censure by the SFA's disciplinary committee, lamenting the fact that there was no parallel committee capable of dealing with the Rangers board, which, *The Herald*'s opinion piece maintained, 'in its overweening way claims control over all published material about its affairs'.

The article continued, 'It is well known that football managers try to intimidate sports writers by withdrawing contact, if the scribe offends them. This explains why so much sports writing draws on platitudinous managerial comment quoted with excessive respect. Rangers have now brought this system to its apogee and in the process made themselves petty and ridiculous.' The author of the piece believed that this 'compounds all the things that have made Rangers disliked down the years, their arrogance and triumphalism ... Rangers have ambition but they have no style. Their high-handedness makes them disliked wherever they go in Scottish football,' before the editorial concluded with a final harrumph, 'We do not think our readers will be greatly deprived by not being privy to the latest *dicta* from Ibrox. They will at all times prefer independent comment to propaganda.'

How things had changed in just a little over a decade. It would be wrong to assume, however, that *The Herald*, by criticising and opposing Rangers in a way that would have seemed unimaginable during the Murray era, was somehow at the time a Celtic-sympathising newspaper, or a bastion of liberal or pluralist values. On the contrary, in fact *The Herald*, a paper with a long and honourable history from as far back as the 1920s of openly contesting some of the widespread views and prejudices in Scotland on issues such as Irish immigration, was itself still not employing Catholics in any capacity, a policy that persisted up to the 1980s, when the paper was owned by Lonrho, part of the business empire of the controversial tycoon and media baron, Tiny Rowland.

The editor of the day, Arnold Kemp, one of Scotland's most highly regarded and successful journalists, later recalled how his appointment in 1981 was greeted by some of the paper's long-serving staff: 'A board member, evidently confused by the fact that I was a Hibs supporter, had insisted on knowing whether I was a Catholic. When I answered in the negative, a cloud lifted from his brow. Some days later, I was visited by a rather sinister member of the personnel department, who wished to assure himself that I would observe the company's traditional recruiting policies. This meant that applicants' letters would be placed in three piles – probables, possibles and "those you won't want to see". This last was a euphemism for those whose name or educational history betrayed their religious affiliation.' Any disputes between *The Herald* and Rangers in the pre-Murray era, and there were many, could be characterised as a disagreement between factions of the establishment classes in the west of Scotland, in which Celtic and the club's supporters didn't feature in any way.

By the time of Murray's ten-year Ibrox anniversary, *The Herald* had been acquired by Scottish Media Group (SMG), an ambitious conglomerate of media and other interests, and was now part of the group's portfolio of similar businesses, including STV and the Glasgow-based tabloid the *Evening Times*. SMG, it seemed, were fully signed up to supporting Murray's business protocol, with the Rangers chairman at one point even enjoying the benefits of having his putative girlfriend, Sarah Heaney, fronting STV's flagship nightly regional news programme, *Scotland Tonight*. Heaney's first appearance on the programme, after a brief stint as a presenter on LiveTV, was accompanied by a soft-focus profile piece in the lifestyle section of *The Herald*, in which the alluring presenter assured readers that she had never taken her clothes off for money. In fact, she had, as a lingerie model, and Sarah, STV's apparent answer to Jeremy Paxman, was romantically linked with the Rangers owner in a number of newspapers, although a cynic may have suggested that there was more than a hint of a Max Clifford-style PR stunt about their supposed relationship.

Interestingly, SMG, who had started life as plain old Scottish Television, by now seemed to have their own plans for rapid expansion, not unlike those of Rangers and Murray at the time. The group had bought *The Herald* and *Evening Times* newspapers in 1996, and from there had grown quickly, acquiring Pearl and Dean, the cinema advertising company, Ginger Media Group, which owned Virgin Radio, and Grampian Television, as well as flirting with two other TV franchises, Border and Ulster. They later also acquired stakes in Scottish Radio Holdings, the parent company of Radio Clyde, as well as in GMTV and Heart of Midlothian FC, owning part of a football club being the ultimate corporate media vanity project in the late 1990s.

After the bursting of the dotcom bubble in early 2000 and the subsequent economic downturn, the company, again much like Rangers, appeared vulnerable, and over the next few years, with spiralling debts reaching £380m, the group began to break up. Even Ms Heaney, now Mrs Ed Adams after marrying a jewellery designer from London, wasn't safe, and the presenter eventually accepted a redundancy package from STV in 2006. In 2008, SMG changed its name to STV Group, with the company announcing its intention to concentrate on its television business in the years ahead, which to be fair was more or less all it had left by then.

With Dick Advocaat now installed as part of the new regime at Ibrox following Walter Smith's drawn-out departure, Murray afforded his new manager an almost unlimited budget, as Rangers turned their attention towards the tantalising but hopelessly unrealistic prospect of bringing the Champions League trophy to Ibrox. The chairman had already indicated where the club's priorities would now be channelled, stating in May 1997, shortly after the record-equalling ninth title was secured, 'We have to deliver a European trophy within three or four years, or be challenging regularly in the Champions League. If we are not doing well in that timescale, I will consider my tenure to have been a total failure.'

With the club's immediate priorities re-orientated towards Europe, Advocaat now added, at enormous expense and in addition to the vast outlay of Smith's final season in charge, players of the required calibre and quality, whom he hoped would take the Ibrox side close to its ultimate goal. These included Arthur Numan, Andrei Kanchelskis, Giovanni van Bronckhorst, Gabriel Amato, Lionel Charbonnier, Daniel Prodan, Stefan Klos and Claudio Reyna, as well as, in the Dutch trainer's second season at the club, Michael Mols and Tugay Kerimoğlu. Neil McCann and Billy Dodds signed up too. On the domestic front at least, the strategy was immediately and irrefutably successful in the initial stages, as Rangers regained the title from Celtic in Advocaat's first season at the club, with the championship finally clinched on a dramatic day at Celtic Park on Sunday, 2 May 1999.

It had been an exhausting title race in which the Parkhead side, ten points behind their rivals at the turn of the year, had tried to reel in Advocaat's men with an impressive display of consistency following the winter break, introduced for the first time in Scotland as part of several new arrangements for the domestic game, including the establishment of a reconstituted Scottish Premier League (SPL). At one stage an unlikely fightback appeared possible, as a combination of Celtic's good form and their rivals' complacency had seen the gap at the top of the table reduced to just four points, but at the end of April the Parkhead club lost to St Johnstone in Perth, a result which, with just four games now remaining, afforded Rangers the opportunity to regain the championship by extending their lead to an unassailable ten points once more with victory in their next match in the east end of Glasgow.

It turned out to be an eventful day; on the field, Celtic were hampered by a number of key absentees due to injury, an ordinary problem that all clubs have to cope with in the normal course of events, but the list of Parkhead players rendered unfit to take part in the climactic fixture was particularly extensive, even by the standards of an injury-plagued campaign. It included Gould, McNamara, Rieper, Burley, O'Donnell, McKinlay, Blinker, Moravčík and Mjällby, while captain Tom Boyd was suspended. In contrast, while Celtic were forced to draft in debutants for the crunch game, Rangers were able to draw on the talents of an almost fully fit complement of players, with only Numan and youngster Ferguson missing from the regular matchday squad.

Nevertheless, in the build-up to the match, few neutrals anticipated that the home team would allow the Ibrox men to win the league at their ground, but regrettably events got away from the Parkhead club on the day, on and off the field, as Advocaat's side ran out comfortable 3-0 winners. An early goal by Rangers' winger McCann, quickly followed by a harsh red card for Celtic's full-back Mahé, set the visitors on their way, but the sending-off also had an unfortunate effect on the expectant home crowd, many of whom had clearly been taking advantage of the opportunity to overindulge themselves in the attractions of the bank holiday weekend before the 6.05pm evening kick-off. One supporter, clearly the worse for wear, fell out of the top tier of the North Stand, fortunately with no apparent ill-effects to his overall health.

There can be no excuse, however, for the conduct of a section of the Parkhead crowd, with a number of individuals invading the field and chucking coins at the referee, Hugh Dallas, one of which struck the official on the head and left a trail of blood dripping from his hairline. After being treated on the field for his injury, Dallas probably felt quite within his rights to award Rangers a soft penalty moments later, which Albertz calmly converted to extend the visitors' lead. If the crowd and the referee, who had a poor game, were spoiling the occasion, the Rangers players, by contrast, were keeping their cool admirably; the Ibrox men played well in difficult circumstances, controlled the game and deserved not only to take the three points on the day but also, over the course of the whole campaign, to reclaim the championship from their great rivals.

The match left a sour taste in the mouth, however, with almost nobody escaping censure in the aftermath of the turmoil, as Celtic were hit with a £45,000 fine over the pitch invasions and the coin-throwing incidents, while the Rangers players and staff were also admonished for inciting the crowd further with their celebrations at the end of the game, when they regrouped in front of their fans to form a 'huddle', mocking Celtic's customary pre-match ritual. Even Sky TV, the Scottish game's new paymasters, failed to avoid criticism for scheduling the powder-keg fixture so late in the day on a bank holiday Sunday, a timeslot for the broadcaster's coverage of Scottish football that was soon to be abolished.

In the following days, however, in an atmosphere of general browbeating in the media, Roger Mitchell, chief executive of the newly inaugurated SPL, appeared to be a lone voice calling for calm reflection and a sense of perspective following the events at Celtic Park. In defence of the arrangements that had been made for the match, Mitchell criticised some of the hyperventilating overreaction to the day's disturbances – recorded both during and in the aftermath of the game – citing Feyenoord's recent title win in the Netherlands, which had been marked by a full-scale riot and gunfire on the streets of Rotterdam, in comparison to the serious but relatively minor incidents of disorder that had occurred in Glasgow.

Nevertheless, the repercussions from the fixture were still being felt many years later, with the SPL and, in more recent times, its successor organisation the Scottish Professional Football League (SPFL), determined to avoid a repeat of the scheduling circumstances that occurred at the time. Even today, the manipulation of the fixture card in Scottish football's top division in a way that prevents Celtic and Rangers from meeting in a potential title-deciding match continues, despite the far-reaching interest in the game in Scotland that such an event might generate, with the league's stance facilitated in the modern era by the introduction to the top flight of the league 'split' in 2000, which enables the announcement of the final five fixtures of the season to be withheld until April.

After going on to secure the Scottish Cup by beating Celtic again a few weeks later, 1-0 in the Hampden final, Advocaat's side had claimed a notable Treble in the Dutchman's first season in Glasgow, and his team then comfortably retained the championship the following year in a desperately poor season for the Parkhead club. In addition to their domestic success, there was also an overall improvement, initially at least, in Rangers' European fortunes from the frustrating and often embarrassing ventures on to the Continent that they had endured under Walter Smith. In 1999/2000, Rangers eliminated the Italian side Parma, another overspending sporting institution on the path to self-destruction, in the qualifiers to reach the group stages of the Champions League, before ultimately finishing third in a strong section ahead of PSV Eindhoven, but behind Valencia and Bayern Munich. The Ibrox men subsequently dropped into the third round of the UEFA Cup, where they were only defeated by German cracks Borussia Dortmund after a penalty shoot-out.

It was a similar story the following year, as Rangers again finished in third place in their group, although on this occasion they had faced far less daunting opposition in the shape of Monaco, Sturm Graz and Galatasaray. Just as in the previous year, Rangers were then eliminated from the UEFA Cup by another German team, Kaiserslautern, after a 3-0 away defeat, a result that represented a disappointing return for the ambitious Ibrox side. When Advocaat's men failed to reach the group stages the following year, knocked out in the qualifiers by Turkish champions Fenerbahçe, the club's European ambitions looked to be in tatters. In the end, despite the chairman's pledge that regular progress through to the latter stages of the Champions League was the minimum prerequisite for success, Advocaat's side had been unable to advance beyond the group stages of the competition throughout the coach's time in charge of Rangers, an outcome that, given the club's stated targets and the money that had been spent on the squad, could only be described as a failure.

Rangers' overambition on the Continental front would ultimately come at a cost, as freelance journalist Phil Mac Giolla Bháin later observed on his blog: 'David Murray allowed Dick Advocaat to, in effect, bankrupt Rangers in the period 1998–2001 ... European success eluded the Ibrox club and they never fully emerged from the debt spiral.' With Advocaat setting the terms for what needed to be spent in order to achieve the level of success that Rangers were hoping for, Murray, it appears, was sanctioning every move, allowing the Dutch trainer to shell out a total of £75m in transfer fees during his three and a half years in Glasgow, on top of a wage bill that had reached a staggering £35m by 2003, almost 50 times the figure of 1986. By 2004, with the club no further forward in regard to their European aspirations under the Dutchman's successor, the hapless Alex McLeish, Rangers' excessive spending and the reckless approach of the club's management had seen the Ibrox institution accumulate liabilities totalling almost £80m – *Moneyball*, it certainly wasn't.

* * *

In contrast to the policy of showy expenditure being pursued at Ibrox, by the time Celtic won the league in 1998 and put a stop to their rivals' bid for ten-in-a-row, the Parkhead club was still operating under the tightly controlled financial strictures of Fergus McCann's more restrained and businesslike regime in the east end of Glasgow, which, with the owner's departure from the club scheduled for the following March, was now entering its final few months. The immediate task facing general manager Jock Brown over the summer, however, following the acrimonious departure of head coach Wim Jansen just two days after securing the league championship, was to identify and appoint the Dutchman's replacement and a number of high-profile names were linked with the job in the media.

An early, genuine candidate for the post was Murdo MacLeod, Jansen's assistant, who would have been a popular choice and who offered the prospect of a swift and seamless transition from the title-winning campaign. However, the former Celtic midfielder had allied himself too closely to Jansen, and his relationship with Brown was one of barely disguised and mutual contempt, with the general manager admitting that he didn't believe the former assistant had the slightest chance of being successful when his name was put forward for the board's consideration. When MacLeod's contract was eventually terminated by the club, he sold his story of the season's tumultuous climax to the *Sunday Mail*, a version of events that was so scathing of Brown's involvement and role at the club that the general manager started receiving death threats.

MacLeod was eventually overlooked, to a certain degree for political reasons, in favour of Brown's preferred candidate Egil Olsen, the Norwegian who was currently in charge of his country's national team at the World Cup in France. After lengthy negotiations with his representatives, terms were agreed between the parties, but Olsen's participation in France appeared to complicate matters, and with no assurances being received about a start date and a confirmed commitment to take over at Parkhead, Brown felt compelled to withdraw the club's offer and consider other options. Olsen subsequently spent the next six months out of football recuperating from a hip replacement operation, which he underwent following Norway's eventual elimination from the tournament in the early knockout phase at the hands of Italy. Another name in the frame at the time was Gérard Houllier, but the Frenchman had already pledged his future to Liverpool, a city where he had spent time as a young student, and Brown's advances were politely declined. Nils Arne Eggen, the Rosenborg boss and Swede Tommy Svensson were other names linked with the vacancy at Celtic in the media, but both were reported to have turned the job down.

Brown was now working under considerable time pressure, with Celtic set to be involved in the Champions League qualifiers as early as 22 July. At some stage during his frequent trips to France over the summer, the name of Dr Jozef Vengloš was put to Brown, and although he was by no means the club's first choice, inquiries immediately began to be made into Vengloš's background and track record. The Slovak was best remembered within the UK for a short-lived spell at Aston Villa in the wake of the 1990 World Cup in Italy, where he had led home nation Czechoslovakia to the quarter-finals. Brown appeared to convince himself, however, that Vengloš's seemingly unsuccessful tenure at Villa Park was a misleading oversimplification of the Slovak's time in Birmingham, and that he had in fact impressed everyone at the club whom he had come into contact with and departed with his reputation intact; he was ahead of his time, he had won a manager of the month award, he was held in the highest regard internationally and was frequently delegated by FIFA to lecture on the game to academics.

Nobody, it seemed, had a bad word to say about the Slovak's qualities as a man and as a coach, and as the tournament in France, where he had been working as a FIFA representative, drew to a conclusion, it wasn't long before things began to crystallise around a potential Vengloš appointment at Parkhead, as permission to pursue the new preferred candidate was sought and obtained from the Celtic board. With everything agreed in principle, work permit delays held up the official announcement even beyond the end of the World Cup, but on 17 July 1998, just five days before the club's opening competitive fixture of the season, Vengloš was officially named and unveiled as Celtic's new head coach. Brown defended the appointment at the ensuing press conference, pointing out that foreign coaches such as Arsène Wenger, who had previously been almost unknown to the domestic game but was now working wonders at Arsenal, were currently fashionable in British football, although McCann at the same time had the presence of mind to concede, 'Jozef might not have been top of the list at the start, but he became the best person for the job as we carried out our investigations.'

Perhaps more than any other foreign manager who had worked in British football up to that point, Vengloš appeared to represent the divergence that had developed down the years between the British and Continental approaches to football. Outside of the UK, Vengloš's credentials seemed impeccable; he held a PhD, no less, in physical education, was fluent in several languages, although his English at times appeared halting, and he boasted an indisputably impressive track record in top-level club and international coaching, stretching back over several decades. But to aficionados of the peculiarly British game, more used to a taskmaster or rabble-rousing-type manager, he seemed suspiciously overqualified.

Mainland European coaches, on the whole, expected football players to be fully in charge of their own professionalism and motivation, relying on their knowledge of the game to figure out how best to deploy and set up their team based on the relative strengths and weaknesses of their own squad and that of their opponents; among their British counterparts, however, the emphasis traditionally depended more on team spirit, an elusive quality, which as often as not required frequent and excessive drinking sessions before it could be fully and properly deployed. When it worked, the stereotypically British style could be effective, with English teams, for example, dominating European football at the highest level in the late 70s and early 80s, but by the end of the century these methods appeared quaint, ridiculous even, especially when compared to the ascetic professionalism and the nuanced tactical thinking behind the latter-day success of the Continent's top sides.

So, when the 62-year-old Venglos eventually turned up at Celtic Park in the middle of July a matter of days before the start of the season and appeared to fit easily into neither the taskmaster nor the rabble-rouser category of coach, many of the Celtic players at first appeared confused and underwhelmed by the appointment. Perhaps the squad's recollections of the previous season with the foreign Jansen at the helm might have helped to manage their expectations of the new coach's methods, but the emotions were still raw regarding the circumstances of the Dutchman's departure, and, in addition, there were other factors in the air around the club at the time, which were causing disruption and unrest within the dressing room.

Much of the blame for the tensions around Parkhead can be attributed to influential sections of the press, who once again, just as they had the previous summer, ridiculed the appointment of another Celtic head coach, whose announcement was accompanied by the seemingly inevitable 'Doctor Who?' headlines, as the media continued their campaign of open hostility towards Brown and McCann. The general manager in particular was subjected to twisted and inaccurate headlines following Vengl#'s surprise arrival. On one occasion, Brown was accused by the *Sunday Mail* of describing Celtic supporters as 'ignorant', after he made the not unreasonable point in a press conference that Scottish football can be insular at times, with many in the country unaware or underappreciative of the qualities of a figure such as Venglo#. Perhaps unsurprisingly, no other paper's journalists who attended Brown's briefing picked up on the 'ignorant' inference and the headline didn't appear in any other publication.

In addition, Brown and McCann were being pilloried in certain quarters over their apparent reluctance to spend money and bring in new players to the club. Part of this issue stemmed from Venglo#'s initial determination, following his appointment, to take time to assess the squad he had inherited so that the correct signing targets could be identified and the key positions in the team strengthened. None of this of course made it into the pages of the newspapers, who were ruthless in their comparisons between Celtic's perceived inaction and the exorbitant sums being simultaneously shelled out by free-spending Rangers, who were restructuring their entire playing staff over the summer. When the new head coach at Parkhead did eventually produce a list of three or four players whom he thought would strengthen and add a new dimension to the group, the selling clubs were unwilling to release their key assets and the European transfer deadline eventually passed without any new acquisitions arriving at Parkhead, although the club did manage to retain all of their title-winning squad.

In addition to these external pressures, however, a significant row erupted within the club itself at this time between the players and the management over the issue of the team's bonuses for qualification for the Champions League. Collectively, and speaking through captain Tom Boyd, the squad had rejected the club's offer, quoted as £280,000 to be distributed as the players saw fit, for successfully negotiating the preliminary rounds and achieving entry into the group stages of the lucrative tournament. It was a significant sum of money that was on offer, but in terms of the potential earnings that qualification would have brought into the club's coffers, the amount still represented a relatively meagre percentage of the total revenue, particularly, from the players' point of view, if they decided to split the cash evenly among participating and non-participating members of the squad. As an act of protest, the group then collectively took the unprecedented step of boycotting a pre-arranged photo shoot with kit manufacturer Umbro, with the three players who had been nominated to model the club's new away strip instead being instructed by their colleagues not to turn up, a decision that, amid the inevitable talk of 'turmoil' and 'crisis' in the press, allowed the story to become public just days before the first leg of the decisive qualifier with Croatia Zagreb.

McCann was angered by the players' actions, believing that the unilateral decision to veto the Umbro event and allow their grievance to be widely reported was taken at a time when he had already agreed to meet and negotiate with the squad over the issue. As a result, in a short, tense meeting between the parties, the owner informed the playing staff that the available bonus was being reduced by £50,000, an amount that he would instead be donating to the children's wing of Yorkhill Hospital in the south side of Glasgow. The squad responded by suggesting that this was a matter of principle and promised to commit the entire fee to charity, an offer that, regardless of the result in the final qualifier, McCann immediately took up. In the end, however, the matter became something of a moot point, as predictably perhaps, following a 1-0 win at Celtic Park, the Parkhead men were thoroughly outplayed by a Robert Prosinečki-inspired Zagreb side in the second leg in Croatia and lost 3-1 on aggregate. The players were so upset over the subsequent coverage of the whole situation in the media that they effectively withdrew their co-operation, refusing to deal with the press on any subject for several months thereafter.

Prior to the bonus dispute, Celtic's new league campaign had opened with a routine 5-0 home victory over Dunfermline Athletic on 1 August, with Burley scoring a notable hat-trick. However, the result was overshadowed by the reception afforded to McCann, as the general sense of frustration around the club was exemplified by a section of the crowd, who jeered the owner at the unfurling of the championship flag ceremony before the match. Although Celtic historian David Potter felt that the heckling was limited to 'a few boneheads' in the stadium, now expanded to a 60,000-capacity all-seater venue with the completion of the new Jock Stein stand in the west end of the ground during the close season, McCann was said to be disappointed and upset at the clearly audible reaction that had been aimed at him.

Despite the triumph of winning the league, the discontent among supporters had been growing over the summer and, for the first time perhaps, the man in charge of the club was forced to confront the reality of a negative backlash towards the management duo of himself and Jock Brown. McCann had previously shown an admirable disregard for the machinations of the media and for the forum of public opinion generally, but it now became clear to the Celtic owner that he could no longer dispute the power of a hostile press to influence a significant section of the fanbase, who up to that point had shown tremendous backing for his regime, most notably when supporters invested their money in his record-breaking share offer in early 1995. The fans' commitment was also illustrated, perhaps most ironically of all in the circumstances, by an estimated crowd of around 60,000, including 53,000 season ticket holders, who were populating the revamped ground on the day.

The supporters were upset in particular over the loss of Wim Jansen, who somewhat tactlessly had returned to Celtic Park as a guest of disgruntled former director Brian Dempsey for the opening fixture of the season and, along with Murdo MacLeod, was sitting in the main stand at the start of the match and witnessed the incident. Another ongoing gripe, which was still in the public domain at the time, centred on the apparent reluctance of the board and owner to spend money on strengthening the squad. Nevertheless, the reaction was poor and over the top from supporters now housed in the fully rebuilt and impressive Celtic Park at a time when the long-awaited success of the previous season was being marked and, as if to prove that there were fans who were disappointed and embarrassed by the barracking he had received, McCann was given a warm reception by the crowd the following week during a friendly against Liverpool, when the new Jock Stein stand and the completed stadium were formally opened.

With Scottish football's top division now operating under the auspices of the SPL, Celtic's positive start to the defence of their title on the field quickly evaporated as, following the win over Dunfermline, Venglos's side subsequently recorded only one victory in their next eight domestic fixtures. The run had started with a 3-2 reverse against Aberdeen at Pittodrie in a match that saw the visitors awarded three penalties, two of which were missed, and in addition to an inauspicious 1-0 home defeat to St Johnstone, the sequence also included a meek loss to Airdrieonians in the Parkhead men's short-lived defence of the League Cup. Against Rangers at Ibrox, however, the coach displayed his tactical intelligence by asking inside-forward Simon Donnelly to man-mark the home team's deep-lying playmaker Barry Ferguson, with the Rangers youngster going on to have one of his more ineffective games against the Parkhead side in an absorbing game, which nevertheless finished in a goalless draw. Wins over Motherwell and Aberdeen in October offered Celtic some encouragement, but by the end of the month the Parkhead men travelled to Rugby Park, Kilmarnock and suffered a 2-0 defeat, leaving Vengloš's side well off the pace in the defence of their title, seven points behind Rangers and with the Ayrshire club sitting comfortably in second spot.

With his doctorate in physical education, Jozef Vengloš was only too aware that Celtic's players were insufficiently rested after their exertions at the World Cup over the summer, and he was able to predict that injuries were likely to be a disruptive factor for his side over the course of the season. The Scotland national team under Craig Brown had called on eight Celtic players for the squad that went to France, and with the Danish duo of Morten Wieghorst and Marc Rieper joining up with their own international camp, Celtic had more players at the tournament than any other club in the world with the sole exception of Barcelona. Although the Scots' campaign was predictably short-lived, it wasn't long before the injuries began to accumulate once the new season got under way, with Wieghorst damaging his knee on the day after the new manager's appointment during a pre-season testimonial game against Kilmarnock at Rugby Park, a setback that resulted in the Danish midfielder being unavailable for most of the season. In addition, by the end of October, Jackie McNamara, Marc Rieper and Craig Burley had all suffered serious knocks and, although McNamara's condition was treatable, he required constant periods of rest and recuperation, while the two other important players would be out for much of the campaign. As Vengloš observed, 'If you are missing top players … it's difficult to maintain the balance within the team because you are giving a chance to young players. After two or three months the players were responding to me with a beautiful passing game that was attractive to the supporters.' Unfortunately for Celtic, by the time the team started playing in the manner in which they were expected, they had wasted almost half the season and a realistic challenge for the league title was beyond them.

The league defeat to Kilmarnock at Rugby Park was followed by a tame elimination from the UEFA Cup at the hands of the mediocre Swiss side FC Zürich, as a Celtic team crippled by injuries lost 4-2 in the second leg and, following a 1-1 draw at Celtic Park, failed to progress to the third round. The match witnessed the last active involvement at Parkhead of general manager Jock Brown, who stood down from his role at the club on Saturday, 7 November, just hours before a scheduled home game against Dundee. Brown had become a lightning rod for all the negativity swirling around the club at the time, and although some of the criticism was undoubtedly deserved, the level and intensity of the campaign that had been conducted against him in the media was out of all proportion to the errors of judgement that had been made. Brown himself observed, with a level of overstatement that only reflected his increasing exasperation at just how untenable his situation had become, 'If I had rescued a toddler from a burning building, certain elements of the press would portray me [sic] as a child molester.'

Once his relationship with the media had broken down entirely, Brown acknowledged that it was inevitable he would eventually have to be 'sacrificed', as he put it, and with a protest against the general manager being planned by a group of supporters and set to go ahead at the home match with Dundee later that afternoon, it was announced at lunchtime that Brown had resigned. As if in celebration of the news, a patchwork Celtic side put their poor recent form behind them and proceeded to set about the Taysiders with a swagger, eventually running out 6-1 winners, with Henrik Larsson, whom Vengl`os was in the process of converting into a world-class centre-forward, helping himself to a hat-trick, and young striker Mark Burchill scoring two goals on his full debut for the club.

Larsson's skills and burgeoning self-confidence were again in evidence two weeks later when the Swede netted twice in a 5-1 home victory over Dick Advocaat's Rangers, although on this occasion the limelight was stolen by 33-year-old L'ubomír Moravčík, who also scored two goals in the game, his first for the club since his £300,000 move from MSV Duisberg in Germany at the start of the month. Many in the media had ridiculed the arrival of the unknown and ageing midfielder, acquired by Celtic for such a modest fee, and with the manager interpreting for his countryman at his unveiling, some sections of the press had claimed with an undisguised sense of mischief-making that 'Uncle Joe', as they were by now habitually referring to Vengl`os, had in fact indulged in an act of nepotism by signing his nephew for the Parkhead club.

One noted hack was even moved to lambast the club for apparently not being able to 'find £500,000 from their biscuit tin to sign a proven talent like John Spencer' in preference to the unheralded Slovak, a view that later provoked Jock Brown to observe of the newspapers' criticism and reaction to Moravčík's arrival at Celtic Park, 'It told you a great deal about the media in Glasgow. [Recent Rangers signing] Colin Hendry was born in exactly the same year [as Moravčík]. He has approximately half the number of international caps held by Lubo and he was reported to have cost in excess of £4m. Yet his arrival in Glasgow was heralded as a major coup for Rangers and he effectively arrived to a fanfare of trumpets.' Such discrepancy, of which the signing of Moravčík by Celtic provided only the latest example, spoke volumes for the patent lack of objectivity and balance being evinced by sections of the media in their coverage of football in Glasgow at this time.

On the day, with Larsson and Moravčík scoring two apiece and the home-grown Burchill adding a fifth goal after being introduced from the bench, Rangers' multimillion-pound side, albeit reduced to ten men midway through the first half following the dismissal of defender Scott Wilson for a rash tackle from behind on the wily Slovak, had been undone by three men who cost less than £1m between them. Moravčík, it turned out, was a footballing genius with 73 international caps to his name, many of them gained as captain of Slovakia, who had helped Vengloš's pre-Velvet Divorce Czechoslovakia side reach the quarter-finals of the World Cup in 1990. One of the greatest foreign imports to Scottish football, along with Larsson and Laudrup, he lit up the game in Scotland over the next four years with his mesmerising skills, enjoying a spectacular Indian Summer to his career in front of an audience in Glasgow who proved, after he had been asked to play as a defensive midfielder with his German club, to be altogether more appreciative and befitting of his undeniable talents.

The victory over Rangers, however, proved to be something of a false dawn for Venglos's side, and there was no immediate return to form for the Parkhead club following the unexpected win. Achieved with debutant Johan Mjällby playing in defence alongside the returning Alan Stubbs, and with Liverpool's fourth-choice goalkeeper Tony Warner drafted in as emergency cover for the injured duo of Stewart Kerr and Jonathan Gould, the result nevertheless failed to provide Celtic with the boost in confidence they required. It wasn't until around Christmas time, in fact, that the Parkhead men began to discover their true form, at which point they were finally able to set out in pursuit of a Rangers team that had already opened up a ten-point gap at the top of the league in their bid to regain the title. Unfortunately, however, there was more trouble in store off the field for Celtic, as their drawn-out pursuit of the Australian striker Mark Viduka took a bizarre twist in January, with the player, just four days after eventually completing his move to Glasgow from Croatia Zagreb, departing for his antipodean homeland and claiming that he needed a break from football due to stress.

Celtic had already added Norwegian international Vidar Riseth, from Austrians LASK Linz, as well as Mjällby, the Swedish international defender from AIK Stockholm, to their squad in the autumn, players who could play in a variety of different positions and who added, with the injury list lengthening, some much-needed versatility to the group. Their pursuit of Viduka, however, stretched back to Jock Brown's time at the club and the aftermath of the Champions League qualifier in Zagreb, when Celtic had first made contact with the Croats over the striker's availability. Brown had travelled to the Balkans on more than one occasion to try to put together a deal for the player, but the selling club appeared to prevaricate, changing their mind on several occasions over whether to release the striker while their Champions League campaign was still ongoing. Several months later, after a further lengthy delay over the player's work permit, Celtic had finally landed their man following a £3.5m transfer, but Viduka, with no credible explanation for his behaviour, had fled the scene almost immediately, leaving the Parkhead club's fans and officials alike feeling deflated and confused by his behaviour.

Croatia Zagreb were nevertheless demanding that Celtic should hand over the transfer fee in full, as agreed, and they were reportedly calculating the interest accruing on the outstanding amount while McCann was pondering his options over the situation with his wayward striker. After much negotiation, however, mostly conducted via late-night phone calls to the other side of the world, Viduka eventually returned to Scotland, although his relationship with McCann seemed damaged beyond repair. The Australian eventually made his Celtic debut from the bench in a 2-1 win over Dundee United in February and then, the following week, he scored two goals on his first start for the club in a 5-1 defeat of Aberdeen at Pittodrie.

The big Australian had, at last, settled into his surroundings on his return to Glasgow, and with injuries continuing to affect the team, he added some much-needed firepower to Celtic's front line, as Venglos's men embarked on an impressive run of results either side of the winter break in an effort to try to make up ground on runaway league leaders Rangers. The Parkhead side won 11 of 13 matches, drawing the other two, including a pulsating 2-2 share of the spoils at Ibrox at the turn of the year, but the pursuit of their rivals ultimately ended in failure after the 3-0 loss to Advocaat's team in the decisive and incident-packed fixture at Celtic Park on 2 May. Before the season reached its controversial denouement, however, Fergus McCann, chairman, chief executive, managing director and majority shareholder of Celtic plc, completed his five-year turnaround operation at Parkhead and, just as he had stated he would do at the outset, he stepped down from his position and took his leave of Celtic for the last time in a position of responsibility at the club.

McCann's departure came on 3 April, when he left his seat in the directors' box and, to polite applause, strode out of the stadium with 15 minutes remaining of his team's 5-0 win over Dundee. It was a typically unfussy farewell from the man who had revitalised and restored the fortunes of the Parkhead institution since his initial takeover of the club in March 1994. With a new acting CEO, Allan MacDonald, already in place, a significant number of McCann's shares in the club were eventually acquired, following the offer for sale later in the year, by the Irish billionaire Dermot Desmond, who had been a non-executive director of Celtic since the takeover, and who would now become the new majority shareholder, investing £4m to increase his stake by 6 per cent to just under 20 per cent of the company.

With a large proportion of McCann's shares now made available to season ticket holders, staff and other supporters, fan ownership of the club rose following the chairman's departure to 63 per cent of the total holdings, with the remaining 17 per cent acquired by institutional investors. It had been an eventful five years for McCann and Celtic, but for everything that had happened, the Canadian exile had kept all of his promises –

rescuing the club from looming bankruptcy, wiping out the debt, building a new stadium, delivering success on the field and bequeathing ownership of the club to its supporters, all achieved within his originally declared timescale.

Throughout this period, however, it was noticeable how the mainstream media in Scotland had chastised and lampooned McCann, particularly in regard to his painstakingly prudent, low-key stewardship of Celtic, while at the same time vaunting David Murray on the other side of the city, despite the recklessness and the self-indulgence that had characterised his chairmanship of Rangers. The approach of the two owners could hardly have been more different, as SPL chief executive Roger Mitchell later noted with some insight: 'The old journalists got sweeties from David and hence David was king; and David's challenger, Fergus, was the village idiot. Fergus was never prepared to try and compete by giving sweeties to the media, and if you don't give sweeties to the media, they don't like you and they hurt you and they treat you badly.'

The mischief-making on the part of the local press had started shortly after McCann's takeover of Celtic, when the tabloids began sending so-called investigative reporters to his homes in North America, not to check on the exiled entrepreneur's business credentials, but to dig for dirt on the seemingly eccentric bachelor. At almost every point over the next five years, in a concerted and sustained campaign, which abandoned all pretence of objectivity, the media in Scotland sought to outflank McCann, doing down the good work he was involved in at Parkhead and successfully turning a large section of the club's supporters against him.

Perhaps the apex of media criticism towards the Celtic owner came after a bruising court case with former Parkhead boss Lou

Macari, who was suing the club for wrongful dismissal following McCann's decision to remove him from his post in the summer of 1994. Almost four years later, however, in February 1998, the presiding magistrate at the Court of Session in Edinburgh, Lady Cosgrove, dismissed Macari's claim against the club for more than £400,000 in damages, chiding the former manager in a lengthy written judgement as 'an amiable but not particularly astute individual', but nevertheless pointing out in regards to the confrontation that he had provoked with his employer, 'The fact Macari insisted in carrying on as he saw fit seems to me to be a further example of his attitude and of a rather stubborn refusal to change his ways. His view of himself as a professional who would not in any circumstances take instructions from an employer did not allow him to acknowledge the reality of life embodied in the maxim: "he who pays the piper calls the tune".' Historian Bill Murray also offered a view concerning Macari's short-lived reign at Celtic and McCann's decision to dispense with his services, stating that, 'Lou Macari ... gave some people the impression that he wanted to run the club from England and with as little disruption to his leisure pursuits as possible.'

The judge, meanwhile, also offered a mild rebuke to McCann's high-handedness and his inflexible style of management, claiming that during the case she had formed the impression of 'a rather devious individual' and of 'an uncompromising and somewhat arrogant employer' in the person of the Celtic chief executive, whose dealings with Macari were described as 'extremely demanding and even dictatorial'. It was this latter assessment that moved the *Daily Record* to compare the Celtic supremo, unfavourably, with Saddam Hussein, president of Iraq and at the time the western world's public enemy number one. 'Dictator' screamed the paper's front page headline the next day, with a head-shot of McCann alongside the despised Middle Eastern leader and war criminal, above a by-line that read, 'One of these men was branded "a devious, arrogant, uncompromising dictator" by a judge yesterday. The other one is Saddam Hussein.'

The main problem with the headline and with the subsequent coverage in the paper was that it didn't seem to convey an accurate assessment of the judgement. As website thecelticwiki.com pointed out: 'She [Lady Cosgrove] did not say he was a dictator and in any case, being dictatorial hardly singles out McCann among management, something that is a trait of practically all major leaders in industry. It's one hell of a leap to jump to then say he is like "Saddam Hussein". It was offensive, crude, pathetic and downright nonsense.' Needless to say, the fact that McCann won the case barely got a mention.

Then, as the approaching hour of his departure loomed, certain tabloid journalists, most notably Hugh Keevins and James Traynor, two former broadsheet football reporters who seemed to believe that a move into the wacky world of the redtops represented some sort of career advancement from the work they had been producing at *The Scotsman* and *The Herald* respectively, appeared to almost hound McCann out the door at Celtic Park, claiming that unless he instigated a clear-out and a wholesale change of attitude at the club, he risked being despised by the fans and leaving a toxic legacy behind him. 'Celtic's irksome managing director has overstayed his welcome. Mr McCann, it's time for you to be somewhere else,' Traynor announced in *The Record*, knowing full well that McCann's departure was already imminent, before continuing, 'Pretty soon his stock among the rank and file will be so low he may be allocated a place in the club's hall of infamy alongside those directors who ruled before him. If he is not careful the mere mention of his name in crowded Celtic strongholds … might cause a silence to fall over the places.' Even Rangers chairman David Murray had offered a contribution to the campaign against his rival, claiming somewhat patronisingly in an interview carried by *The Record* in November 1998, amid all the eulogising that accompanied the tenth anniversary of his acquisition of Rangers, that McCann ought to be a bit nicer and even show more humility!

Curiously, however, this antipathy and lack of appreciation towards McCann and his work at Celtic didn't appear to exist outside of the bubble of the west of Scotland mainstream media, as Patrick Glenn later noted in *The Guardian*: 'Rangers' predominance, founded on a willingness to spend untold millions … blinded the majority of fans to the long-term wisdom of McCann's policies. They were not helped by a disgracefully hostile majority in the media, who portrayed the managing director as a tight-fisted, bumbling, dithering, self-seeking capitalist who knew nothing of football.' Lawrence Donegan, meanwhile, writing in the same blatt after being conducted on a tour around the impressive new Celtic Park, finally completed at a cost of £41m, noted brusquely, 'No one apart from Camilla Parker Bowles has had a worse press than Fergus McCann.'

In the end, however, his antagonists in the media could hardly have been more wrong with the line they were taking against the Celtic owner; following the Rangers boardroom coup in the mid-80s and McCann's takeover at Parkhead in the early 90s, the two clubs had come under enormous pressure to adapt to the changing face of the modern game, while at the same time trying to keep a winning team on the park. Regardless of the fluctuating fortunes of their respective teams on the field, however, McCann would ultimately be considered one of the most important and significant figures in Celtic's history, while his counterpart Murray would justifiably be labelled one of the most pernicious and damaging in Rangers'. As Glenn Gibbons noted in *The Scotsman* in 2014, with the 20th anniversary of McCann's takeover approaching, 'We will witness a predictable, spreading rash of revisionism among many, from supporters to media, who passed most of his five years in Scotland casting the entrepreneur as a figure of ridicule and who now clamour for his immortalisation in marble or bronze.'

McCann made mistakes along the way, most notably by embroiling himself in a bonus dispute with his players when he refused to stump up the going rate, as the team was trying, and inevitably failing to qualify for the group stages of the Champions League in August 1998. Fastidious and curiously lacking in emotional involvement, McCann took the decision from the outset to run Celtic strictly as a business, surrounding himself with people, it appeared, whose most notable attribute was an obvious lack of empathy for the team on the field. The last thing McCann needed, from his point of view, was the involvement of Celtic partisans pointing him in the direction of what the fans desired or trying to deflect him from his primary purpose of being able to sell his shares after five years, having turned a profit, while getting the club back on its feet. It was an approach that brought him criticism from within the club as well as without, but with almost his entire fortune invested in Celtic at the time of his takeover, McCann's methods were understandable, perhaps even necessary, and certainly in the end fully justified, despite the often legitimate concerns that were being expressed along the way.

The 'Bhoys Against Bigotry' initiative, introduced and championed by McCann after his takeover, was a well-meaning but ill-conceived campaign to counter sectarianism by banning from Parkhead, in an apparent effort to present a clean image of the club to his new, expanded customer base, the singing of Irish political songs, which had often been mistakenly referred to by elements of the press who should have known better as 'IRA chanting'. The campaign at times seemed to lend legitimacy to the argument that the Old Firm clubs were no more than mirror images of one another, each as guilty as the other over sectarianism and prejudice, a position that was stridently refuted by most Celtic supporters. The fans felt that McCann was demonising them through the scheme for his own strategic, commercial purposes and they were quick to point out the inconsistencies and the hypocrisy contained within its adopted parameters, a point of view that even the club's manager at the time, Tommy Burns, eventually agreed with.

The loss of manager Wim Jansen, after a single, successful season at Parkhead, the result of a personality clash with his outspoken general manager, Jock Brown, led to the heckling incident at Celtic Park and a moment that perhaps marked the apex of hostility from the club's fans towards the owner, as a section of the Parkhead crowd, taking their cue from the press, jeered McCann as he unfurled the championship-winning flag at the start of the new season. It was a ridiculous, embarrassing reaction from fans sitting in a now completely rebuilt colosseum of a stadium, after the league title had been won for the first time in ten long years. However, with the tabloids continuing their vendetta, it was perhaps inevitable, in the days before internet bloggers and alternative media, that their relentless campaign against the Celtic CEO would wash off on some, a testament to the power of an influential media to befuddle the thinking of otherwise rational people.

It wasn't just the press and the more credulous element within the fanbase, however, who appeared to be on McCann's case, as the Canadian also found himself coming into conflict with the game's administrators on a number of occasions during the period of his stewardship of Celtic. The £100,000 fine imposed by the Scottish League for the illegal approach to Kilmarnock manager Tommy Burns in McCann's first few months in Glasgow, when he was still perhaps naïve to the ways of football administration, proved to be an early indication of how the relationship would develop between the Parkhead CEO and those charged with running the game in Scotland. On that occasion, the League's decision was later ratified by the SFA's meddlesome chief executive, Jim Farry, whose judgement and competence would later be called into question when McCann successfully sued the governing body over the delayed registration of the striker Jorge Cadete in April 1996.

McCann had a slightly odd manner; he could be ill-mannered, obstinate, and disarmingly abrupt to the point of discourtesy, and even well beyond. He had a typically North American fondness for recourse to his lawyers. There was little warmth in him, but neither was there any spite or malice, only a steely professionalism. McCann himself observed of his time at Celtic: 'Of course I have regrets and of course I have made mistakes, but football is a very strange business compared to anything else.' There were bust-ups and fallouts all over the place, but as respected journalist Kevin McCarra later noted, 'He always seemed to be at war, but with the passage of time, the smoke of those battles drifts away and he can be seen clearly as one of the greatest figures in the club's history.'

Even among McCann's apologists, there were those associated with the game who had genuine and justifiable regrets over the gentrification and the commercialisation that was taking place in football at this time, and McCann, with his share issues, his corporate hospitality and his appeal to middle-class consumers was undoubtedly a part of this process. In the years since his departure, however, Celtic has seemingly managed to bridge the divide between brand and identity, so often seen as mutually exclusive in today's football, and the club continues to celebrate and reflect, as part of its image, the charitable roots and Irish heritage of its early years. To that extent, McCann can perhaps be seen as an unlikely compromise figure, at Parkhead and in Scottish football generally, between those who believed that Celtic, under the old board, were stuck in the past, swimming laboriously against a tide of modernisation, and the understandable reluctance of others to see their cherished football club surrender its soul to the contemporary game, with all its glaring and obvious faults.

McCann's early business partner, Brian Dempsey, walked away from their association after a row over the direction in which the new CEO was taking the club, believing that in the end, in that dreaded phrase that he often used, 'corporate interests' would eventually determine Celtic's future. In addition, European Cup winner Jimmy Johnstone decided not to turn up for the ceremony that marked the completion of the rebuilt stadium in August 1998, blaming McCann and his policy of taking the club away from its roots as the main reason for his non-attendance. Johnstone's former team-mates, however, the other ten 'Lisbon Lions', didn't appear to have the same misgivings as the legendary winger and all were present on the day to celebrate the occasion. In the end, the Canadian found a voice of support from a former rival, when erstwhile Ibrox director Hugh Adam, who would later be a lone voice warning of Rangers' looming insolvency, told the BBC, 'Fergus McCann … came in when the club was on the verge of bankruptcy. From there he has built a European-class stadium, you just cannot argue with that. His football team won the league after a period they hadn't looked like winning anything, so you just cannot fault the man.'

Fergus McCann was Celtic's saviour; if he hadn't been there and stepped up with his money in 1994, investing in the club the lion's share of the small fortune that had taken him most of his adult life to accumulate, at a time when success was far from guaranteed, it seems likely that Celtic would not have survived in its present capacity. While there were other people with money who were around at the time and who were interested in buying the club when the old board were finally forced out, such as Gerald Weisfeld and Brian Dempsey, it still seems highly likely that there would have been an insolvency event somewhere down the line at Celtic, such was the condition of the company's finances and the known intransigence of the club's bankers.

McCann proved that football clubs don't need philanthropists, or knights in shining armour, mythical figures who supporters are often told will one day arrive on the scene and invest millions in their team for purely altruistic reasons. The most important factor that's required for any club to be successful over the longer period is for the owner and board of directors to ensure that it's run properly, and McCann provided that good governance. He came in, turned the ship around, made his money, retired and left the club in a far healthier position than when he found it. A Celtic furnished with a 60,000-capacity all-seater stadium, regularly watched by 53,000 season ticket holders, majority-owned by shareholding supporters and managed by such luminaries as Martin O'Neill, Gordon Strachan and

Brendan Rodgers would have been all but inconceivable without McCann's intervention.

Perhaps most crucially of all, were it not for McCann's turnaround of Celtic, David Murray on the other side of the city would have been able to comfortably oversee his club's continuing dominance of Scottish football for many more years against an emaciated and troubled Parkhead outfit. The Rangers chairman, with his notoriously brittle ego, would never have been cajoled into over-inflating Rangers' transfer policy and subsequently risking everything by allowing the Ibrox club to fall heavily into debt in an effort to stay ahead or even just to keep up with a flourishing, post-McCann Celtic. As things turned out, however, faced with a reinvigorated, determined and superior Parkhead side over the ensuing years, it was Rangers, rather than their eternal rivals, who eventually went bust.

Following a boardroom coup, David Holmes (right) was named Rangers' new chief executive officer in February 1986. He appointed Graeme Souness as manager and Walter Smith (left) as his assistant. It was the start of a new era for Scottish football.

Other suitable footballers had baulked at the idea of becoming the first Catholic to play for Rangers in the modern era, but Maurice Johnston had no such scruples. As historian Bill Murray observed, 'With an interest in life's issues that barely went beyond the most basic, Johnston was the ideal man to bear the brunt of the moral outrage his signing had provoked.'

The 'dream-ticket' appointments, Brian Dempsey and Michael Kelly celebrate their nominations to the Celtic board, May 1990. The pair later fell out, and when Dempsey's ratification as a director was blocked in October, the battle lines for control of the club had been drawn.

Fergus McCann at McDiarmid Park, Perth on the day after his takeover of Celtic, 5 March 1994. Celtic beat St Johnstone 1–0 on the day thanks to a goal from Paul Byrne. It would be the start of a long, slow journey back to the summit of Scottish football for the Parkhead club.

Men at work. The task of reconstructing Celtic Park's three main stands got underway in July 1994. The club endured a miserable season as tenants at Hampden Park, before the ground reopened with a limited capacity for the start of the 1995/96 season. (courtesy of Tom Grant)

Rangers were the dominant force in Scottish football in the 1990s, but often appeared naive and predictable in Europe. In August 1994, AEK Athens got the better of Walter Smith's side at Ibrox despite, or perhaps because of, the strike partnership of Mark Hateley and Duncan Ferguson, 'a double act that died on the big stage' (Neil Drysdale).

Rangers' spending rocketed during the David Murray era. Here Paul Gascoigne, signed from
Lazio for £4.5m in July 1995 is unveiled, flanked by the chairman and manager Walter Smith
(right). Few questions were asked about where all the money was coming from and, even as the
club's debts rose alarmingly, Murray continued to enjoy favourable coverage in the local press.

McCann with general manager Jock Brown and new signing Paul Lambert, November 1997.
Brown later denied that he had tried to block the transfer because he did not rate the Champions
League-winning midfielder.

Celtic head coach Wim Jansen and assistant Murdo MacLeod celebrate winning the league championship, 9 May 1988. Jansen became the first foreign coach to win the title in Scotland, preventing Rangers from claiming a tenth consecutive crown. Three days later he resigned, citing a clash of personalities with general manager Jock Brown.

The completed Celtic Park, in use for the start of the 1998/99 season. With 53,000 season ticket holders, Celtic were now the fifth best supported club in the world behind Real Madrid, Borussia Dortmund, Inter Milan and Barcelona. 'When we look at the stadium, all of us, every Celtic supporter, must feel a little pride.' (Fergus McCann)

Alan Thompson volleys home to help Celtic knock Barcelona out of the UEFA Cup, 11 March 2004. After years of underachievement on the continent, manager Martin O'Neill transformed Celtic Park into a European fortress during his five-year spell in charge of the club.

After plans for an SPL TV channel were rejected by Celtic and Rangers, the nascent Irish broadcaster Setanta Sports covered Scottish football for most of the 2000s. The company's UK operation later folded, inflicting further financial hardship on the Scottish game.

Rangers owner Craig Whyte leaves Ibrox accompanied by a security guard, 13 February 2012. Earlier in the day, Rangers had lodged legal papers at the Court of Session in Edinburgh signalling their intention to enter administration. The club was later liquidated.

Callum McGregor scores a last-minute penalty to complete a 5–0 win over St Mirren in Celtic's final match before the COVID-19 shutdown, March 2020. When Celtic were named champions in May, the club had claimed their ninth title in a row, completing a remarkable turnaround in fortunes of the two Glasgow sides since the 1990s.

8.

The Bhoy From Brazil

IN October 1999, Fergus McCann completed the sale of his 50.3 per cent majority shareholding in Celtic Football Club plc, dispersing the ownership of the club, just as he had always intended, among the Parkhead institution's season ticket holders, existing shareholders, staff, players and other supporters. The previous month, 14,400,000 of McCann's 14,600,000 ordinary shares had been made available, with a minimum block of 250 shares costing investors £700, although for purchases of 500 shares or more, McCann and his brokers, Williams de Broe, had put in place an instalment plan that potentially allowed more ordinary supporters to be able to afford the package, with the cost split into four staggered payments over the course of the financial year. The offered price of £2.80 per share was 37p below what the club's stock was trading at on the open market at the time, but the sale still valued the business at roughly £135m, an astonishing increase in the net worth of the financially stricken institution that McCann had acquired in 1994.

Returning to Glasgow almost six months after his initial departure from Celtic in early April, McCann stated at the launch of the share offer on 20 September, 'What I want to achieve is ideally no dominant shareholder, with a substantial amount of shares, perhaps even a majority, held by the supporters. Whether that happens is up to the fans as a whole.' To incentivise supporters to buy into the scheme and meet his target for fan ownership, McCann offered to provide a donation of up to £1.5m towards a proposed new football academy and training facility at Celtic – still much in need at the club with the old Barrowfield site near London Road starting to show signs of age and increasingly being seen as unfit for the requirements of a modern club of Celtic's size and stature – if the total number of fan applicants exceeded the 10,000 mark.

Despite the overall success of the sale, however, which saw more than 75 per cent of the offered shares taken up by fans and the remainder sold on by underwriters Williams de Broe, in the end the final tally of individual small investors fell short of the stipulated target and, rather than magnanimously provide the club with the funds for the academy in any event, McCann stayed true to his word and held on to the cash. A total of 5,300 subscribers had applied to buy shares, including 3,000 who had made use of the interest-free payment plan, somewhat fewer than McCann had hoped, but many of the applicants had bought in bulk so that in the end the total investment by the club's fans exceeded McCann's initial, record-breaking share issue in the winter of 1994/95, leaving Celtic supporters now with an ownership stake of 63 per cent of the club's total holdings.

The disposal of his shares represented the formal end of McCann's involvement with Celtic, as the now former owner of the club confirmed once the take-up and transfer of his stake had been completed. 'I now look forward to once again being a full-time supporter and hopefully watching the team and club progress to realise its true potential, which I believe is considerable,' he announced. Asked in a final TV interview what he would miss most about owning Celtic, the former CEO replied, 'All the free advice.' In total, McCann had raised approximately £40m from his share offer, a healthy profit on his original £9m investment in 1994 and, perhaps inevitably, he was obliged to defend himself from accusations in the press in regard to the amount of money he had made personally, with the departing owner somewhat irascibly pointing out that he could in fact have increased his profits if he had sold his shares to financial institutions or other commercial consortiums with no association to the Parkhead club.

McCann also referred to the long hours he had put in, on a relatively modest salary, over a period of 'five years which nearly blew my brains out', while in response to some of the carping that had been directed towards him by David Murray, the departing Celtic owner couldn't resist firing back a valedictory rebuke concerning the very different off-field position of the two Glasgow rivals. 'I think I leave this club in a sound financial situation,' he said as he spoke to the board for the last time. 'The club has no debts, is beholden to nobody and is primed to move ahead. Unlike other clubs who have a win-at-all-costs policy, we have based ours on financial stability.'

McCann had successfully bequeathed overall control of Celtic to the Parkhead institution's supporters, guaranteeing that no individual or company could arbitrarily determine the club's future or take it into private ownership unopposed. Of the total number of offered shares, 4,402,272, or just over 30 per cent of McCann's assets, had also been made available to institutional investors, and the Irish billionaire, Dermot Desmond, already a substantial stakeholder, now took on the challenge of becoming the company's majority shareholder by increasing his level of ownership of the club to almost 20 per cent. Joining Desmond on the new-look plc board were Frank O'Callaghan, a former chairman of the MacDonald Hotels group, and Allan MacDonald, the ex-managing director of British Aerospace's Far East operation, who were approached and subsequently appointed by the Board's Appointments Committee in early 1999. With McCann's duties at the club being divided up following his departure in April, O'Callaghan and MacDonald were subsequently named non-executive chairman and chief executive respectively, while other directors already at the club included Brian Quinn, a former Acting Deputy Governor of the Bank of England, who had joined the board in March 1996 and who ultimately became a long-serving chairman in 2000 when he succeeded O'Callaghan in the role, as well as Sir Patrick Sheehy, who was named a director at the same time as Quinn after a spell as chairman of British American Tobacco in the early 1990s. For the most part, Sheehy's main role was in an advisory capacity to the board, using his experience, expertise and contacts in the City of London to guide the club during the difficult transition process, as the owner prepared to hand over the reins and head home to Canada at the end of his five-year plan.

At last, it seemed that the long-term wisdom of McCann's strategy was becoming increasingly clear, as it soon emerged that the board of Celtic plc, in the wake of the Canadian's final disengagement from the club, now consisted of a group of men who possessed the useful combination of the necessary financial clout and commercial expertise to take the club forward. As McCann later noted, 'We were able to attract some top quality individuals as board directors, such as Brian Quinn, Sir Patrick Sheehy and Dermot Desmond. I think some fans underestimated their value to the club in providing benefits not available to our competitors.'

This last point was the key, and another unmistakeable sideways swipe at Murray's Ibrox operation; the strategy of the Celtic directors was now to run their club smartly and in accordance with sound commercial principles, and by doing so, to outflank Rangers, who were still subject to the consequences, for good or ill, of Murray's one-party state regime at Ibrox. Now established as a properly constituted plc and controlled by a board of directors who considered that the showmanship and the courting of media gratification for which Murray had latterly become notorious were nothing more than economic irrelevancies, Celtic appeared, as the century drew to its close, to be the better placed of the two clubs to face the challenges posed by the uncertain economic times that lay ahead. Whereas all commercial decisions at the Parkhead club would now be taken in concert by the plc board, Murray by contrast, according to Rangers historian Robert McElroy, was still in such an unchallenged position at Ibrox 'that he could dismiss concerns raised at one annual general meeting over liabilities in the balance sheet with a wave of the hand'.

Financial stability on its own, however, is no guarantee of sporting success and, following the departure of manager Dr Jozef Venglos over the summer of 1999, the Parkhead club failed to move forward in the area that matters most to any football club, namely on the field of play. With the ageing Slovak leaving Glasgow after only one year in the job – although he remained loosely affiliated to the club with a remit to scout players from central and eastern Europe – Celtic demonstrated over the following season the importance to any well-run sporting institution, no matter the size, of appointing the right people to positions of responsibility not just in the boardroom, but also further down the chain of command, within every department of the organisation's structure, and how rapidly and painfully the situation can unravel if these basic requirements are not met.

The new chief executive, Allan MacDonald, a lifelong Celtic supporter with an impressive CV, had already arrived and taken up the reins at Parkhead in March in anticipation of McCann's much-heralded departure, but the new CEO's first appointment was to reopen the director of football vacancy at the club and offer the position to his friend and occasional golfing partner, the former Parkhead forward, Kenny Dalglish. The nepotism within the new regime at Celtic continued when Dalglish then approached John Barnes, a long-term associate whom he had managed at Liverpool and whose playing career had latterly been winding down at Charlton Athletic, and invited the former England winger to come up to Glasgow and coach Celtic's first team. Barnes's subsequent appointment to the role on 10 June 1999 saw him become the first black manager in the history of top-flight Scottish or indeed British football, a notable feather in Celtic's cap, but the job offer had apparently been made by Dalglish on the basis of a couple of training sessions that Barnes had put on while the pair were working together during a brief spell at Newcastle United. As if the old pals act at Parkhead hadn't already gone far enough, a few weeks into the season Barnes signed his close friend Ian Wright to play centre-forward.

Perhaps surprisingly in the circumstances, the campaign started well for Celtic under their new head coach, the club's third in as many years, with Barnes's side recording victories in eight of their first nine league fixtures, including two thrashings of Aberdeen, 5-0 and 7-0, and a 4-0 home win over Hearts, while the Parkhead men's 3-0 defeat of St Johnstone on the opening day of the season at Celtic Park was watched by 60,282 spectators, the biggest crowd of the decade for a league game in Britain. Any perceived risk undertaken by the club in appointing another rookie manager to the position at Parkhead, after the relative failure of Liam Brady's tenure in the post earlier in the decade, was mitigated, so the fans were assured at any rate by the presence of Dalglish in a 'mentor' capacity, with the legendary forward and experienced former boss of a trio of EPL sides remaining in the background at Celtic Park to assist the 35-year-old Barnes as and when required. Nevertheless, following the announcement of the new manager in June, the *Scotland on Sunday* had warned, 'There must be Celtic supporters this weekend who are still numb at the shocking risk being embarked upon by this rebuilt and revitalised club. In an age when strategy is said to be everything, it beggars belief that the club will place its rich investment in players in the hands of an untried trainee coach. There are many who have grave doubts about the appointments of Kenny Dalglish and John Barnes, and others willing to go further in thinking that this initiative will end in tears.'

So it proved as the season progressed, with Barnes's side undoing all their early good work by inexplicably losing 1-0 at home to Motherwell on Wednesday, 27 October, missing out on the opportunity to return to the top of the league table in a match that had seen the visitors reduced to ten men after the first-half dismissal of defender Shaun Teale. Manager John Barnes was forced to admit following the defeat, 'That was our worst performance of the season. We couldn't pass the ball straight. After about 25-30 minutes of the second half, we knew we could have been there all night and not scored. I can only hope it was a one-off.' Sadly, however, things were about to go from bad to worse for Celtic, and Barnes's sanguine expectation that the result and performance against the Fir Park side would prove to be nothing more than a blip in his team's form turned out to be an unfortunate case of misplaced optimism on the manager's part.

At half-time during the game against Motherwell, the Celtic Park crowd had been introduced to former England centre-forward Ian Wright, who had arrived at the club on a free transfer from West Ham 24 hours earlier. Wright was signed as emergency cover for star striker Henrik Larsson, who had suffered a broken leg the previous week during a 1-0 defeat in the first leg of the Parkhead side's UEFA Cup tie against Lyon in France. Two weeks later, in early November, Celtic were eliminated from the competition after a second 1-0 loss in the return match at Parkhead, in a game that bore an uncanny resemblance to the Motherwell fixture. The French side comfortably made off with the spoils following another lacklustre display by Barnes's men, who had failed to put up a proper challenge over the 90 minutes. From there, the season unravelled with alarming alacrity for the rookie manager and his team, as three days after their European exit the Parkhead side travelled to Ibrox and lost 4-2 to Dick Advocaat's Rangers, despite a brace of first-half goals from new signing Eyal Berkovic.

By now, sections of the Celtic support were beginning to turn on Barnes, and there were already signs of a loss of faith in the 'dream team' appointments – as they had cringingly been labelled at the outset of the campaign – of the manager and his mentor on the golf course, sporting director Kenny Dalglish. Following the defeat at Ibrox, Tom Shields reported in *The Herald*, 'Mingling, as we do, with the ordinary Celtic fan, we hear words which are quite clear. The new regime will not do.

If Barnes is a football prophet, he is too far ahead of his time. His system, whatever it is, does not work. Good players have become bad. Moderate players have become worse … The lack of leadership is also apparent on the field. The pass back rather than the searing run forward is the leitmotif of this Celtic team. There is a lack of heart and spirit in the squad which is unacceptable.' Just to twist the knife in further, Shields then concluded his excoriating piece with the following riposte, 'What the team needs is a couple of sure hands on the tiller. Fergus McCann and Wim Jansen spring to mind.' Coming barely a fortnight after the former owner had formally severed his ties to the club and the new share certificates had been dispatched to supporters and other investors, it seemed that the revisionism in the press regarding McCann's stewardship of Celtic was already under way.

The dispiriting defeat to Rangers at Ibrox, during which another important player, Paul Lambert, had been carried off with a serious injury, was followed later in the month by a second loss to Motherwell, on this occasion by a 3-2 margin at Fir Park, a result that subsequently allowed Celtic historian David Potter to reflect on the prevailing mood around the club at this time: 'The main cause for concern was not so much results as the way the team was playing. Players were seen to argue with their colleagues, passes went astray, the defending was naïve and the forward play ineffective.' Although the form of Barnes's side eventually picked up in December, with Viduka and Berkovic playing the best football of their short spells at Celtic, as the Parkhead men notched up encouraging 4-0 and 4-1 wins over Hibernian and Dundee United either side of a 6-0 trouncing of Aberdeen at Pittodrie – seemingly Celtic's favourite opposition at the time with an aggregate scoreline of 18-0 in the three games between the sides so far that season – nevertheless an important chance to exert their authority and reduce the gap at the top of the league was missed in the final game prior to the winter break. After Viduka had given the home team the lead against Rangers, they allowed the Ibrox side to escape from Celtic Park with a draw, following an equalising strike by Billy Dodds.

It was a case of another missed opportunity for Barnes's men and, as if to confirm the wayward thinking and the erroneous practices that were being implemented by the club at this time, a few days before the contest against their rivals at Parkhead, Celtic had announced the completion of the £5.5m transfer of defender Rafael Felipe Scheidt from Brazilian side Gremio. At first glance, the purchase of the 23-year-old Scheidt may have looked like a positive piece of business by the club, with the new regime at Parkhead apparently prepared to flex their financial muscles and match, or at least rival, Rangers' outlandish levels of spending on exotic foreign talent, but sadly for the club's fans, the Brazilian stopper turned out to be no better than his name suggested.

Now free of Fergus McCann's scrupulous penny-pinching, new chief executive Allan MacDonald had already indicated his willingness to endorse a more free-spending approach within the club, and the plc board had earlier sanctioned the £5.75m signing of Berkovic, an Israeli international, from West Ham in a deal that broke the Scottish transfer record at the time, as well as the acquisitions of Ivorian defender Olivier Tebily from Sheffield United, Bulgarian midfield prospect Stiliyan Petrov from CSKA Sofia, whom the manager misused by fielding at right-back, Dutch winger Bobby Petta from Ipswich and Russian Dmitri Kharine as a back-up goalkeeper from Chelsea.

The arrival of Scheidt – by now known, thankfully, as Rafael – in Scotland was held up by the customary work permit and other bureaucratic delays and, coupled with injuries, including a case of appendicitis that struck the player almost as soon as he touched down in Glasgow, the defender was only able to make three appearances for the Parkhead side before the end of the season, by which time he had become nothing more than a figure of fun. Scheidt had previously featured three times for the Brazilian *seleção*, all in friendly games, but it was later suggested that his country's celebrated national team were at the time handing out unmerited international caps to local players in an apparent attempt to entice less than meticulous and slightly desperate European clubs to part with overgenerous sums of money in exchange for average players. Celtic, in their vulnerability and with their flawed modus operandi behind the scenes, were seemingly taken in, with Barnes later admitting that he had only ever watched the player on a couple of occasions on ESPN. In addition, when contracts manager Jim Hone flew down to Porto Alegre in the hope of watching the player in action for his club, he discovered, rather unfortunately, that he had arrived in South America during a mid-season break in the Brazilian league.

Nevertheless, the positive sequence of results in December had seen Barnes pick up the final 'manager of the month' award for the year, but few were convinced that the rookie head coach's side had turned the corner. The winter break allowed divisions within the squad to fester during a close-knit training camp in Portugal, and no sooner had the football returned following the January resumption, than further calamity struck the ailing Parkhead outfit. Barnes's side had already suffered a 3-2 defeat to Hearts at Celtic Park, in a match that had seen the home side squander a two-goal first-half lead, when plucky Inverness Caledonian Thistle came calling to the east end of Glasgow for a third-round Scottish Cup tie on 8 February.

The game had originally been scheduled for 29 January but rain and high winds had caused some minor damage to the guttering on the roof of the new Lisbon Lions stand, resulting in a postponement of the fixture on safety grounds. In the meantime, the result and performance against Hearts had left many supporters at the end of their tether. It was becoming increasingly evident by this stage that the team had stopped playing for the manager and that Barnes, in turn, had run out of ideas in his efforts to try to resolve the situation.

Inverness proved to be a disaster waiting to happen for the manager and his misfiring Parkhead side. The visiting club had only been in existence since 1994, when Highland League teams and former local rivals Inverness Caledonian and Inverness Thistle merged and were admitted to the senior Scottish Football League as the domestic game's newest and most sesquipedalian outfit, Inverness Caledonian Thistle. For some weeks already, by the time the tie was eventually played, the young team had been looking forward to the biggest night in their relatively short history after the draw had paired them with Celtic, whom they would be taking on in the Parkhead club's splendid new stadium. As early as the 13th minute, the First Division side took the lead through Barry Wilson, and although Burchill quickly equalised, the visitors were again in front when a set -piece header from Mann was deflected into his own net by the unfortunate Moravčík. For the remaining 20 minutes of the first half, Celtic seemed to have no idea how to extricate themselves from the ever-deepening hole in which they were now floundering, and with the jeers cascading down from the stands as the players trooped off at the interval, Barnes's fate as manager of Celtic was about to be sealed.

A full-scale dressing-room bust-up ensued, with assistant manager Eric Black, in an apparent effort to try to provoke a reaction from Viduka, effectively accusing the big Australian of a lack of effort. The striker's response to the allegation, instead of going out and rescuing the game by scoring a hat-trick, which is presumably what Black was anticipating, was to take off his boots and throw them in the bin, in essence refusing to take the field for the second half. Berkovic was also accused by certain team-mates of a conspicuous reluctance to fight for the team's cause, while the whole episode was reportedly played out to the sound of Ian Wright cackling with laughter. Barnes, meanwhile, rather like Captain Smith of the *Titanic*, appeared to witness the unravelling of his career in front of his eyes with a kind of passive immobility that bordered on mental paralysis.

Inverness scored a further goal in the second half, from the penalty spot, to win the match 3-1, a deserved and noted triumph for the Highlanders, who would soon complete their journey through the divisions of the Scottish Football League and take their place in the top-flight SPL. For Celtic, however, it was a seminal moment. *The Sun* urged manager Barnes to immediately 'get lost' on its back page, while the banner above the match report inside the paper evoked childhood memories for those supporters who had grown up in happier times for the Parkhead club during the 60s and 70s: 'Super Caley Go Ballistic Celtic Are Atrocious'. The gleeful headline subsequently became a part of tabloid folklore, but Celtic would need more than the magic nanny Mary Poppins and her catchy songs to turn their season around. Barnes was immediately sacked, leaving the club the following day along with two key members of his backroom staff, assistant coach Eric Black and 'social convener' Terry McDermott, with his mentor, Kenny Dalglish, summoned home from a trip abroad to take charge of the first team at Parkhead and see out what was left of the league campaign. It would not be long, however, before Dalglish, along with his boss Allan MacDonald, would follow the rookie manager out of the exit door at Celtic Park.

Managing Celtic's first team on a day-to-day basis wasn't what Dalglish had in mind when he took up the rather loosely defined position of 'director of football operations' at Parkhead the previous summer. His role initially allowed him to combine work and leisure pursuits, such as the golfing-cum-scouting trip he had undertaken to La Manga, Spain when Barnes's regime finally imploded against Inverness. Dalglish had been one of the best and most successful players in the history of Scottish football, winning an unequalled 102 caps for Scotland and scoring 167 goals in 320 appearances for the Parkhead side between 1968 and 1977, when he was eventually transferred for a British record-breaking, but still relatively modest, transfer fee to Bob Paisley's Liverpool. In England, he found success equally easy to come by, scoring the only goal of the game in the European Cup Final against Bruges at Wembley in his first season at the Anfield club, before reclaiming the Continent's most prized trophy with two further victories over the course of his career against Real Madrid in 1981 and Roma in 1984. In addition, Dalglish's Liverpool were crowned champions of England on five separate occasions during his spell as a player at the club, before the Anfield side promoted the Scot to the dugout and claimed three more titles in the late 80s with Dalglish as their manager.

Dalglish's time at Anfield, however, was also marked by tragedy, as he witnessed events at the Heysel Stadium in Brussels in 1985, when 39 Italian fans were killed after a wall collapsed before the European Cup Final between Liverpool and Juventus.

Then, in April 1989, the Scot was in charge of the Liverpool side that took to the field at Hillsborough, Sheffield to play an FA Cup semi-final against Brian Clough's Nottingham Forest. The match was soon abandoned after 96 Liverpool fans suffered fatal injuries after being penned in and crushed on a section of the ground's Leppings Lane terrace, despite other areas of the stand remaining far from over-occupied. Dalglish eventually resigned as Liverpool manager in February 1991, before returning to the dugout a few months later to take charge of cash-rich Blackburn Rovers, whom he led out of the second division to the Premier League title in 1995, plundering steel tycoon Jack Walker's millions to oversee the Lancashire side's first English championship success in 81 years.

After his most recent, unhappy experience in charge of Newcastle United, however, Dalglish had little appetite for a return to front-line management and he made it clear that, following the dismissal of John Barnes, Celtic would now be embarking on a process of identifying a suitable replacement for their now former manager on a permanent basis. While he accepted his own role and responsibility in the ultimately mistaken decision to appoint such an inexperienced head coach, Dalglish also responded to suggestions that some of the players may have contributed to Barnes's downfall by their failure to show the required levels of commitment and dedication to the team's cause in the manner expected of any professional footballer. 'We need players here who will wear the jersey with pride,' the interim boss told a hastily assembled press conference. 'If they don't want to wear it, they needn't bother coming to work. Players can make mistakes and have poor performances and results and that is acceptable, but if there is not 100 per cent commitment they'll be in trouble. I don't think our club or our supporters deserve people like that. If there are any here like that they won't be here long.'

Throughout his short spell as interim manager, Dalglish appeared to retain an obvious disdain for some sections of the press and the role they had allegedly played in contributing to the failure of Barnes's tenure at Parkhead, particularly in regard to the cynicism they had displayed from the outset towards the former England man. On the eve of one Old Firm game, he invited the media to Bairds Bar, a Celtic supporters' pub on the Gallowgate with a lively reputation, where in lieu of the customary facilities at Celtic Park, he held his pre-match press conference. Dalglish claimed at the time that he wanted to get out among the supporters and bring the club closer to its fans, but many in the media never forgave him for the stunt, with some of the hacks apparently so upset by the necessity of having to slum it out in the east end that it wasn't long before suggestions began to emerge of how Dalglish had tarnished his reputation as one of the greats of Scottish football.

A further altercation between the former Parkhead forward and the media occurred following the capture of the CIS League Cup, the first trophy to be won in the new millennium, which Dalglish's side claimed in March with a 2-0 victory over Aberdeen in the Hampden final. The Dons had previously knocked Rangers out at an earlier stage of the competition, while Celtic had progressed to the final at the expense of Ayr United, Dundee and, latterly, Kilmarnock in the semi-final, after Dalglish had taken over from Barnes and, with Eric Black and Terry McDermott having also left the club, appointed former manager Tommy Burns as his assistant.

The final itself was a largely unmemorable occasion, with the destination of the cup seemingly secured on the hour mark following the dismissal of Aberdeen's Norwegian defender Thomas Solberg only moments after Tommy Johnson, who had been controversially named in the starting line-up at the expense of promising youngster Mark Burchill, had given Celtic a two-goal lead, vindicating his selection by the interim boss and doubling the advantage established by Riseth's first-half strike. Asked after the game about his plans for next season and whether the capture of the trophy might influence his thinking regarding the permanent position, Dalglish told STV reporter Peter Martin, 'We get asked this every time; you're getting like Chick Young. We told you it'll be the end of March. I don't think this is the end of March yet. But certainly, every decision we make, we take the supporters into consideration.' To a rival broadcaster, being compared to Young, the much lampooned BBC Scotland newshound, was surely the ultimate insult.

The margin of victory in the League Cup Final had extended the aggregate scoreline for the season between the two teams to fully 20-0 in Celtic's favour, although a 5-1 defeat at Celtic Park in early May, while only extending the agony for the Pittodrie men, at least allowed Aberdeen to belatedly break their duck against the Glasgow side. By then, however, Celtic's season was limping to a sorry conclusion, with Dalglish's team at one stage in April accumulating a mere three points from a run of four games, allowing Rangers to coast to a 49th league title without ever facing a sustained or credible challenge from their rivals. Advocaat's side, meanwhile, were motoring along nicely, it seemed, and although the spending at the start of the 1999/2000 season wasn't as exorbitant as the previous year, the Ibrox club, as chairman David Murray had vowed, were nevertheless still burning through enormous amounts of cash in an effort to stay ahead of the pack.

In addition, the Ibrox chairman by now was already experimenting with an alternative method of meeting his responsibilities to the taxman, by allowing a select number of his most highly paid employees, including manager Dick Advocaat and Champions League-winning goalkeeper Stefan Klos, who was reported to be earning more than David Beckham at Ibrox, to receive a portion of their salary in the form of a loan, through controversial tax avoidance schemes such as Employee Benefit Trusts (EBTs) and the Discounted Options Scheme (DOS). These so-called loans, none of which were ever paid back, allowed employees to take home huge wads of tax-free income in addition to their regular wage, a ruse that went undiscovered for several years. Over the ensuing decade, Murray expanded the trust payment scheme and used it to meet the salary demands of dozens of the club's most highly paid players, a significant number of whom, had Rangers been paying their taxes lawfully and fully, the club would not have been able to afford.

In the meantime, the relative ease with which the Ibrox side were able to defend the title was emphasised when, just a week after lifting the League Cup, Celtic travelled across the city and were thumped 4-0 at the home of their rivals, with Rangers not flattered by late goals from Albertz and Van Bronckhorst, as the Parkhead men found themselves on the wrong end of an ignominious Ibrox rout. The result provoked the headlines 'Men against Bhoys' as well as, even more unkindly, following the interim manager's decision to hold his pre-match presser in a well-known Celtic hostelry, 'Dalglish staged his press conference in a bar on Friday and turned out a pub team yesterday!' With David Murray announcing his three-for-one rights issue in the immediate aftermath of the result at Ibrox, and considering in particular the gushing coverage that his proposals to raise some much-needed capital were greeted with across a range of media outlets, it appeared that a morose sense of doom and gloom had once again descended over the Parkhead club, whose eternal rivals, having swatted aside a brief threat to their hegemony the previous year, now seemed set to embark on another new era of glorious and unprecedented success.

When Rangers eventually won the league by fully 21 points from a distant and forlorn Celtic, it looked to all intents and purposes as though the Fergus McCann era at Parkhead had ended in failure. Murray, by contrast, was portrayed as having effectively seen off his brash adversary on the other side of the city and had seemingly emerged from the McCann challenge with his reputation enhanced and his club poised to establish themselves in an even stronger position at the summit of Scottish football. One radio pundit even suggested at the time that it would take the Parkhead club 20 years to catch up with their traditional rivals, while Glenn Gibbons in *The Scotsman* noted that the new Celtic manager, whoever he may be, would have to 'accept a challenge so daunting that it would make James Bond choke on his martini'.

The reality was somewhat different; behind the bombastic façade, Rangers and the Murray empire were walking a financial tightrope, teetering on the brink of catastrophe, particularly after the bursting of the dotcom bubble in March 2000, which caused uncertainty and instability in stock markets around the world. The effects of the subsequent economic downturn would be felt most severely across the global economy by indebted and other reckless sectors of industry, including Rangers, and with their cross-town rivals having at last, over the summer of 2000, made an astute managerial appointment, the Parkhead men were finally ready to test the almost unchallenged assertions of the Ibrox club's assumed supremacy of the Scottish domestic game.

9.

A Turning World

FOLLOWING his takeover and turnaround of Celtic Football Club, the success of Fergus McCann's departing share issue in October 1999 had left the Parkhead institution in a secure and very much strengthened off-field position. On the field, however, converting their new-found financial security into sporting success had proved too difficult a task for the untried managerial partnership of John Barnes and Kenny Dalglish, and despite the capture of the League Cup in March 2000, only the fourth trophy to be won by the Parkhead side in 11 years, by the end of the season the doomwatchers and naysayers were out in force once again. Many even suggested that, after finishing the campaign fully 21 points behind Rangers, the Parkhead club was no further forward than it had been during the miserable years of the old board back in the early 1990s. Such a perception was false, however, and easily disprovable, if only by pointing to the evidence of the vast sums of money that Celtic had misspent in season 1999/2000 on players such as Rafael Scheidt and Eyal Berkovic, two expensive misfits who had cost the club over £10m between them. By contrast, in the early part of the decade, before McCann's arrival and intervention, the club had been struggling to buy any players at all without having to rely on then manager Lou Macari's specialist knowledge of bargain signings from the lower reaches of the English Football League.

What seemed clear was that Celtic, and chief executive Allan MacDonald in particular, had made poor recruitment choices when filling the key positions at the football club following McCann's departure, but with rookie manager John Barnes relieved of his duties after the Inverness debacle and his interim replacement Kenny Dalglish also leaving the club over the summer, it now fell to the under-fire CEO to identify once again a suitable candidate to step into the role, as for the fourth year in succession Celtic found themselves obliged over the close season to embark on the task of recruiting a new head coach. Names linked with the Parkhead job in the media over the summer included Gordon Strachan, the former Scotland international midfielder then in charge of Coventry City, Wim Jansen, inevitably, who was still out of work at the time, with one radio pundit suggesting that Celtic might never again be able to win the league unless the Dutchman was reappointed to his former role at Parkhead, and Joe Kinnear, who in 1994 had led unfashionable Wimbledon to a sixth-place finish in the EPL and whose use of colourful expletives was so profuse that it wasn't long before people within football started referring to him as JFK.

MacDonald's preferred candidate, however, was the experienced Guus Hiddink, who had been linked with Celtic in the past but was now a free agent after recently parting company with Real Betis. Majority shareholder Dermot Desmond flew out to Spain to discuss the vacancy at Parkhead with the Dutchman and his representatives, but in the end the Celtic kingmaker left the meeting underwhelmed and unconvinced that the much-travelled coach was aware of the scale and significance of the post he was being considered for. 'I looked into his eyes and didn't see it,' Desmond later remarked, '... didn't see an understanding of the whole history.' Perhaps betraying a loss of faith in his CEO that would soon result in MacDonald's departure from the club, Desmond then furtively consulted with Manchester United manager Alex Ferguson, who offered the club his own list of candidates, based on his view of the three best managers currently working in British football. With one name standing out above all others on Ferguson's three-man shortlist, Desmond made a final intervention in the recruitment process and came to a decision that would ultimately have a profound bearing on the history not only of Celtic, but also of Scottish football.

As a player, Martin O'Neill had enjoyed considerable success at both club and international level, winning the English First Division with Nottingham Forest in 1978, before, two years later, adding his name to the elite group of footballers to have won the European Cup, when Brian Clough's motley crew of mostly former Second Division players defeated the German side Hamburg 1-0 in the final in Madrid, with the only goal of the game scored by Scotland international winger and long-term O'Neill associate John Robertson. Clough's side, featuring the dependable O'Neill on the right side of midfield, had managed to retain the trophy they had captured the previous year with a similar result in Munich against the Swedish champions Malmö, a game that had seen the Irishman relegated to the bench by his manager after he failed to fully recover in time from a niggling injury. O'Neill also earned 64 international caps for his native Northern Ireland and captained Billy Bingham's side to great success at the 1982 World Cup in Spain, but after failing to regain his fitness in time for the 1986 event in Mexico, for which the Irish had also qualified, he retired shortly before the tournament at the age of 34.

Realising that he was a very different character from the brusque and confrontational Clough and perhaps feeling slightly daunted at the prospect of following in the footsteps of his renowned former boss, who at times during their relationship displayed a mistrust typical of many old-style British managers towards educated, intelligent men such as O'Neill, the Irishman's first tentative steps into management came in the lower reaches of English football. The inexperienced O'Neill was keen to gauge his aptitude for the job during short spells at non-league sides Grantham Town and Shepshed Charterhouse, before taking over at Wycombe Wanderers in 1990. He then led the Buckinghamshire side into the Football League, where they won promotion to the Third Division at the first attempt before he returned to the Midlands, following a brief spell in charge of Norwich, to take up the reins with Leicester City in December 1995, succeeding the former Celtic forward Mark McGhee in the role. At Filbert Street, just as he had done at Adams Park, O'Neill guided his team to unprecedented levels of success, as the Foxes won promotion to the Premier League in 1996 after a dramatic play-off final victory over Crystal Palace at Wembley. Leicester then claimed the Coca-Cola League Cup the following year, a trophy that at the time came with the added bonus for the winners of a place in European competition.

Leicester's attempt on the UEFA Cup was ended at the first hurdle by Atlético Madrid, but in February 2000 O'Neill's side repeated the feat, winning the then Worthington Cup with a 2-1 victory over Tranmere Rovers in the Wembley final, before completing their season by attaining a creditable eighth-place finish in the Premier League. By then, however, tentative approaches were starting to be made by Celtic, with the club already on the lookout for a suitable candidate to become the next permanent manager at Parkhead following the dismissal of John Barnes, who, unlike O'Neill, had been casually thrown in at the deep end in his first managerial appointment.

Celtic had to pay compensation to Leicester, reported as £1.25m, for the loss of their highly regarded boss, with Filbert Street chairman John Elsom reluctant to sanction O'Neill's departure from the club after four and a half successful years. 'I spent one week trying to dissuade him from going,' Elsom acknowledged, before adding, somewhat unwisely, 'In the end the pursuit of a personal dream related to his Roman Catholic heritage seems to have won the day.' The Leicester chairman continued to prove difficult to deal with even after his manager had left Filbert Street, with the Midlands club playing hardball over the positions of assistants Steve Walford and John Robertson, who were wanted by O'Neill in Glasgow. It wasn't until almost the end of August before both O'Neill's coaches had joined him at Celtic Park and his backroom team was complete.

'What took you so long?' O'Neill was reported to have quipped when Desmond eventually reached out and offered him the job, promising his fellow countryman full control of all aspects of the football operation at Celtic Park. This arrangement would render redundant the director of football position at the club and ultimately confirmed the departure of Kenny Dalglish from Parkhead, although his interim assistant, Tommy Burns, was retained by the new manager as a youth development coach, a role that seemed to be more suited to his talents. Hiddink would potentially have been the more eye-catching appointment, but after being relieved of his duties at both Betis and Real Madrid in a short space of time, his star appeared to be on the wane in comparison to the ebullient Irishman, as Desmond explained, 'It wasn't about raising the profile or anything else … There was only one simple reason for hiring Martin O'Neill – he will win trophies and he would help the performance of Celtic.'

If Fergus McCann put things right behind the scenes at Celtic, laying the foundations and securing the Parkhead club on a solid commercial footing, then Martin O'Neill, it could justifiably be claimed, did the same thing for the team on the field. One of his first acts, after meeting the players for the first time, was to lock the entire squad up in the dressing room together for 45 minutes, after nobody had been able to give a satisfactory answer to his question about why the league hadn't been won the previous season. When O'Neill eventually returned and unbolted the door, he explained to the group that the previous season's frustrations were the responsibility of everyone at the club and that he would not tolerate less than 100 per cent from every player in order to ensure that the failings were not repeated. It was an act of pure theatre on the new manager's part, but the message of unity and a new-found sense of purpose had been effectively conveyed.

The difference in Celtic was immediate and irrefutable; at the start of the season O'Neill's team had already won six matches out of six, albeit some more convincingly than others, so when Dick Advocaat's Rangers arrived in the east end of Glasgow at the end of August, the match was seen as the first real test of this new Celtic side's credentials. In the end, the game went down in the Parkhead club's folklore and proved to be a turning point in the fortunes of the two sides, with videos featuring edited highlights of the game being produced by Celtic's commercial department and appearing for sale in the club's shops within a matter of weeks. After 11 minutes of play, Celtic had already raced into a three-goal lead following strikes from Sutton, Lambert and Petrov, with Jozef Vengloš's best signing, Ľubomír Moravčík, preferred to Eyal Berkovic despite recently passing his 35th birthday, having a hand in all three. Rangers pulled a goal back before half-time and had a second ruled out after a marginal offside call, before Larsson scored a majestic fourth shortly after the interval, rounding the Rangers defence and chipping Klos from the edge of the 18-yard box. Again Rangers kept themselves in the contest with a penalty converted by Billy Dodds, but a Larsson header sealed victory for Celtic just after the hour mark, with a late effort from Sutton crowning the occasion and ensuring that Celtic had scored six goals against their rivals for the first time since the celebrated 7-1 success in the League Cup Final of 1957.

If ever there was a game that signalled a changing of the guard in terms of one team's dominance over another, it was this 6-2 victory at Celtic Park. Rangers even won the reverse fixture by a similar scoreline, 5-1, when the sides met at Ibrox at the end of November, but it was merely fleeting revenge that Advocaat's side had gained over their rivals on that occasion and the result had no significant consequences beyond the allocation of the three points on the day, which in any event only reduced the lead Celtic had accumulated in the title race by that point from 13 to 10 points. The balance of power in Glasgow had shifted and thereafter Rangers would forever be playing catch-up, with Ibrox chairman David Murray left desperately trying to cut corners in a futile attempt to reverse Celtic's ascendancy to the summit of Scottish football.

The seminal win over Advocaat's Rangers was, in part at least, a result of O'Neill's shrewd dealings in the transfer market over the summer, with the club shelling out a then Scottish record £6m fee on Chelsea striker Chris Sutton, adding to the £3.5m they had parted with to acquire defender Joos Valgaeren from Roda JC, a player whom the manager had scouted while the Belgian was representing his country at Euro 2000. In addition, with no transfer window in place at the time, O'Neill continued to invest in his playing squad as the season unfolded, bringing in Alan Thompson from Aston Villa, who made an immediate contribution by scoring on his debut against Raith Rovers in the League Cup, and Didier Agathe from Hibernian on 1 September, while goalkeeper Robert Douglas was signed from Dundee in October before Neil Lennon arrived from Leicester two months later, with the additional signings costing the club a combined fee of around £9m.

Rangers had been floundering badly since their defeat at Celtic Park, and the Ibrox club's last throw of the dice, effectively, was the headline-grabbing £12m purchase of Tore André Flo from Chelsea in November. The Norwegian striker had been a more effective forward than Sutton for the west London side the previous year, so his signing seemed logical, if rather extravagant, with the country's transfer record smashed by the Ibrox club in a predictable blaze of publicity. Flo failed to produce the goods in Scotland, however, and Rangers' downward trajectory couldn't be halted, despite the arrival of another expensive recruit, Ronald de Boer, who had joined Advocaat's side from Barcelona in a reactive move by the club following the 6-2 game at Celtic Park. De Boer had added to the growing Dutch contingent at Ibrox, but despite his obvious quality, the midfielder was another who ultimately failed to live up to his billing in Glasgow, due mainly to the length of time he would spend on the treatment table.

Shortly after De Boer's arrival, Rangers' domestic form collapsed, with the Ibrox side racking up a miserable run of results over the autumn, culminating in a 2-1 loss to St Johnstone in Perth on 22 October. After that setback, Advocaat had publicly branded some of his players 'fat-necks', a Dutch phrase that appeared to have been lost in translation until the manager admitted that he had been trying to point the finger of blame for the defeat at the inflated egos and the growing levels of conceit within his squad, and should more accurately have used the term 'big-heads'. Despite refusing to single out individuals, the press seemed convinced that Advocaat was referring in particular to Barry Ferguson and Ronald de Boer for their role in the McDiarmid Park reverse, although it was generally accepted that the expression could equally have been applied to almost any member of his underperforming side.

Ferguson was the only Scottish member of Walter Smith's ageing team whom the manager had retained following his arrival in Glasgow, and Advocaat would later promote the midfielder to the captaincy of the club, stripping the position from the vain Lorenzo Amoruso, whom the other Rangers players had lost confidence in. Ferguson's relationship with the Dutchman seemed fractious, however, with the Scot at times having difficulty adjusting to the new manager's methods, as he later admitted in his autobiography. 'We all ate at the same time every day, and you couldn't leave the table until Dick had finished every last scrap. You couldn't even start until he had – it was like boot camp,' the midfielder complained, adding, 'There were times when he would mop up his gravy with his bread or have a final Kit-Kat just to wind you up. I'd be sitting there thinking, "Hurry up, you little Dutch bastard, I want to go home."'

There were one or two additional grumbles that, perhaps inevitably, started to surface now that the team was struggling – issues that had been seen as secondary and unimportant during Advocaat's first two seasons in Glasgow. Under the Dutchman, the high-earning foreign players were no longer available for supporters' club functions, with fans' groups for the most part having to rely on a back catalogue of Ibrox old-timers for their gatherings and events. Meanwhile, the media were largely left disappointed by Advocaat's wary remoteness, finding it almost impossible to get to know the inscrutable Dutchman, who turned out to be quite a boring individual, unwilling to interact with the press, rival managers or even his own players – a footballing anorak with no other interests in life.

At times he appeared to find it difficult to understand why his players didn't share his same obsession with the game, berating them during the autumn slump for behaving like film stars, having other priorities during the week and only thinking about football when there was a match on. He was seen as a disciplinarian, but Advocaat felt that his strictness as a coach was overemphasised, admitting that he treated his players like children at times, but claiming at the same time that he was only enforcing professional standards, such as turning up for training on schedule, something that, in his opinion, he was perfectly entitled to expect. 'It is like a family and children,' he explained. 'You give your children some rules to work to and they adhere to that. It is quite simply the framework that we all have to work within.'

As Advocaat's side stumbled, Celtic continued to press home their advantage, with the first defeat of the season for the Parkhead men not arriving until they suffered the jolting 5-1 loss at Ibrox at the end of November against a Rangers team augmented by the costly addition of Flo, who made a scoring debut for his new club. It must have seemed to many around Ibrox, not least the manager and chairman themselves, as if the spending strategy at the club was paying off once more, particularly when a run of nine wins from the next ten league matches appeared to have finally put an end to the fall-out from the 'fat-necks' controversy. Rangers' recovery was eventually halted, however, by a trip to Celtic Park in February, when Alan Thompson scored the only goal of the game for the Parkhead side, four days after a 3-1 victory for O'Neill's men in a League Cup semi-final between the teams. By the time O'Neill and his men visited Ibrox again, when they exacted a measure of revenge for the 5-1 capitulation by winning 3-0 at the home of their rivals at the end of April, the Parkhead side had already won the league and, with the first trophy of the season already in the cabinet after a 3-0 victory over Kilmarnock in the final of the League Cup, O'Neill's team were on course for a first domestic Treble since 1969.

It was a case of more of the same the following season, as Celtic successfully defended the title for the first time since 1982, racking up an astonishing total of 103 points from 38 matches, a tally that was only beaten by Brendan Rodgers's 'invincible' Parkhead side of 2017. By the end of the season, Advocaat would be long gone from the Ibrox dugout, flummoxed by O'Neill's revival of Celtic, departing in December 2001 in a manner that would bring criticism from fans and press alike, with Hugh Keevins reporting in the *Daily Record*, 'He was running away from the problems and I don't think you can dress it up any other way.'

The Dutchman was replaced in December by Hibernian boss Alex McLeish, who steadied the ship at Ibrox, winning all five of the first domestic trophies that were realistically available to him, including a clean sweep Treble in season 2002/03, when McLeish's side took the title on goal difference on a dramatic final day of the season. Rangers, it was clear, were in no mood to meekly give up the ghost, and for a while it may have seemed as if the hegemony of the Scottish game was once again up for grabs. A more established pattern was restored in 2004 when Celtic cruised to another wide margin league championship, taking the title by 17 points from McLeish's team after a run of 25 consecutive victories, which followed a disappointing goalless draw against Dunfermline on the opening day of the season. O'Neill's men then secured the Double after beating the Fife side once again in the final of the Scottish Cup, in a match that marked Henrik Larsson's final competitive appearance for the Parkhead club.

In Europe too, O'Neill had re-established Celtic as a credible force, with the newly crowned Scottish champions reaching the Champions League group stages in only their second appearance in the competition, after qualification was secured on the back of a convincing 3-1 first-leg victory over Ajax in Amsterdam in the play-off round. Despite winning all three of their home games, Celtic could only finish third in the section behind Juventus and Porto, and dropped into the UEFA Cup, where after two hard-fought games, both of which finished 1-0 to the home team, O'Neill's side were eventually eliminated by Rafa Benítez's Valencia, one of the Continent's top sides, following a penalty shoot-out.

Season 2002/03 began with the disappointment of failing to match the previous year's progress to the Champions League group stages, after Celtic suffered a narrow defeat to Christian Gross's FC Basel in the play-off round. The decisive goal of the tie, it turned out, came in only the second minute of the first leg, when Gimenez scored for the Swiss champions at Celtic Park, and although O'Neill's side fought back and won 3-1 on the night, a 2-0 defeat in Switzerland two weeks later meant elimination for Celtic on the away goals rule. The setback proved to be the inspiration for an extraordinary sequence of results, however, which eventually took Celtic all the way to their first European final in 33 years, with top sides from England, Spain and Germany being dispatched along the way. The club's first victims were the hapless Lithuanian side FK Sūduva, who bore the brunt of Celtic's obvious frustrations and were routed 8-1 in Glasgow, with the Parkhead side completing a 10-1 aggregate win following a run-out for some of O'Neill's fringe players and youngsters in the away leg.

This brought Blackburn Rovers to Celtic Park, the English side managed by former Rangers boss Graeme Souness, who arrived in Glasgow by train and, in the end, headed back south of the border after suffering a rather unfortunate 1-0 defeat, the result of a late strike from Larsson. Before the second leg two weeks later, however, Souness's comments about the match, intended to be in-house and for the benefit of his players, describing how his team had dominated the game at Celtic Park for long spells and referring to the contest, despite the defeat, as being like 'men against boys', were rather loosely repeated in public by certain members of his squad. The ill-judged remarks proved to be all the motivation that Celtic required, with O'Neill's side emerging from Ewood Park as comfortable winners, following a 2-0 away victory, with goals either side of half-time from Larsson and former Blackburn forward Chris Sutton.

The Galician team Celta Vigo, enjoying the best period in their history as one of Spain's elite teams, were Celtic's next opponents, and following another hard-fought 1-0 win at Celtic Park, with Larsson again the goalscorer, the Parkhead men appeared to have given themselves the opportunity, if a decent result could be obtained at the Estadio Belaídos, of securing European football beyond Christmas for the first time since the club had faced Real Madrid as long ago as March 1980. In those less complicated days, wins over Partizan Tirana and Dundalk could take a team into the quarter-finals of the European Cup, but 23 years later, progress on the Continent could only be attained via a more circuitous route, with Celta, in December, already the fourth opponent that O'Neill's side had faced. In the much-anticipated second leg, the home team took the lead through Jesuli, but Hartson equalised before half-time with a shot from the edge of the box, and although the Spaniards scored again in the second half through South African striker Benny McCarthy, Celtic held on and, thanks to the away goals rule, progressed to a meeting with German side Vfb Stuttgart in the new year.

Prior to the first leg of the last-16 tie on 20 February, star forward Henrik Larsson had suffered a broken jaw in a match against Livingston, and with Hartson, Mjällby and goalkeeper Magnus Hedman also unavailable, *The Scotsman* had taken the view that Celtic were 'as prepared as the American Navy before Pearl Harbour' for the tie against the Bundesliga outfit. The Parkhead side looked to be in trouble when, despite being reduced to ten men after Stuttgart defender Bordon was ordered off by Italian referee Pierluigi Collina for a professional foul on Petrov, the visitors took the lead on the night through Brazilian-born forward Kevin Kuranyi. A splendid fightback ensued, however, and following Lambert's equaliser, young forward Shaun Maloney, whom O'Neill had decided to partner in attack alongside Chris Sutton, scored a vital goal just before half-time to put Celtic ahead. After the interval, Petrov added to the home side's advantage with a raking shot from a narrow angle, allowing the Parkhead men to take a 3-1 lead into the second leg, and the tie was essentially secured after 11 minutes of the return match in Germany, by which time early strikes from Thompson and Sutton had given O'Neill's men a 2-0 advantage, ultimately rendering Stuttgart's late fightback and 3-2 win on the night ineffective.

The glamour ties kept coming for Celtic, when the Parkhead side were paired with Gérard Houllier's Liverpool at the tournament's quarter-final stage. Larsson marked his return to first-team action by scoring in only the second minute of the game at Celtic Park, but the Merseysiders appeared to have emerged from the first leg with the advantage after Emile Heskey's equalising strike secured a 1-1 draw. In the Anfield return, however, despite help from Rangers when Sandy Jardine provided Liverpool first-team coach and former Ibrox team-mate Alex Miller with a detailed dossier on Celtic's strengths and weaknesses, the Parkhead men took the spoils with a deserved 2-0 win, clinched by a late, long-range effort from John Hartson, which sealed the tie and ensured the club's progress to the semi-final.

The eye-catching result had come just days after an unfortunate and contentious 2-1 defeat to Rangers in the final of the League Cup, a game in which Hartson had seen a late strike wrongly disallowed for offside, before the Welsh forward then missed a last-minute penalty. Despite the disappointment of seeing the trophy being lifted by their rivals, who themselves had crashed out of Europe in October with a first-round UEFA Cup loss to Czech side Viktoria Žižkov, midfielder Neil Lennon, in his autobiography and elsewhere, pointed out the enormous sense of belief that O'Neill had been able to transmit to his players before the return match against Liverpool, convincing them that, even on the back of such a recent and bitter defeat, they could travel down to England with confidence and overcome one of the country's best teams.

Following their win, the English media were quick to acknowledge the merit in Celtic's victory, with *The Guardian* picking up on the sense of accomplishment that was surrounding O'Neill, and the difficulty he faced in trying to earn respect both in England and in Europe with a Scottish side: 'That success testifies to Martin O'Neill's remarkable feat of leading his club so far beyond their meagre environment in the Scottish Premier League. The adjustment needed whenever they face clubs from the strongholds of European football is radical, yet the transformation is being made regularly. Liverpool join Blackburn Rovers, Celta Vigo and Stuttgart in the distinguished list of the vanquished.' Celtic chairman Brian Quinn, meanwhile, summed up the result at Anfield more succinctly, 'It's the greatest night since Lisbon,' he remarked afterwards.

Celtic had progressed to their first European semi-final since an infamous running battle of a contest against Atlético Madrid back in 1974. Their opponents 29 years later, however, Boavista of the Portuguese league, presented the Parkhead club with the unwelcome opportunity to revive the old failing of many Scottish club and international teams down the years of being able to produce the goods against the strongest opposition, but then witnessing their best form evaporate when confronted with the game's lesser lights. Boavista were a strong team but could hardly be described as possessing the same quality as Liverpool, and even in Portugal, whose league was traditionally dominated by the big three clubs of Sporting, Benfica and Porto, they were not considered to be one of the country's top sides.

Both matches were tense, vapid affairs with a Valgaeren own goal at Celtic Park giving the Iberians the lead early in the second half, before Larsson swept home an immediate equaliser. The chance to take a lead to Portugal was then squandered when goalkeeper Ricardo saved the Swede's penalty, and with an away goal secured, Boavista sat back and defended deep at home in the second leg, successfully preserving their narrow advantage until 11 minutes from the end of the tie, when Larsson, in attempting to play a one-two with Hartson, received the ball back from a Portuguese defender and scooped it into the net. It was a goal which, in the end, proved to be the winner, despite a late, heavy bombardment of the Celtic penalty box by Boavista, who were forced to radically alter their tactics for the last ten minutes of the match, but when the final whistle was eventually blown by Russian referee Valentin Ivanov, it was the cue for the Parkhead celebrations to begin in earnest.

The venue for the final was the Estadio Olímpico in Seville, with the city in the Andalusian region of Spain at least providing a bit of continuity, as the tabloids cheerfully pointed out, by extending the connection to Celtic's defeated rivals over the course of the campaign, all of whose names contained the letter 'V', prompting headlines such as 'Here V Go', 'V Day' and 'Celtic's V for Victory' on the morning after the elimination of Boavista. The Parkhead side's opponents in the final, Porto, were managed by one José Mourinho, then a largely unknown figure outside of the Iberian Peninsula but who would soon achieve international recognition as arguably the coach of the decade, given the success he would subsequently enjoy with Chelsea and Inter Milan.

The Portuguese side also possessed a group of players, including the likes of Deco, Paulo Ferreira, Nuno Valente and Ricardo Carvalho who, one year later, would go on to lift the Champions League, as Mourinho's team became the only club in the new century from outwith the 'big five' European countries to be crowned champions of Europe. They had already secured the Portuguese league title on the back of a 27-week unbeaten run and had recently demolished Lazio 4-1 in the first leg of the semi-final, a game that was followed by a goalless draw in Rome, as Porto progressed to a meeting with O'Neill's men at the expense of the Italian side, which had previously been favourites for the tournament with most observers.

An estimated 80,000 Celtic fans made the trip to southern Spain, described by UEFA as 'the largest travelling support to have assembled for a single game'. A total of 33 charter flights took off from Glasgow airport alone, with another nine departing from nearby Prestwick, alongside many more supporters who were travelling on scheduled flights, meaning that the Celtic exodus accounted for an estimated 20 per cent of all traffic leaving Britain on the day of the game. In addition, many others flew in from around the world, most of whom had little chance of obtaining a ticket for the showpiece. Just being there seemed to be the most important thing for the majority, along with a determination to enjoy themselves, with supporters putting on a show that variously included sombrero hats, masks of Zorro, Manuel from *Fawlty Towers* moustaches, as well as kilts, wigs, beach balls, polka dot bikinis and giant sunglasses, all blending in with the ubiquitous green and white hoops.

Amid the carnival atmosphere, celebrity Celtic fan, Rod Stewart flew in on a private jet from Los Angeles and performed an impromptu concert in Seville city centre, while one Irish bar, a focus for the travelling army of fans, managed to sell over 300 barrels of beer in one day. What the locals made of this green-and-white invasion was anybody's guess, with Celtic historian Pat Woods later noting of the supporters' good-natured occupation of the Andalusian capital, 'The citizens of Seville were bewildered – it was as if they had woken up to find themselves strangers in their own city.'

The match itself kicked off at 8.45pm local time on Wednesday, 21 May 2003 in sweltering, Mediterranean heat, a factor that seemed to slow the tempo of the contest in the initial stages, as both teams struggled to impose their natural game on their opponents. Just before half-time, the match was brought to life when Derlei fired home the opening goal after Russian international Alenichev's shot had only been parried by Robert Douglas, but within minutes of the restart, Celtic were level when a trademark header from Henrik Larsson, who out-jumped Ricardo Costa to meet Agathe's cross, saw the ball nestle inside Vítor Baía's far post. It was a more open contest now, and Mourinho's side soon re-established their lead with a clever bit of play from the influential Deco, who teed up Alenichev to restore Porto's advantage, but Larsson once again soon restored parity with another towering header, as the Swede notched up his 11th goal of the competition when he latched on to Thompson's corner to beat Baía again, this time at his opposite post.

In many ways, the match appeared to be reflecting the clash of cultures between the southern European and British styles of football, with Porto's eye-catching combinations contrasting with Celtic's more dynamic and direct approach, which, along with the fluctuations in the play and the goals at each end, made for a fascinating contest. Less appealingly, however, the comparisons between the two teams' methods also extended to some of the Iberian side's play-acting and other antics, as increasingly lengthy delays began to accrue due to time-wasting and other dubious stoppages, with particular cause for complaint, certainly from O'Neill's perspective, being the time required to restart the match after the goals that put Porto in front were scored. As commentating guru Archie Macpherson later noted of the Porto players' blatant diving and their apparent inability to get back on their feet in a timely fashion, '[Porto] could play some excellent football but betrayed histrionics which went beyond even the style of those crowd extras in John Ford movies, ten of whom could fall from a horse after only one rifle shot by John Wayne.'

With no further goals during the 90 minutes, the knife-edge contest moved into extra time, when the scales tipped once more in the Portuguese side's favour after Celtic defender Bobo Baldé received a second yellow card from Slovakian referee Ľuboš Micheľ and was ordered off. Now a man down and exhausted both by their efforts on the pitch and by the balmy, late evening temperatures, O'Neill's men looked to be holding out for a penalty shoot-out, but hopes were finally dashed when Derlei capitalised on an iffy bit of defending in the Celtic rearguard and shot past the floundering Douglas. With his 12th goal in the tournament, the Brazilian had edged ahead of Larsson as the competition's top scorer, but more immediately he had restored Porto's lead with just five minutes of the UEFA Cup Final remaining. Still a man short as the seconds ticked by, Celtic were unable to respond, despite a late red card for Porto's Valente, and the trophy was won by Mourinho's side.

It had been a tremendous campaign by O'Neill's men and the disappointment of ultimately failing to lift the trophy was mitigated by the fans, who were up for a party at any rate, and whose good-natured annexation of the Andalusian capital was later rewarded with the FIFA Fair Play award, in recognition of the way they had conducted themselves collectively as a body of supporters while following their team abroad in such extraordinary numbers. Recommending the club's fans for the award, UEFA spokesman Mike Lee noted, 'We felt it right that when FIFA came to us for nominations for the world award, we should nominate them. The whole of that week they were just magnificent, even after their side was defeated.'

The club's followers also received praise from across the British media, who were, on the whole, generous in their assessment of the Celtic players' efforts, on the night as well as across the whole campaign, in addition to their compliments towards the support that the team had received. *The Scotsman's* Stuart Bathgate, it seemed, summed up the general consensus when he observed following the result of the final, 'If this was disappointment and dejection, it was the sort that most clubs would die for.' The mayor of Seville, meanwhile, Señor Alfredo Sánchez Monteseirín, also registered his approval in a letter to Glasgow's Lord Provost Liz Cameron. 'You should feel proud to have fans such as these in Glasgow, who give their city and country a good name … We hope to see you again in Seville on a similar occasion, when you will surely be luckier on the playing field,' he wrote.

Much of Mourinho's subsequent success in charge of some of the Continent's top clubs can be traced back to his Porto side's victory over Celtic in the UEFA Cup Final of 2003. A man who had hidden his light under a bushel during a short, uneventful career as a player in his country's lower divisions, the young Portuguese coach was previously best known, certainly within the UK, as Bobby Robson's translator at Barcelona, but he would later go on to win the Champions League on two occasions as well as claiming numerous domestic trophies in England, Italy and Spain. Looking back, Mourinho remembered, 'I've played three European finals since, two in the Champions League. I've won a lot of titles, been involved in so many incredible games. But in terms of living with tension, intensity, with emotion raised to the limit, that game against Celtic beat them all.' Goalkeeper Vítor Baía also reflected, when looking back on his playing days, that the match against Celtic in Seville was the most emotionally charged game of his career.

The following season, O'Neill's side came close to doing it all again and almost reprised their successful campaign of 2002/03 with another strong run in the UEFA Cup, including a further notable scalp along the way, as the Parkhead men attempted to reach a second consecutive European final. After qualifying for the Champions League group stages, where they finished third behind Bayern Munich and Lyon, Celtic once again found themselves playing in the UEFA Cup beyond Christmas, when a routine victory over Czech side FK Teplice set up a meeting with Frank Rijkaard's Barcelona in March 2004. By then, the Catalan giants were arguably the form team in Europe, with the club's fortunes transformed behind the scenes by a dynamic young president, Joan Laporta, after the three years of stagnation and failure that had marked Joan Gaspart's disastrous regime at the Camp Nou.

With several key players missing for the first leg at Celtic Park, O'Neill deployed the energy and dynamism of youngsters

Stephen Pearson and Craig Beattie on the flanks against the Catalan side, who included such luminaries as Carles Puyol, Xavi and Ronaldinho in their line-up. Beattie, in fact, was making his first home start for Celtic, with his only previous experience of European football coming against the Lithuanian side FBK Kaunas in the Champions League qualifiers, and the manager was also forced to bring on 19-year-old goalkeeper David Marshall at half-time following a fracas in the tunnel as the players left the field, which saw Robert Douglas ordered off by German referee Wolfgang Stark. The same incident had also resulted in the dismissal of Barça's Brazilian-born Italian international midfielder Thiago Motta, and when Javier Saviola joined his team-mate in receiving a red card early in the second half, Celtic found themselves operating against their illustrious opponents with a one-man advantage. The only goal of the game then came when Petrov's cross was headed back across goal by Larsson, allowing Alan Thompson to volley the ball emphatically into the net to give Celtic a narrow first-leg lead.

Celtic Park was now gaining a reputation as a European fortress under O'Neill, with the Parkhead side having already notched up a 74-game unbeaten run at the venue by the time they added Barcelona to the roll call of impressive names to have left the east end of Glasgow with nothing. The list, since the completion of Fergus McCann's rebuilt stadium in the late 1990s, now included teams such as Juventus, Porto, Valencia, Celta Vigo and Lyon, alongside the Catalan giants. The second leg in the Camp Nou presented an altogether tougher assignment, however, with the Parkhead side's away record nowhere near as impressive as their home form, but a tremendous defensive display in Catalonia saw Celtic keep the home side at bay, despite O'Neill being forced to draft in another youngster, as 20-year-old John Kennedy made a telling contribution at the heart of central defence alongside Stanislav Varga in only his second European start for the club. Sadly for Kennedy, however, his career as a professional footballer would effectively be over by the end of the month, as just seven days later the defender suffered a horrendous knee injury after only 14 minutes of his full debut for Scotland, the result of a late, high tackle by Romania's Ioan Ganea.

The man of the match award in the Camp Nou, however, was reserved for Marshall, standing in for the suspended Douglas and making his first European start for the club, with the teenage goalkeeper, from as early as the second minute, making a series of increasingly astonishing saves to keep the scoreline blank and allowing Celtic to progress to the quarter-final. Perhaps inevitability, however, having eliminated the best team in the competition, Celtic came a cropper against a lesser side in the following round, losing 3-1 on aggregate to small-town club Villarreal and ensuring that the citizens of Gothenburg, whose Ullevi stadium was hosting the 2004 UEFA Cup Final, would not be treated to the same experience as the residents of Seville 12 months earlier.

Celtic won the league in 2004 by fully 17 points, but after relinquishing the title to Rangers on another dramatic final day in 2005, just as they had two years earlier, O'Neill left the Parkhead club, securing the Scottish Cup with a 1-0 win over Dundee United in his final match, to tend to his sick wife Geraldine, who was suffering from lymphoma. He was replaced by Gordon Strachan, the tenacious former Scotland international midfielder, who won consecutive league titles in his first three seasons at Celtic between 2006 and 2008, a feat not achieved by the Parkhead side since the days of Jock Stein.

Between 2009 and 2011, Rangers matched Strachan's accomplishment, taking three titles in a row under the returning Walter Smith, who had answered Murray's call following the Frenchman Paul Le Guen's short-lived reign of error at Ibrox in January 2007. By then, however, even the traditional power struggle for the supremacy of Scottish football had been overtaken by more significant events. The tawdry secret behind Rangers' success on the field had been laid bare, while, behind the scenes, the company's finances were now in such a desperate state that the imperilled Ibrox club was on course for oblivion.

10.

When the Sky Deal Fell In

IN July 2002, David Murray announced suddenly that he was stepping down from his position as chairman of Rangers Football Club, with his successor and deputy, vice-chairman John McClelland, set to take up the reins in charge of the Ibrox club with immediate effect. Murray would retain the title of honorary chairman as well as his 66 per cent majority shareholding in the company but, after almost 14 years at the helm of one of the country's most high-profile sporting institutions, his day-to-day involvement in the running of Rangers was now effectively over, at least for the time being.

Many explanations were cited for the possible reasons behind his decision to step back from a prominent role at the club, both from Murray himself, as well as from media commentators and former colleagues, although none sounded particularly convincing. There was the expected stuff from Murray about wanting to spend more time with his family, including his two upwardly mobile, 20-something sons, David and Keith, who were branching out on their own at the time, with his eldest boy heading up Charlotte Ventures, the private equity and investment arm of MIH, which controlled the group's non-core businesses. 'Young David is running a fund worth £25m – maybe I'll be able to spend more than two minutes discussing it with him without having to rush off to sort out some football player's contract,' the departing chairman suggested.

Murray also intimated that he just felt the time was right to take a break from it all and that he was looking forward to spending his Saturday afternoons doing something altogether more relaxing, such as shooting grouse on his Perthshire estate, for example, rather than submitting himself to the emotionally draining highs and lows that were inevitably involved in looking after the fortunes of a famous football team. Elsewhere, meanwhile, the general consensus seemed to accept that Murray's tactical retreat from front-line duties at Ibrox represented the ideal opportunity for a re-evaluation in the immediate priorities of the 50-year-old business, as former Ibrox vice-chairman Donald Findlay told *The Herald*, 'David has built up a very successful business, he has his estate in Perthshire, houses elsewhere and his private plane. But the time must come in life when you want to enjoy these things a bit. There's no point in working away all your life not to enjoy the fruits of your success.' The problem with this rather disingenuous soul-searching argument, about Murray simply fancying a change of emphasis in his lifestyle choices, was that it didn't seem to sit too well with known aspects of his personality, and the departing chairman was never able to fully shake off the notion that he was simply bailing out just as the going was getting tough, as Findlay admitted, 'David may find it difficult … He has always been very hands-on in everything he has done in life, so he will not find that easy.'

One issue that received very little attention or coverage in the press following the announcement of the chairman's departure was the increasingly perilous condition of the Ibrox club's finances, despite Murray hinting at a more realistic motive behind his decision to quit, when he conceded, 'Football is entering a very difficult period. The game is not going to be as expansive as it was and cutbacks and penny-pinching are not my style.' It was an effective admission that his Parkhead rival, Fergus McCann, the bungling fool who couldn't seem to do anything right during his time in charge of Celtic, had in fact been years ahead of him all along in his approach to running a football club. As a result of McCann's tightly controlled fiscal policies, unpopular though they often were at the time, the former Celtic chairman and managing director had left the Parkhead club well equipped to face the challenges of tougher economic times ahead, and although Celtic had accumulated debts since McCann sold up and returned to Canada, these liabilities were seen as manageable, and were in fact a short-term strategic necessity in order to try to compete on the field with Murray's prodigal club.

Rangers subsequently found themselves in the unfortunate position of being caught in a pincer movement, outflanked by their rivals both on and off the field; the Ibrox club no longer had the financial muscle to swat aside a Parkhead institution whose standing had been completely transformed behind the scenes by the actions of Fergus McCann, while at the same time they were coming up against a Celtic side that was led and inspired by a supremely talented coach in Martin O'Neill. In the circumstances, to make matters worse, Murray found that he was no longer able to produce any more rabbits from the hat, having scared off any potential new investors with his mishandling of ENIC's money and the cash generated from his spring 2000 share issue, which had seen Dave King buy into the club and take up a seat on the board, but ultimately lose another £20m to the chairman's profligacy. By 2002, with the club having lost a staggering £80m in their pursuit of domestic and European glory over the previous five years, Murray had brought the club to the brink of collapse, a position that led another of the chairman's colleagues, former director Hugh Adam, who had raised an estimated £18m for the club in the 1970s through the Rangers Pools, to admit for the first time in February 2002 that the possibility existed at some undetermined point in the future of an insolvency event at Ibrox. It was a prospect that Adam claimed Murray was ill-equipped to try to avert. 'He's not a businessman in the long-term sense of planning and prudence,' the former Ibrox director told *The Scotsman*. 'He's more of an impresario.'

Murray's decision to stand down had also been hastened by the retirement of his old friend at the bank, Gavin Masterton, following the HBOS merger in 2001 between the Halifax and the Bank of Scotland, a move that had come as a direct consequence of the financial crisis caused by the bursting of the dotcom bubble around the turn of the century. Masterton had loaned absolute fortunes to Scottish football clubs during his time with the Bank of Scotland before his eventual resignation as the bank's treasurer, a policy that in the harsher economic climate of the post-dotcom slump contributed to Murray's assessment of the new reality that was hitting Scottish football, when he observed in 2001, 'If you were to do a financial analysis on Scottish football as a business, it is basically bankrupt.' Surveying the traumatised landscape of the game in Scotland at the time, it was an assessment that was difficult to argue with.

Scottish football's financial predicament and the tensions created by the game's relatively impoverished condition had in recent years been an increasing cause of friction behind the scenes in the country's top division, between Murray's club and Celtic on the one hand, and some of the other chairmen of the smaller clubs in the SPL on the other. These squabbles and disagreements, which had been brewing away in the background for some time, finally came to a head in the months leading up to Murray's decision to stand down, when events on the field in Scottish football were overshadowed by the collapse of the proposed plans for SPL TV, as the game north of the border, already struggling, suffered a further serious financial setback.

The idea for a new subscription-based television channel dedicated to top-flight Scottish football was the brainchild of SPL chief executive Roger Mitchell, who seemed to have secured broad support for his initiative from the member clubs following the failure of the League to agree a new deal with their broadcast partner Sky, whose four-year contract to cover the SPL had come to an end. Many of the clubs felt that they were being short-changed by the Sky deal, valued at £45m over four years, which represented a relatively modest financial commitment by the broadcaster in comparison to its eye-watering levels of investment in both the Premier League and the lower divisions of the Football League in England, with Scottish football very much relegated to third place by the Rupert Murdoch-backed company.

In June 2000, Sky, by now the effective paymasters of the British game, had agreed a new £1.2bn deal to cover the Premier League between 2001 and 2004, a figure that, when compared to the SPL contract, was out of all proportion to the size of the market in the two countries, meaning that Scottish subscribers to the satellite provider were effectively subsidising the broadcaster's lavish funding of English football at their own game's expense. Sky had offered the SPL a new four-year deal, on terms that were roughly equivalent to the current contract, but despite Mitchell and his colleagues' own research suggesting that they could earn almost double what the broadcaster was currently paying, Sky, believing that they were operating in a buyers' market in which they could dictate the terms, refused to increase their bid. As a result, in December 2001, the SPL clubs turned their noses up at Sky's offer, branding it 'insulting' to the Scottish game, and walked away from the only deal on the table.

SPL TV was Mitchell's proposed solution, and it looked all set to happen in time for the new season, but with an 11 to 1 voting majority required to take the proposal forward, Celtic and Rangers combined in April 2002 to pull the plug on the idea. The Glasgow sides, between them, had initially been asking for a 40 per cent share of all revenue received from the proposed channel, but they had reduced their demand during the negotiations to one third. The other ten clubs in the division wanted them to accept a still smaller slice of the pie, leaving David Murray exasperated. 'The other clubs are all demanding that we reduce our claim to 28 per cent, while playing in 100 per cent of all televised games,' he complained. 'It's madness. We have lost Sky TV money, pay-per-view TV has come and gone and now every last penny of broadcasting money is about to vanish.' The Glasgow sides subsequently withdrew their support for the new channel idea, citing the high level of business risk involved and 'a lack of firm substantiation of the plan assumptions'. The executives of Celtic and Rangers, in other words, refused to believe that enough people would sign up for the channel, with Mitchell's plan based on a one-third uptake from all satellite TV subscribers in Scotland.

British Satellite Broadcasting, known as BSB, one of the merged partners in BSkyB, which was eventually rebranded as Sky, had been covering Scottish football since 1990, two years before they had bludgeoned their way into people's homes in the south by securing the first broadcasting rights deal with the new Premier League in England. But whereas the 'whole new ball game' Americanisation of the coverage of English football had been backed from year zero by colossal levels of investment, Sky quickly developed an altogether different attitude when it came to dealing with football north of the border. The pretext was simple and summed up by Andy Melvin, deputy managing director of Sky Sports, who claimed, 'People in Scotland love to watch English football. I'm not sure people in England love to watch Scottish football.' It was a disingenuous argument; Sky had invested billions in the English game, increasing the profile and reinvigorating the awareness and popularity of English football around the globe, while delivering a quality product by attracting some of the best players in the world to even some of the nation's more remote footballing outposts.

Clearly, nobody was suggesting that Scottish football could match its larger neighbour to the south pound for pound, but given the traditional levels of interest and support for the game in Scotland, there was the potential for growth in the game north of the border too. In particular, the reputed international appeal of the Old Firm fixture was something that was constantly trumpeted by Sky. A more appropriate offer for the television rights, which reflected the popularity and cultural significance of football in Scotland, would have been welcome, and almost certainly would have led to the development of the game and an increase in the standard and appeal of Scottish football, as former Sky Sports presenter Richard Keys, who was sacked by the broadcaster along with his sidekick Andy Gray in 2011, subsequently pointed out in an interview with the *Daily Record*: 'I don't buy into the theory they won't pay proper money for it [Scottish football] because it's not a very good product, because when we set up the Premier League in England it wasn't a very good product either.'

Sky's investment had transformed English football, whether for weal or for woe, but there was no way the broadcaster was going to show an equivalent level of commitment to the Scottish domestic game. Following the SPL's failure to agree a new deal with the company, Sky Sports' managing director, Vic Wakeling, took the unprecedented step of refusing to allow any references to Scottish football on the rolling news channel Sky Sports News, as Keys confirmed: 'The instruction was "Scottish football doesn't exist. Shut it down. We don't talk about it until they come back to the table on our terms."' To some, it seemed that Sky's manifest reluctance to treat Scottish football fairly was from the start a quasi-political decision, with the broadcaster clearly wary of the Scots' dogmatic regard for the game's plebeian heritage and its working-class roots, something which, over the years, the organisation had been instrumental in dragging English football away from. Ever since the game was first handed down from the public schoolboys and the university alumni teams of the mid-Victorian period to the clubs that sprung up in urban communities across the country, British football had been associated with the leftist ideals of shared identity and solidarity among working people, out to enjoy a bit of leisure time at the weekend, something which Sky, with its Tory boy presenters and its indulgence of the culture of the super-rich in football, quite apparently abhorred.

Sky's interest, it seemed, was in deliberately keeping the game north of the border weak, for strategic, political reasons, and while there were many genuine football fans in England, especially among those old enough to remember the pre-Sky years, who lamented the declining standards in Scottish club and international football in recent times as something of a sporting tragedy, there were also those who, for whatever reason, tended towards scorn and ridicule of the game in Scotland. A strong Scottish game might have been culturally powerful enough to provide an alternative, more traditional narrative to the course that football in Britain had taken in recent decades, but instead Sky was content, it appeared, to have Scottish football remain where it was, little more than an impoverished laughing stock in comparison to the riches available in England. As a result, it was generally the wind-up merchants and the mickey-takers down south, rather than the true supporters, who were getting what they desired from Sky's condescending coverage, and its lack of commitment and restrictive investment in the Scottish game.

Meanwhile, in a busy summer for Scottish football, the SPL now found itself in the horns of a dilemma as a result of the failed deal with Sky and the subsequent collapse of its intended replacement, SPL TV, with the very real possibility now looming that the League would be left without a broadcast partner for the 2002/03 season. In the end, however, an 11th-hour deal with the BBC, which allowed Gary Lineker and chums to travel north four times a year to cover the Old Firm fixture for a UK-wide terrestrial audience, ensured that Scottish football continued to be available to armchair viewers across the country. However, the contract, agreed jointly with the nascent Irish-based broadcaster Setanta and valued at £8m per annum over just two years, was worth barely two thirds of what Sky had initially put on the table. The decision of Celtic and Rangers to jointly reject the plan for SPL TV plunged Scottish football into chaos, with the other member clubs immediately signalling their intention to resign from the League, a threat that was carried out when ten letters of resignation were duly received by the SPL, days before the 2 August deadline, triggering the two-year notice period.

This left the Glasgow sides potentially isolated, faced with the amusing but unrealistic prospect of having no one to play but each other every week, and consequently rekindling speculation over the pair's quixotic plans for a lucrative relocation to the south, but the intention had always been to invite the two clubs back into a new league on terms set by the other ten members. Inevitably, there followed months of bitter recriminations and protracted negotiations over voting rights and the distribution of income, before the resignations were eventually withdrawn in January 2003, with a new 8-4 voting structure agreed. By then, Roger Mitchell had been forced to resign as the League's CEO and, with Scottish football apparently floundering in the mud, he wasn't replaced, as his executive duties passed to SPL chairman Lex Gold.

As a direct result of the collapsed proposal for SPL TV, Motherwell FC, in April 2002, were forced into administration. In a bid to establish themselves as the 'best of the rest', or perhaps even to challenge the Glasgow giants, the Lanarkshire club, since the arrival of owner John Boyle in 1998, had been following the Rangers model and overspending heroically on players such as former Scotland international goalkeeper Andy Goram, John Spencer, Rangers' pre-Maurice Johnston schoolboy Catholic, and former West Brom and Wolves centre-forward Don Goodman, racking up millions of pounds in debt each year before the inevitable crash-landing. Boyle blamed the economic downturn and the resulting reduction in income from gate receipts and corporate hospitality, as well as the demise of Motorola, the club's sponsor, for his decision to put the business up for sale, but he admitted that the collapse of the Sky TV deal and the subsequent failure of the proposal for an in-house television channel had been the tipping point.

As well as swingeing cuts to the non-playing staff, 19 players were immediately made redundant, with 'Well's Spanish midfielder Roberto Martínez lamenting, 'It's like business is just running all over football and that's hard to understand.' Others such as Andy Dow, having just seen his contract ripped up, were less equivocal, as the defender was left fuming by the owner's decision to trigger administration, telling the *Daily Record*, 'John Boyle has shafted every single one of us ... Now we are all out of a job at the very end of the season. And what chance do any of us have of getting a new club right away? I have two kids to support and have just bought a new house. I'm not going to have any income over the summer months.'

The experiment of appointing a former footballer to the role of chief executive had clearly failed, with Pat Nevin immediately resigning from the position, citing his disagreement with Boyle's decision to file for insolvency and his preference instead for a 'soft landing', involving a gradual reduction in the owner's investment. In December 2003, with the club still looking to exit the period of interim administration, former director John Swinburne described Nevin as 'the biggest culprit' in the whole affair, telling *The Scotsman*, 'He was awarding extended contracts to guys who were under-achievers. The result was that Motherwell ended up in huge debt and going nowhere. Our annual debt figure was £2m-£3m per annum, and rising. John

Boyle had no option but to put the club into administration and get things back on an even keel. The root cause was the ludicrous contracts given to players nearing the end of their careers. They were given seven or eight thousand pounds a week and three-year contracts. We could not afford it.' Nevin, for his part, maintained that Boyle was aware of the risks from the start and that he had nevertheless agreed the strategy and given the green light to the overspending.

After the departure of manager Eric Black, who immediately resigned along with Nevin, his assistant Terry Butcher took charge of the struggling club and handed an opportunity to an emerging group of youngsters, including Steven Hammell, Stephen Pearson and David Clarkson, all of whom went on to play for Scotland, as well as James McFadden, who became the Tartan Army's talisman and scored 15 international goals, a total that has been surpassed only by Kenny Miller in recent years. After a relegation reprieve in 2003, when Motherwell finished in last place but were spared demotion due to the failure of First Division champions Falkirk to meet the SPL's stadium grading criteria, which required all top-flight grounds to be able to seat a minimum of 10,000 spectators, the Fir Park club finished in the top six group of clubs in 2004 and 2005, a feat that they had previously been unable to achieve under Boyle's stewardship since the introduction of the end-of-season league split in 2000.

Over the next few years, a number of other Scottish clubs followed Motherwell into administration, or worse, such as Dundee, who under the management of the enigmatic Bonetti brothers brought Caniggia and Ravanelli to Tayside, as well as the former Celtic international midfielder Craig Burley, but the spending was unsustainable and the club eventually gave up the ghost, filing for insolvency in November 2003. Partick Thistle boss Gerry Collins described the Dens Park club as 'cheats', after they spent beyond their means and then simply went into administration when it suited them in order to cut costs and shed the unwanted baggage, while most of their rivals were still playing by the rules and trying to balance their books, despite their evidently meagre circumstances.

Others to feel the effects of the financial ill-wind blowing through Scottish football included Airdrieonians (liquidated, before reforming as Airdrie United after taking the place of another liquidated club, Clydebank, in 2002), Dundee United (supported by soft loans from rich shareholders), Aberdeen (almost ruined by their reliance on expensive foreigners before changing tack and starting again with Scottish youngsters), Livingston (only formed in 1995 but in administration by 2004 and demoted to the bottom division in 2009 for another breach of insolvency rules), Dundee (again, suffering a second insolvency event in October 2010 and consequently being deducted 25 points), Hearts (selling out to an eccentric Lithuanian banker before finally going into administration in 2013), Gretna (a meteoric rise through the divisions was followed by an equally catastrophic collapse after owner and backer Brooks Mileson became ill in 2008), Dunfermline (entered administration in 2013, with majority shareholder and former banker Gavin Masterton eventually declared bankrupt) and of course Rangers, the architects of the culture of overspending in Scottish football, who were eventually liquidated in 2012, owing tens of millions to the tax authorities as well as to hundreds of other creditors.

Ibrox chairman David Murray was undoubtedly at the epicentre of the financial earthquake afflicting the Scottish game over this period, but he tried to deflect the focus from Rangers and his alternative business practices at the club, with his 'basically bankrupt' remarks, spreading the blame around the other clubs for the financial insanity that had gripped the Scottish game. Certainly, the problem seemed to be, more generally, that there were too many people in positions of responsibility at long-cherished Scottish football clubs, who in the expectation of popular acclaim, were gullibly following the Murray agenda. With the media howling them on from the sidelines, slaughtering any directors in the Fergus McCann mould who showed the slightest inclination towards responsible custodianship as penny-pinching cheapskates only out to fleece the fans and make money for themselves, it's hardly surprising that certain owners and chairmen allowed their ambitions to override all sense of caution, leading to the inevitable consequences once economic reality eventually took hold.

In among the financial carnage, Scottish football appeared to have lost almost an entire generation of footballers of international quality, with the cut-off point seemingly apparent from the last Scotland squad to qualify for a major tournament, the World Cup of 1998 in France. Of manager Craig Brown's 22-man selection for the competition, Gallacher, Hendry, Collins, Jackson, Boyd, Calderwood, Lambert, Durie, McKinlay T, McKinlay W and Whyte were all born in the mid to late 1960s, as were Englishmen Elliott and Gould. Londoner Sullivan was a child of the early 1970s, as were Booth, Weir, Burley, Gemmill and McNamara, but even from that group, the latter three were from footballing families and may well have emerged in any era. From there, things tail off very quickly and there are very few international-class Scottish footballers down to the Darren Fletcher, James McFadden group, born in the mid-1980s, many of whom, including McFadden, only emerged once the mercenaries and other chancers at clubs such as Motherwell had been cleared out of the way.

The country of Baxter, Law, Johnstone and Dalglish produced only one real international footballer of note who was born in the fallow period between the early 1970s and mid-1980s, namely Barry Ferguson (born February 1978), another player who came from a footballing family and might well have come to prominence during any time period. Adding to these players who were schooled at home, Simon Donnelly and Christian Dailly can be included, who both went to France, as well as internationals Neil McCann (born August 1974), Gary Naysmith (November 1978), Kenny Miller (December 1979) and maybe one or two others, although few would argue that such a bunch constituted a golden generation.

After the Motherwell fiasco, however, the penny seemed to drop at clubs such as Aberdeen, who began to introduce and develop young Scottish talent under the Dane Ebbe Skovdahl, and Hibernian, where an extraordinary batch of youngsters were nurtured through their ranks, first under Bobby Williamson, then by Tony Mowbray, including future internationals Gary Caldwell (born April 1982), Gary O'Connor (May 1983) and Scott Brown (June 1985). Darren Fletcher (February 1984) was taken to England as a youngster by Alex Ferguson, who after conferring the 'class of 92' on the English and Welsh international teams, was determined to bequeath a genuine Manchester United player to the Scottish game, after trying and failing with Michael Stewart.

Players were emerging at other clubs too, although the problem seemed to be that the better individuals would ultimately end up at Celtic and Rangers, or because the league was so destitute, they would be snapped up by lower division English clubs, where they could earn comparative fortunes and where they were largely forgotten about. Later in the decade, in 2006, a group of Scottish youngsters managed by Archie Gemmill reached the final of the U19 European Championships, where they lost narrowly to a Spain side that included players such as Gerard Piqué and Juan Mata. However, having had a sniff of success, the same group embarrassed themselves at the U20 World Cup in Canada the following year, and only Steven Fletcher (March 1987) and Robert Snodgrass (September 1987) went on to enjoy notable success.

It's notoriously difficult to ascribe any sort of national narrative to the fluctuating fortunes of a country's international football team, but it seemed undeniably the case in Scotland that the emergence of the culture of showy over-expenditure in the game, combined, perversely, with a startling lack of real money, coincided with the inversely proportional and tragic decline in the overall quality and standard of play. Of all the countries to emulate or be influenced by, the example of England, with Sky implementing its transformation of the game south of the border, was probably the least appropriate model that could have been applied to Scottish football, both because of the traditional rivalry and defiance towards English methods that had served Scotland so well over many years, but also, more importantly, because the source of the strength of the game in England was now money, the one commodity that was conspicuously lacking in Scotland. Scottish football had lost its defiance, its traditional strength, and in its place it appeared that the game north of the border had now become all about its greatest weakness.

11.

Fade to Whyte

B Y January 2004, 18 months after announcing his resignation as Rangers' chairman, David Murray felt compelled to emerge from his self-imposed exile and respond to a new wave of criticism directed at him over the way he had run the Ibrox club's affairs, which was coming chiefly from the newly constituted body, the Rangers Supporters Trust. The fans group were unhappy about the mounting debt, which was now in the public domain and being regularly cited as the reason behind the stringent cutbacks at the club, but more significantly, despite winning the Treble in 2003, the supporters were also upset with the team's performances on the field, as season 2003/04 was already unfolding as a barren year for Rangers.

The Ibrox side had finished bottom of their Champions League section and soon found themselves effectively out of contention for the league title by the time of a 3-0 New Year defeat at Celtic Park, a result that left the team 11 points behind their rivals, with a trophy-less campaign confirmed for McLeish's side when they were also beaten by the Parkhead men in the quarter-finals of the Scottish Cup in March. Perhaps betraying an oversensitivity towards criticism for which he had already become notorious, the *in absentia* former chairman eventually reappeared and spoke to the media, vigorously defending his record at Rangers and seeking to spread around the blame for any admitted mistakes.

In particular, Murray responded to accusations that some of his subsidiary businesses, including the direct marketing company Response Handling, Azure Catering and the IT consultancy firm Carnegie Information Systems, which were all owned by Charlotte Ventures as part of the wider Murray Group, still had their fingers in the pie at Rangers, and were taking money out of the club. 'I'm the major shareholder of Rangers so why on earth would I try to take advantage of the club?' Murray retaliated. 'I'm disappointed I have to answer a question like this but if it helps the fans understand then I'm happy to do it. I've been with Rangers for over 15 years and I have never taken a penny out of the club,' he affirmed.

It was this latter claim that in time would be called into question, after the list of beneficiaries from Murray's EBT tax avoidance scheme at Rangers became public in 2012. Only then was it revealed that the chairman had personally requested more money from the trust than any other individual, including some of his best-paid players and managers, with the owner found to have plundered a total of £6.3m in tax-free income from the scheme during his time at the club, apparently for his own ends. Regardless of his customary bombast, however, Murray couldn't really offer the disgruntled supporters anything substantial, admitting that he had been reluctant to pop his head above the parapet once more and sticking to his line about how he had had enough of it all. 'The last round of interviews, I didn't really enjoy,' he confessed some time later. 'Everybody's got a shelf life and I don't want to end up like Doug Ellis or Ken Bates, old fogeys in their 70s still running clubs. I want to enjoy my life.'

The grumbles from supporters caused by the team's poor form on the field were understandable and predictable, given the unhealthy sense of entitlement that the fans often betrayed. More worrying for those concerned with Rangers' future wellbeing, however, were the losses that the business was still accumulating and the lack of improvement in the precarious financial predicament at Ibrox, even in the face of the downsizing measures that chairman McClelland had belatedly introduced. Throughout the period of Murray's absence, Rangers had continued to sink deeper and inexorably into the red, with the club somehow contriving to lose £30m in 2003, pushing the debt figure up to £68m, an unsustainable number for a company of Rangers' size. Worse was to follow in 2004 when the liabilities in the balance sheet peaked at £74.9m, a figure that, by anyone's calculations, was very close to the value of the business, a sobering reality that left McClelland and Rangers frantically trying to re-evaluate the net worth of the company's tangible assets, chiefly the stadium and training complex, so that the club would not be declared technically insolvent.

Legacy issues from Murray's time at the club were hampering McClelland's efforts, with the problem rather neatly summed up by the De Boer twins, as Frank joined his brother Ronald at Ibrox on a six-month deal in January 2004 following his release by Galatasaray; Ronald was still earning the weekly sum of £35,000 from his four-year Ibrox contract, which dated back to Dick Advocaat's extravagant Champions League-chasing days at the club, whereas his brother Frank, another big name in world football who had earned 125 caps for the Netherlands, was picking up a comparatively modest £5,000 per week during the austerity-hit McLeish era for doing more or less the same job.

With no end in sight to the club's financial problems, Murray eventually returned to a hands-on role at Rangers in September 2004, after McLeish's side had failed to capitalise on the potential availability of an extra place in the Champions League group stages for the SPL runners-up by losing to CSKA Moscow in a play-off and missing out on an estimated £8m in revenue that qualification for UEFA's flagship competition would have brought. Murray's solution to the crisis in the balance sheet was to offer a rights issue, in which existing stakeholders and other interested parties would be allowed to invest in newly issued shares in the company. Before he could return to his previous role at the club, however, the once and future chairman first had to buy out ENIC, who were unwilling to see the value of their stock further diluted by the rights issue, so Murray paid £8.7m for the shares that had been acquired by Joe Lewis's company for £40m back in 1997, taking his total ownership of Rangers up to almost 92 per cent of the total holdings, further eroding the influence of the club's small shareholders. The returning chairman, who resumed his position on 1 September 2004, hoped to raise up to £57m through the issue of new shares, but in the end only just over £1m was taken up by outside investors and existing shareholders, meaning that the underwriters, Rangers' parent company MIH, had to make up most of the not inconsiderable shortfall.

Murray had wiped out a significant chunk of Rangers' debt, but he had only achieved it by moving over £50m from other, less toxic areas of his business, an outcome that left the club's bankers happy in the short term, but which was only storing up future problems for MIH, the cornerstone of Murray's entire business empire and an organisation that was also now living on borrowed time. HBOS in fact, yet another firm associated with Rangers with a short and bleak future ahead of it, agreed to restructure the remaining £23m of Rangers' debt, rolling over the sum into a new financial product and agreeing to provide further capital for the club's day-to-day overheads. These 'rollovers' would come back to haunt HBOS within a few years, as during the financial crisis, or 'credit crunch' of 2008, the bank was found to have exposed itself to an unsustainable level of toxic debt, meaning that it couldn't continue trading in its present form. Only a merger, hastily completed on 17 September 2008, with former competitors Lloyds TSB, a less recklessly exposed and better capitalised bank, funded at an extortionate cost to the UK taxpayer, prevented the bank from collapsing entirely.

As an indication of how volatile and unstable the previously sedate world of banking and high finance had become by the time of the credit crunch, the tie-up of two organisations, who were themselves the offspring of recent mergers, resulted in the creation of a single, giant financial institution, where, in the middle of the previous decade, five separate banks had once existed – Lloyds/TSB/Cheltenham & Gloucester/Halifax/ Bank of Scotland – with the new organisation, known as Lloyds Banking Group, holding a combined 28 per cent of the UK mortgage market, far more than would normally be allowed under competition law.

In an article on his blog entitled 'The Worst Bank in the World? HBOS's Calamitous Seven-Year Life', financial journalist Ian Fraser, who wrote the book on Rangers supporter Fred Goodwin's disastrous chairmanship of the Royal Bank of Scotland, summed up the short seven-year period of HBOS's existence, pointing out the catastrophic mismanagement that had been at the heart of the bank's ruinously short lifespan: 'At worst, the bank was dangerously out of control and riddled with fraud and alleged criminality, having been pump-primed by its management to deliver maximum short-term profits, growth and maximum rewards for executives, irrespective of whether its lending was reckless or whether the bank had a chance of surviving long-term – or whether its shareholders, creditors, depositors, customers and staff got burned. Throughout the bank's calamitous seven-year life, the Financial Services Authority (FSA) and other authorities, for the most part, turned a blind eye or even sought to cover up the bank's blatant wrongdoing and recklessness.' It was a damning indictment of the cultural flaws at the heart of the organisation and an assessment that could, in certain aspects, just as easily have been applied to Murray's stewardship of Rangers.

The credit crunch hit Rangers hard, chiefly because, unforgivably, having brought the debt down to a more sustainable level, thanks to the rights issue and a lucrative run to the last 16 of the Champions League in 2005/06, the recklessness and extravagance for which the Ibrox club had earlier become synonymous returned during the second coming of manager Walter Smith, who was reinstated to his former role at Ibrox after the brief experiment with Frenchman Paul Le Guen in the job came to an abrupt end in January 2007. It seems that Smith was either unaware or unconcerned about the new financial reality at Rangers, as by the end of the summer transfer window, the returning manager had splashed out relative fortunes on a total of 18 players, including David Weir, Ugo Ehiogu, Kevin Thomson, DaMarcus Beasley, Steven Whittaker, Lee McCulloch, Carlos Cuéllar, Daniel Cousin and Steven Naismith, none of whom came cheap.

By the end of the following summer, despite being knocked out of the UEFA Cup at the first hurdle by Lithuanian minnows FBK Kaunas, Smith had also added, at further great cost to the club, Kenny Miller, Andrius Velička, Madjid Bougherra, Kyle Lafferty, Pedro Mendes, Maurice Edu, Andy Webster and Steven Davis. It was almost like the good old days at Ibrox once again, but on this occasion the party was short-lived, as following the collapse of HBOS and the subsequent acquisition by Lloyds TSB, the fun would soon be over for free-spending Rangers.

In October 2009, the club's new bankers appointed company man Donald Muir to the Rangers board with a remit to keep a watchful eye on the financial affairs at Ibrox and, if possible, with David Murray already indicating his eagerness to sell up, to facilitate a change of ownership at the club. As part of the merger process with HBOS, Lloyds had also taken on the historic debt, a figure that, since Smith's return to Ibrox, had climbed back up to £30m, thanks to the increased number of player acquisitions and the trebling of the club's wage bill. Lloyds immediately made every member of Smith's squad available for transfer, but given the inflated wages at Ibrox, which other clubs were reluctant to match, in the end most of the players couldn't be sold.

Rangers enjoyed a terrific run in the UEFA Cup in season 2007/08, however, reaching the final and matching Celtic's achievement of five years previously, although the club's financial situation was only modestly improved by the success of making it through to the showpiece in Manchester, where they lost to Dick Advocaat's Zenit St Petersburg, due to the extraordinary mega-bonuses that were paid to the players with each round of progression. Nevertheless, by winning the league in three consecutive seasons, Rangers were able to benefit from direct entry into the Champions League group stages, which was perhaps the strategy all along, and the subsequent financial windfall that came with qualification, along with the austerity measures put in place by the bank, allowed the debt figure to come down to £18m by the time the club was eventually sold in May 2011.

By then, two significant changes had occurred in the life of David Murray; firstly the industrialist had been knighted in the 2007 New Year's honours list for 'services to business', although it seems unlikely that the Queen realised, when she tapped Murray on the shoulder with her ceremonial sword, just how much money his companies still owed her. At the time, HMRC were being frustrated in their inquiry into Rangers' covert use of the EBT tax avoidance scheme, which allowed the club to buy and retain players who they would otherwise have been unable to afford, by the refusal of the club's management to cooperate with the investigation, with Rangers' oily CEO, Martin Bain, instead continuing to issue denials and withholding evidence from the revenue service.

Secondly, in August 2009, Murray had stepped down once again from his role as Rangers' chairman, leaving the club for good this time and being replaced by Alastair Johnston, a 61-year-old accountant and sports management executive, who had been a non-executive director at Ibrox since February 2004. Ruling out another potential comeback somewhere down the line and emphasising the finality of his decision on this occasion, following his earlier departure in 2002, Murray again reiterated his previous statements about wanting to concentrate on other things, both personal and professional, free from the disproportionate demands on his time and attention that

Rangers had been taking up, and he stressed that the club's conscientious new bankers, Lloyds, hadn't influenced his resolve to quit in any way.

Manager Walter Smith paid tribute to Murray on his resignation, admitting that he owed his career as a top-level coach to the long-serving chairman, who had promoted him to the manager's office at Ibrox in 1991 after the unexpected departure of Graeme Souness to Liverpool. 'I had no track record as a manager and he could have gone for someone with a track record behind them,' Smith emphasised. 'He took a chance on me, gave me an opportunity to get into management, the opportunity I wanted, which could not have been an easy decision to make … There was no guarantee of a job here at that stage. Maybe I would be back in my old job at Dalmarnock power station now if I had not been kept on.'

Smith also pointed to the number of trophies that had been won under Murray's stewardship, but the club's fans were more ambivalent about his time at Rangers, and for all the praise and adulation that had come his way during the nine-in-a-row years of the 1990s, the latter stages of Murray's tenure at Ibrox had seen an increasing number of protests and voices of opposition being expressed against the chairman, with a section of the crowd unveiling a 'David Murray Must Go' banner during a home game against St Johnstone in the Scottish Cup in January 2009. Betraying that sense of entitlement again, the fans had also launched a 'We Deserve Better' campaign around this time, with one spokesman complaining, 'At the end of the day Rangers FC is a business. There is no other business in the world that would receive such a high level of complaints from their customers and then ignore them … This campaign has struck a chord with ordinary Rangers fans who are fed up with the club accepting second best all the time. It's not the way Rangers fans were brought up.'

Smith countered, showing an admirable sense of loyalty, by dismissing the criticism that had been directed towards his now former boss, when he noted, 'The campaign we saw last year is maybe indicative of what Rangers is all about; it doesn't really matter what you do for a lot of people, that will not be good enough.' In the end, though, the fans were right to feel concerned over the situation at the club and the way Rangers was being run as a business, and vindication over at least some of their grievances would soon arrive when the full effects of the seeds of destruction that Murray had sown during his time at Ibrox were eventually exposed.

Meanwhile, a few months before Murray's final farewell at Ibrox, the financial woes for Scottish football had been exacerbated by the collapse of the SPL's broadcast partner Setanta in June 2009. The Irish network had been covering Scottish football since the failure of the League's proposal for an in-house television channel in 2002, acquiring the rights exclusively in 2004, and with the contract up for renewal in 2010, the SPL had moved early to agree a new deal with the company, which would earn the League £31.25m per season, a considerable increase on the current £13.5m and potentially the most lucrative television deal in the history of Scottish football.

With Setanta ready to invest and show their commitment to the Scottish game, it looked as if football in Scotland would at last be offered the kind of financial package that it deserved, but a year before the contract could kick in, the broadcaster's UK operation folded, allowing the League's former partners, Anglocentric merry-andrews Sky, to pick up the rights to cover the SPL once more and rejoin Scottish football's meagre party, in partnership with the Disney-owned channel ESPN. Sky's schedules were already crammed full of English football, so instead of a bidding war with ESPN, the two firms agreed to table a joint take-it-or-leave-it offer to the now desperate Scottish League, dividing the 60-game timetable equally between their organisations. The combined bid was worth just £13m per season over five years, less even than the value of Setanta's current contract, but in the absence of any other offer, and with a new season fast approaching, the SPL's executives bit the broadcasters' hands off and took what they were being offered.

In February, Setanta had lost out in the latest round of bidding for the rights to show the EPL, winning only one of the six 23-game packages that were available, compared to Sky's five. Ever since the European Commission introduced competition laws in 2005, ending Sky's monopoly of Premier League coverage, bids were invited for these bundles of matches from other broadcasters, with Setanta currently owning the rights to two of the six packages and showing 46 EPL games per season. The loss of the second package, however, meant that their schedule was now reduced to a total of only 23 matches and, as a result, Setanta couldn't pick up enough subscribers in England. The company's UK operation quickly became insolvent, defaulting on their payments to both the English and Scottish Premier Leagues and subsequently going off the air, meaning that Sky, who paid a total of £1.62bn for their five EPL packages, had once again contributed, albeit indirectly, to the further impoverishment of the Scottish game.

Although buffered by the same financial ill-winds that were blowing through the rest of the domestic game in Scotland, Celtic's position proved to be more robust than many of their rivals, and Rangers in particular, in the face of the economic and commercial turmoil that was afflicting Scottish football at this time. Despite the increasing problems in the environment in which they were operating, the integrity of the Parkhead company was never seriously threatened, due to the sustainability and strength of their revised business plan, which had been put in place by the club earlier in the decade following a brief, free-spending era during the early years of Martin O'Neill's time as manager at Parkhead. By 2003, Celtic had run up considerable liabilities, roughly £20m, since the days of Fergus McCann, who had left the club in a debt-free position in April 1999, but the shortfall had been made up by further rights issues, offering more shares in the club to the public and to the existing investors. The subsequent uptake had allowed Celtic to splash out on the kind of transfer fees and players' wages that had helped O'Neill's side to topple Rangers from their previously unchallenged perch at the summit of Scottish football, but the cost was considerable and the Celtic board eventually decided that a change of policy was required.

Since McCann's departure, the Parkhead side had enjoyed considerable on-field success, but the directors concluded that the cycle of debt and the accumulating losses in the balance sheet were not sustainable, with Celtic running at a deficit even in season 2002/03 when the club had profited from its extraordinary run to the UEFA Cup Final in Seville. Accordingly, chairman Brian Quinn held an impromptu meeting of the plc board in a hotel in Donetsk following a 3-0 Champions League defeat to Ukrainian champions Shakhtar in October 2004. Quinn put it to the other directors, including majority shareholder Dermot Desmond and new chief executive Peter Lawwell, that the present situation couldn't continue indefinitely and that it was necessary for the club to take immediate steps in order to reduce costs. Commenting on the need for a change of policy at the club, Quinn observed, 'When you raise money from shareholders it should be for capital expenditure, such as building a training ground and improving the scouting structure ... We cannot keep going back to shareholders to cover current expenses.'

Celtic eventually finished bottom of their Champions League section that season in an admittedly difficult group, which also contained Barcelona and AC Milan. The squad was ageing, with many players edging past the peaks of their careers, having been lured to Celtic or retained by the Parkhead club on wages that were competitive with the going rate in the EPL. As a consequence, despite participation in three Champions League group stages during O'Neill's time as coach in addition to the UEFA Cup campaign in 2003, the club was still haemorrhaging cash far more quickly than it was being earned. Quinn's new strategy, which was approved by the board, involved going after younger, fresher, largely undiscovered talent and offering these scouted players a lower basic wage, which would then be supplemented by larger bonuses for success on the field. The Parkhead side's new recruits could then either be retained and developed by the club, perhaps spending much of their careers at Celtic on manageable wages, or sold at a profit to teams operating in a more affluent footballing environment.

A key feature of the new strategy was that Celtic had to be economically self-sufficient, with the club setting out to spend no more than it earned over the financial year, balancing the books and trusting that the strength of the business model would yield sustainable sporting success over the longer term. Rather than simply relying on the power of the chequebook, the new policy, if it was to work properly, also depended on the talents of the individuals behind the scenes at the club, with particular need for scouts and coaches who were capable of successfully implementing the strategy by identifying and developing the right type of player. At times the new fiscal restraints were so tight that they attracted criticism from the club's fans, but overall they were successful, both on and off the field, with any complaints from supporters generally drowned out by the frequent celebrations of success and the *schadenfreude*, richly enjoyed, over the eventual fate of their less provident rivals on the other side of the city.

It was a consequential decision that Quinn had taken on behalf of Celtic, in conjunction with the other directors, because it ultimately cost the club their high-flying coach, Martin O'Neill, who had been the chief architect of his team's extraordinary rise to the summit of the Scottish game in the early 2000s and the reversal in the fortunes of the two Glasgow teams on the field. O'Neill initially agreed to stay on and oversee the change of policy, but with his wife Geraldine suffering from lymphoma, he took the decision in the spring of 2005 that he could no longer continue dealing with important family matters while facing up to the arduous task of trying to keep Celtic ahead of the pack on a reduced budget. O'Neill was subsequently replaced in the summer by Gordon Strachan, who was more amenable to the club's new business model and who surpassed his predecessor by winning three consecutive titles, but in reality Celtic would never again be able to assemble such a strong squad of players as they had in the peak years of O'Neill's time at the club.

Despite some of the criticisms over the club's perceived parsimony, which on occasion may have been justified, particularly in regard to the board's apparent reluctance to expand when successful – a sound principle of business – the new strategy proved to be an insightful and courageous step forward. It allowed Celtic to remain competitive on the field while effectively downsizing, and the policy of buying players at the comparatively cheaper end of the market and then selling them at a profit continues to this day to be the basis of the club's operational model, as shown by such recent examples as Ki Sung-yueng, Victor Wanyama and Virgil van Dijk.

Celtic's trophy glut during this period of self-imposed stabilisation was all the more remarkable because of Rangers' use of the EBT tax avoidance scheme, the controversial trust payment system implemented by David Murray in order to meet the financial demands of dozens of the club's players during the 2000s, which finally came to light in April 2010. The revelations showed that for years the Ibrox organisation, in the hope of reducing the club's costs by slashing the overall tax bill, had been inducing a large number of its employees, including many of its most highly paid footballers, to sign up to the scheme and receive a portion of their pay through this alternative method of remuneration. In total, roughly £47m in untaxed income had been plundered from the EBT scheme over the course of a decade or more, allowing Rangers, at a time of almost unrelenting hardship for the Scottish game, to buy and retain players who would otherwise have been beyond the budget of the financially stricken club.

The EBTs were administered through an offshore trust, called the Murray Group Management Limited Remuneration Trust, set up by Rangers' parent company Murray International Holdings. As part of their pay, employees were then able to apply for a notional loan from the trust through their individual sub-trusts, an arrangement that later allowed Murray and Rangers to argue in court that these payments were non-contractual and discretionary, and therefore not subject to income tax. The letters that secured the money from the trust always carefully and politely acknowledged that the beneficiary would not, in legal terminology, 'fetter the discretion of the trustees' and would abide by their fiduciary decision over whether to release the cash. In all cases, however, the sums were paid to the players in accordance with the terms that Rangers had offered them, and it soon became clear that these so-called loans were never intended to be paid back.

In addition, it also soon came to light that another potential problem for the Ibrox club had arisen over the way the scheme was being implemented. A BBC Scotland documentary, *Rangers – The Men Who Sold The Jerseys*, broadcast in May 2012, revealed that, in the case of a majority of the beneficiaries, the extra income provided by the trust had been guaranteed through secretive side-letters, in effect a second contract, which promised large sums of tax-free earnings – not loans – to dozens of Rangers players in addition to their standard wage. The scheme therefore appeared to fall foul of both SFA regulations, which stipulate that all earnings from football must be declared in the relevant paperwork submitted to the governing body with a player's registration, and the revenue service, HMRC, who viewed the sums paid out to players through the trust payment scheme as 'disguised remuneration' and therefore taxable income.

The EBT scheme, which was originally established as a provision to allow companies to aid their employees through finite periods of hardship – not to pay tax-free lump sums to millionaire footballers – was being misused by Rangers in a way that seemed to leave the Ibrox organisation open to accusations of both tax evasion and financial doping. At the very least,

Rangers were treading a thin line between tax avoidance, which is legal but immoral, and tax evasion, which is both immoral and illegal. Following the public revelations that the case was going to court, Murray eventually made the not unreasonable decision to take the club off the market. The former chairman had been trying to sell his majority shareholding in Rangers since 2006, but with the dispute over HMRC's assessment against the club set to begin at the First-tier Tribunal in Edinburgh in October 2010 it now seemed extremely unlikely that any credible party with an interest in acquiring the club would come forward while such potentially toxic liabilities were hanging over Ibrox like the mythical Sword of Damocles.

HMRC were claiming roughly £50m from Rangers in unpaid taxes, including penalties and interest, and with the debt to Lloyds bank still outstanding and running to tens of millions of pounds, the club was facing an existential threat to its viable continuation as a going concern. So desperate was Murray to offload the club, of which he had been the owner and majority shareholder since his £6m purchase in November 1988 and chairman of the board for most of that time, that he was taking meetings and sharing information with virtually any interested party. The media had reported in late 2010 that the club was up for sale at a price of £30m, but in the end, in May 2011, the former chairman accepted the sum of £1 – a quid – for his shares in the club from a certain Craig Whyte. It was Murray's final and perhaps his most heinous act of folly before he ultimately disentangled himself from Rangers for good.

Whyte was an ambitious young entrepreneur, but he was never destined for greatness in life. He had dreamed of making money since he was a boy and had successfully dabbled in the stock market as a teenager, but he seemed to lack the hardheadedness so often associated with the most acquisitive capitalists and, after leaving school at 15 and setting up his own plant hire company, by his mid-30s he had left a trail of failed and aborted business ventures behind him. The Motherwell-born businessman had even been disqualified from operating as a company director for seven years during his haphazard career and his approach to meeting his obligations to the tax authorities appeared even more grudging and half-hearted than Murray's, when he stated in his autobiography, *Into the Bear Pit*, published in February 2020, 'My view on tax is that transactions between people should be voluntary, and that goes for the government as well. Tax havens are completely moral as they stop governments from stealing your money. Governments are basically shakedown operations, like the mafia, but with better manners. They are parasites with no morals whatsoever.' Nowhere in his book did Whyte suggest an alternative means of raising money for schools, hospitals, other public services or Her Majesty's Armed Forces, all of whom, in their desperate desire to stay ahead of their rivals, Rangers were ultimately found to have been cheating for years.

David Murray couldn't believe his luck when he learned of Whyte's interest in gaining control of Rangers. With the club imploding and about to go to the wall on his watch, it appeared that the former chairman had found someone foolish enough to take on the role of the patsy and remove the burden of responsibility from his shoulders, allowing Murray, just in the nick of time it seemed, to jump ship and escape the looming crisis. Perhaps Murray saw something of himself in Whyte, who was of a similar age to the former chairman at the time of his 1988 takeover and, like Murray, Whyte had harboured ambitions of becoming a tycoon since his youth. Regardless, after 22 years of acting and behaving like the club's sovereign, dealing with the media and other parties as a king handles his ministers, Murray handed Rangers over to Whyte for the princely amount of one pound and then headed for the hills.

The club's takeover advisory, or vetting, committee, formed from board members and senior officials, warned Murray not to sell his shares to Whyte. Curiously, they also tried to fob off the prospective purchaser, with Whyte suspecting that some of the incumbent directors such as Dave King, Paul Murray and Alastair Johnston were trying to gain a controlling interest in the club themselves, possibly in a post-administration or post-liquidation scenario, when the business would be clear of its debts. Still holding an 85 per cent stake in the company, however, Murray was able to effectively ignore the entreaties of the vetting committee, who were representing the club's 27,000 small shareholders, with the former chairman claiming in the end that it was 'too late' to prevent the transaction going through and Whyte acquired the club in time to see Rangers clinch their third consecutive league championship with a 5-1 win over Kilmarnock at Rugby Park on the last day of the season.

It was a time of celebration and relief around Ibrox, as the club held off a close challenge from Neil Lennon's Celtic to retain the title and, with veteran manager Walter Smith stepping down, it was an opportunity to savour the long-serving boss's contribution to the Rangers cause as well as to anoint his successor, Ally McCoist, while the club looked forward to a new era under both new management and new ownership. Whyte appeared keen to stress that, under his regime, the profligate days of Murray's earlier stewardship of the club would be a thing of the past, with Rangers now expected to embrace a new future while conducting its affairs in a more prudent and sustainable manner. Indicating the need for a change of strategy at the club, Whyte announced, 'Rangers costs approximately £45m per year to operate and commands around £35m in revenue. From the outset, I have made it clear that I do not think it is in the best interest of Rangers to throw good money after bad. Against a backdrop of falling revenue, costs have to be cut significantly.'

Under pressure from McCoist, however, one of the new owner's first acts over the close season, rather than attempt to bring down the wage bill at the club, was to sanction lucrative contract extensions for seven players, including high earners Allan McGregor, Steven Davis and Steven Whittaker. Despite the obviously precarious conditions under which the club was now operating, these lavish new deals appeared to represent a return to the extravagant spending under Smith and Murray during the pre-credit crunch era, which had seen the club's debts soar back up towards the £30m mark. It was now imperative, purely in order to balance the books, that McCoist's side should qualify for the group stages of the Champions League and bring some much-needed prize money from UEFA into the club but standing in their way in the first knockout round were the experienced Swedish champions Malmö.

Rangers' prospects of advancement looked doomed when the Swedes emerged from the first leg at Ibrox with a 1-0 lead, with the only goal of the game scored by Daniel Larsson, after the forward capitalised on an individual error from the newly re-signed Whittaker, who had lost possession of the ball inside his own penalty box. The situation soon appeared irretrievable early in the second leg at the Swedbank Stadium when Whittaker, in the 18th minute, compounded his error in Glasgow by stupidly throwing the ball at an opposition player, resulting in a straight red card for the Rangers defender. Despite being reduced to ten men, however, and with no away fans in the ground due to a UEFA-imposed ban on the club for sectarian singing the previous season, Jelavić gave Rangers an unlikely lifeline when he peeled away from his marker to volley home the opening goal of the night, equalising the tie on aggregate.

Unfortunately for the Ibrox side, the situation soon became more complicated once again after Bougherra, playing in his last match for the club, became the second Rangers player to receive his marching orders when the defender was dismissed for a flailing elbow in the 66th minute, and despite a third red card of the evening for Malmö's Ricardinho, the Swedes eventually secured a 1-1 draw from the game and knocked Rangers out of the competition. McCoist's side subsequently dropped into the Europa League, but worse was to come for the Ibrox men when they failed to reach the group stages of the secondary tournament following the club's elimination at the hands of the Slovenian side Maribor, who held out for a 1-1 draw in Glasgow in the second leg of the tie after inflicting a 2-1 defeat on Rangers on home soil. Instead of the much-needed financial injection that Champions League or even Europa League participation would have provided, the Ibrox club was now facing up to the prospect of a season without any further European football at all.

If Craig Whyte's intention all along was to put Rangers into administration, clear the club of its debts and start again with a more viable business plan, then this was the time to do it. The reasons and explanations for such a course of action would have been clear from the club's failure to progress in either of the potentially life-giving European competitions, and in a notorious blame culture such as Scottish football, the overall responsibility for the move could have been spread around among many groups and individuals, not least the new owner's

predecessor and culprit-in-chief David Murray, the architect of
the club's EBT scheme and of the high-risk spending strategy
at Ibrox. Instead, despite the absence of any European revenue,
Whyte decided to plough on, and with his lackadaisical
approach towards meeting his tax obligations, the new owner
decided to use money that should have been collected as PAYE
income tax and National Insurance contributions as working
capital to help with cash flow and to meet the club's day-to-day
overheads. It was a disastrous decision, which ultimately pushed
the club's known liabilities to the taxman over the £10m mark,
and coming on top of the already potentially ruinous EBT case,
which was still going through the courts, the accumulation
of another tax debt only strengthened HMRC's resolve and
allowed them to move against the club even while the larger
claim was still in dispute.

After Rangers' elimination from Europe, Whyte had been
holding meetings with HMRC bosses in an attempt to negotiate
a restructured repayment plan on the club's behalf and persuade
the revenue service to allow him, in the worst case scenario, to
pay off the EBT bill and the other outstanding liabilities in
instalments over several years. The Rangers owner was hopeful
that the tax authority would be amenable to his proposals,
but despite First Minister Alex Salmond being drafted in by
Whyte to support the club's cause, HMRC made it clear that
they weren't going to relent from their position of demanding
repayment in full, and such was the revenue service's belief in
the strength of their case against Rangers, they intimated to
Whyte that they would appeal any decision that went against
them all the way, if necessary, to the highest court in the land.
The owner's pleas for clemency and flexibility had effectively
fallen on deaf ears, and it wasn't long before the appalling reality

of the situation began to dawn on Whyte, Rangers and the whole of Scottish football. In the circumstances, there was only so long that the present situation could continue, and despite selling Nikica Jelavić, the club's top scorer, to Everton for £5m at the end of the winter transfer window, Rangers entered administration on 14 February 2012.

Previously, the newspapers had feted Whyte as a billionaire and a lifelong Rangers fan, who was going to torpedo the club's financial difficulties and put an end to the fans' worst fears by ploughing in untold millions to kickstart a new Ibrox revolution. Although some doubts had crept in by the time of his £1 purchase in May 2011, his takeover of Rangers had still been greeted with a fanfare by many who viewed his arrival, in effect, as a turning point in the club's history. Immediately, in order to curry favour with the new big man at Ibrox, sports journalists began to cultivate a cosy relationship with Whyte and some, including James Traynor of the *Daily Record* and Darrell King of the *Evening Times*, would on occasion send over their copy for his scrutiny and approval, so that the new Rangers owner could take out the bits he didn't like before the articles went to press. Gradually, however, the worm began to turn, particularly after Whyte's dubious business record was exposed and his reputation trashed by a BBC Scotland documentary, broadcast in November 2011, in which it was claimed that the businessman could have been sent to prison for acting as a company director while disqualified. Following HMRC's triggering of administration, the media, sensing the anger among supporters at what had happened to the club, now decided that they had their villain.

Particular outrage was reserved for Whyte's use of the financing company Ticketus, whose money the prospective purchaser had borrowed at the time of his acquisition to pay off the £18m debt to Lloyds Banking Group. Whyte had effectively mortgaged three years' worth of season ticket sales through the London-based company, as *The Record* revealed in January, although strangely the paper had apparently been sitting on the story for some time and the use of such financing in football wasn't particularly unusual, with Rangers having previously borrowed money from Ticketus when Walter Smith was the coach, including as part of the funding for the £4m deal that had brought the now offloaded Jelavić to Ibrox from Rapid Vienna in August 2010.

Scottish football had been suffering from financial problems for years and many of the country's lesser lights had already succumbed to the indignity of having to call in the insolvency practitioners, but the shock of seeing it happen to Scotland's most successful club, particularly in consideration of the aura of brash triumphalism with which Rangers liked to adorn the team's on-field achievements, was nevertheless considerable. The Glasgow media may have been slow on the uptake, but the process marked the beginning of a slow, lingering death for Rangers, despite the efforts to rescue the club by the appointed administrators, Paul Clark and David Whitehouse from corporate finance consultants Duff and Phelps, who had initially assisted Whyte with his takeover at Ibrox. The firm eventually identified a 'preferred bidder' for the company's assets in the guise of former Sheffield United owner Charles Green, the Yorkshireman who appeared late in the day and acquired the club, once again, for £1 from the now ostracised Whyte. In spite of Green's entreaties to HMRC, however, the club couldn't be saved and in June Rangers were consigned to liquidation, owing over £14m to the revenue service, with an estimated potential claim for another £75m still going through the courts, as well as £26.7m to Ticketus and a total of roughly £15m to 274 other unsecured creditors.

While HMRC, despite the club's liquidation, continued to pursue their full claim against Rangers all the way to the Supreme Court, which ruled in the revenue service's favour in July 2017 and condemned the club's use of EBTs as an unlawful form of tax avoidance, the governing bodies in Scottish football seemed far less keen to follow the case through to its logical conclusion. In February 2012, shortly after Rangers entered administration, the SFA charged the Ibrox club with bringing the game into disrepute over their insolvency and launched an investigation into Whyte's conduct in office, including his initial failure to disclose his June 2000 disqualification. Two months later, the independent panel imposed a fine and a transfer embargo on Rangers, while Whyte, the man who had been proclaimed by the tabloids 18 months earlier as a billionaire and a lifelong Rangers supporter, was also fined £200,000, an amount that was never paid, and he was banned from Scottish football for life.

A further inquiry was later set up by the SPL into Rangers' alleged breaches of the SFA's Articles of Association over the Ibrox club's use of the indemnifying side-letters, or second contracts, which guaranteed additional income to dozens of Rangers players. The commission, which was chaired by former judge Lord Nimmo Smith, with its parameters defined in consultation with SFA chief executive Stewart Regan, reported its findings in February 2013. The SFA's own inquiry had already determined in relation to Whyte's decision to withhold money that should have been collected as income tax from October 2011 to February 2012 that 'only match fixing in its various forms' would have constituted a more serious breach of the rules, and imposed a commensurate sentence on the former owner, but in relation to Rangers' use of EBTs, introduced by Murray and operated by the club over a far longer period of time, the Nimmo Smith report seemed remarkably mealy-mouthed.

To general astonishment, the commission found that the EBT scheme conferred no 'unfair competitive advantage' on the Ibrox club over the period from November 2000 to May 2011, ruling that the question of the legality, or otherwise, of the scheme was outside of its remit, and with the main case against Rangers brought by HMRC still going through the courts system at the time, the commission found that 'there was no evidence before us as to whether any other members of the SPL used similar EBT schemes, or the effect of their doing so'.

Celtic had used an EBT to top up the salary of the Brazilian playmaker Juninho, following his arrival at the Parkhead club in August 2004, but chairman Brian Quinn, with his background as an even-handed economist at the Bank of England, quickly recognised the dubious legality of the scheme and paid the tax in full. Yet the Nimmo Smith Commission seemed to be saying that such arrangements were open to other clubs, because, with the case against Rangers still under appeal, there was no current definitive ruling on their legality, an outcome that with hindsight could have been predicted in advance and looked for all the world like a happy contrivance.

Rangers were facing the prospect, if found guilty of fielding teams full of improperly registered players for a decade or more, of having trophies and titles struck from the record books, but the Nimmo Smith inquiry absolved them on a technicality, finding that the registrations were valid at the time they were made and that any breaches of the rules that were subsequently discovered were not relevant to that validity. As website wingoverscotland.com commented on this confusing conclusion, 'The Commission found that even if a registration was improper, it nevertheless remained in force unless and until it was explicitly revoked. This interpretation is the core of the Commission's decision to, in effect, not punish Rangers at all. What it says is that although Rangers were registering players illegally, *because they didn't get caught at the time it didn't count* [their italics], and any game in which they played must be allowed to stand. This appears to contradict every existing precedent under the auspices of the SFA.' Elsewhere, Nimmo Smith was critical of Rangers' conduct throughout the whole affair, including over the club's failure to effectively cooperate with the inquiry, an offence for which the 'Oldco' club was hit with a fine of £250,000, an amount that was later transferred to the relaunched 'Newco'.

Meanwhile, HMRC's claim against the club was proceeding through the courts with a painful lack of alacrity. After an initial judgement in favour of Rangers from the First-tier Tribunal, which was upheld at a further hearing in 2014, HMRC appealed the decision to the Court of Session, Scotland's highest civil court, where in November 2015 the original decision was overturned and the appeal upheld, with the panel of three judges considering that the EBTs were 'a mere redirection of emoluments or earnings' and 'thus assessable to income tax', and that it was 'common sense' and 'self-evident' that the payments were linked to contractual employment. In a final, binding decision, the Supreme Court in London confirmed the ruling in the revenue service's favour and, five years on from the club's collapse, the case against Rangers was at last closed.

However, once the final verdict in HMRC's successful appeal was obtained, which condemned the Ibrox club over its irregular and ultimately unlawful tax avoidance strategy, the

SFA refused to revisit the now widely ridiculed Nimmo Smith Commission, claiming that it had no basis in law to do so. In addition, when the amalgamated league body, the SPFL, invited the SFA to take part in a proposed 'review of Scottish football's actions and processes' in the aftermath of the Supreme Court's verdict, to see what Scottish football could learn from the whole Rangers debacle, the governing body declined to participate. It claimed that five years on from the turmoil created by the Ibrox club's liquidation, it would be counterproductive to 'rake over the coals' of the events at Rangers and urging everyone involved in the Scottish game to 'move on' from the whole affair.

By then David Murray would be long gone from the Ibrox institution, his links with Scottish football severed, apparently for good. Liquidation and the disgrace associated with being exposed as a tax-dodging organisation were, in the end, Murray's legacies to the club, although the trophies his teams accumulated during the EBT years were ultimately allowed to stand. The ruinous debts at Rangers had been accumulated at a time when the club's bankers, Bank of Scotland and, latterly, HBOS, were indulging in 'kamikaze lending to the great and the good', as journalist Ian Fraser later noted when reporting on Murray's collapsed business empire, while Murray, and others like him 'had been used to picking up the phone to HBOS and receiving hundreds of millions of pounds within hours'.

In the early 1980s, by contrast, before Murray's involvement with Rangers, banks generally hadn't been keen to lend money to football clubs at all, or to anyone else for that matter, without good cause – house buyers even had to apply to a building society if they wanted a mortgage loan – and with the clubs themselves often exercising painstaking care in order to avoid going into the red, Scottish football was consequently devoid of debt. The culture had changed beyond all recognition from the 1990s onwards, however, with Murray and Rangers riding the bucking bronco of the fickle and erratic financial markets, enjoying the highs and the thrills of success over this period, until they inevitably fell off and suffered a harsh reality check.

Murray was on an ego trip at Rangers, where the ultimate destination would be insolvency. In total, the club accrued losses amounting to £180m over his time at the club, with the apex of irresponsibility coming during Dick Advocaat's spell in Glasgow, when at one point a shortfall of £35m drained out of the club in a single season. Unlike his father Ian, however, the somewhat tragic figure who had gambled away the family silver in the 1960s, Murray's own extraordinary predilection towards risk-taking and rule-bending, fuelled by an unshakeable belief that he could never lose, meant that he was playing fast and loose with peoples' jobs, with their emotional attachment and support for their cherished football team and with the health and prosperity of the Scottish game overall.

If ever there was a man whose reach exceeded his grasp it was Murray. Lessons learned by children at their parents' knees about the pitfalls of showboating and getting too big for one's boots seemed to be lost on Murray even in late middle-age, leaving outside observers often baffled by his attitude and behaviour. In the end, however, the industrialist emerged relatively unscathed from his time at Ibrox, with the blame for the club's collapse almost universally reserved for the renegade Whyte, whom Murray was soon alleging had 'duped' him into selling Rangers. 'I was primarily duped. My advisers were duped, the bank was duped, the shareholders were duped. We've all been duped,' the former owner claimed, laughably, after the club entered administration.

His firm, MIH, which started out as Murray International Metals back in 1974, was itself eventually consigned to liquidation in 2015, with the asset sale, ironically, overseen by Deloitte, an arm of the company that Fergus McCann had once worked for in Canada. MIH went to the wall still owing £348m to Lloyds Banking Group, over a third of the debt that had been accumulated by the time of the HBOS merger, and with Lloyds effectively having written off another £269m through debt for equity swaps – exchanging money owed for worthless shares – it seemed that Murray, following the October 2008 bailouts, had effectively racked up another cost to the British taxpayer, in addition to the bill that he had accrued at Rangers of over £600m.

In the end, Murray was spared the humiliation that befell some of the other indebted HBOS tycoons, an outcome that was attributed, in part, to his belligerent negotiating skills, but one banking insider also suggested that Murray's knighthood may have helped his cause, admitting that the former Rangers owner was considered to be 'one of the great and the good, like [Sir] Tom Farmer and [Sir] Tom Hunter'. Others in a similar position, meanwhile, such as plain old Mr Jonathan Milne, had his FM Developments summarily dismantled by Lloyds, while the bank also took effective control of the property portfolios of other excessive HBOS borrowers, including Ken Ross, owner of the Elphinstone Group, and Geoff Ball, executive chairman of Cala Homes.

Having being allowed to wriggle off the hook by Lloyds, Murray has since concentrated most of his efforts and resources on Murray Capital, the private equity firm formerly known as Charlotte Ventures, which he was permitted by Lloyds to hive away from his deceased conglomerate, as well as on property and

– an indulgence – on his wine-producing vineyards in the south of France. He was even reported in *The Sun* in July 2019 to be dating 50-year-old Sarah Heaney again, the former television presenter, following the couple's recent divorces, although, as the paper perhaps tellingly pointed out, the pair were still living at opposite ends of the country at the time.

In Rangers' wake, a new club started up, with the team, still managed by Ally McCoist, initially playing its football out of the fourth tier of the Scottish game, after fans of the other top-flight sides rejected a bid to parachute the Newco straight into the SPL. Another feature of the obstinacy and lack of contrition over the way the Ibrox club had handled its affairs soon revealed itself when Rangers people started insisting, somewhat tediously and inevitably, that despite liquidation and all it implies, the new entity and the Oldco were one and the same club. Certainly, in regard to the traditions and practices of the old Rangers, the relaunched organisation bore an uncanny resemblance to the former institution and pillar of the Scottish game; the team still wore blue jerseys, with five stars above the same club crest in recognition of the 50th title won in 2003, they were supported by the same fans, they still played out of Ibrox and, unlike other reformed clubs who were forced to change their name, they still called themselves Rangers.

Additionally, and less appealingly, the new club appeared to be wedded to the same profligate spending policy as its predecessor, burning through tens of millions of pounds as it climbed through the lower divisions. Football board chairman, Sandy Easdale, and Isle of Man-based hedge fund, Laxey Partners, the club's largest individual shareholder, found themselves obliged to stump up £1.5m in February 2014 just in order to keep the lights on for the rest of the season, despite a lucrative share flotation in December 2012, which brought £22m into the club's coffers. In addition, the club's directors appeared to have a similar association with tax-fiddling ventures as their former Ibrox counterparts, including Easdale, who had been jailed for 27 months for VAT fraud in 1997, and Dave King, the club's chairman from March 2015 to March 2020, who had been found guilty in South Africa on 41 counts relating to income tax breaches. Finally, the club's supporters couldn't shake off the old issues relating to bigotry and racism, with UEFA ordering a partial stadium closure of Ibrox Park following 'racist behaviour which includes sectarian singing' by fans at a game against St Joseph's of Gibraltar on 18 July 2019.

What happened to Rangers under David Murray should be held up in Scotland, and beyond, as a classic test case of how not to run a football club, but because of the club continuation narrative and the tendency to lay the blame for everything that went wrong at Ibrox at the door of Craig Whyte, the designated patsy, Murray's role in the club's downfall is left largely unexamined. After Neil Lennon's Celtic eventually captured a coronavirus-affected ninth successive league championship in season 2019/2020, however, it seemed that the balance of power between the old rivals was now a mirror image of how things had stood during the early years of Murray's involvement at Ibrox, when Rangers won their nine-in-a-row and Celtic were facing possible insolvency. More than a reversal of roles, with no credible figure to come to their rescue, Rangers ultimately faced the reality of liquidation and, on present form and with the resources that the Parkhead side currently have at their disposal, there is no telling when Celtic's run of consecutive championship titles in Scotland may be interrupted.

Nobody can predict what will happen in football of course. The game's marvellous ability to defy expectations is part of its enduring appeal, but one thing seems certain: thanks to the contrary and very different approaches of Fergus McCann and David Murray at their respective clubs, Celtic are the dominant force in Scottish football once again, and are likely to remain in such a position at least for the foreseeable future.

Selected Bibliography

Bisset, A & McKillop, A, (eds.), *Born Under a Union Flag, Rangers, Britain and Scottish Independence*, Luath Press, Edinburgh, 2014

Brown, J, *Celtic-Minded: 510 Days in Paradise*, Mainstream, Edinburgh, 1999

Burns, S, *Walter Smith, The Ibrox Gaffer: A Tribute to a Rangers Legend*, Black and White, Edinburgh, 2011

Caldwell, A, *The McCann Years: The Inside Story of Celtic's Revolution*, Mainstream, Edinburgh, 1999

Campbell, T (ed.), *Ten Days That Shook Celtic*, Fort, Ayr, 2005

Campbell, T and Woods, P, *Dreams and Songs to Sing: A New History of Celtic*, Mainstream, Edinburgh, 1996

Drysdale, N, *SilverSmith: The Biography of Walter Smith*, Birlinn, Edinburgh, 2011 (revised edition)

Duff, I, *Temple of Dreams: The Changing Face of Ibrox*, Breedon Books, Derby, 2008

Esplin, R (ed.), *Ten Days That Shook Rangers*, Fort, Ayr, 2005

Esplin, R and Anderson, A, *The Advocaat Years*, Argyll Publishing, Glendaruel, 2004

Esplin, R and Walker, G, *The Official Biography of Rangers*, Hachette Scotland, Glasgow, 2011

Ferrier, B and McElroy, R, *Rangers: The Complete Record*, Breedon Books, Derby, 2005